ONCE UPON
A MIDLIFE

OTHER BOOKS BY ALLAN B. CHINEN, M.D.

In the Ever After:
Fairy Tales and the Second Half of Life

ONCE UPON
A MIDLIFE

*Classic Stories
and Mythic Tales
to Illuminate
the Middle Years*

Allan B. Chinen, M.D.

Foreword by Roger Gould, M.D.

JEREMY P. TARCHER, INC.
Los Angeles

Library of Congress Cataloging in Publication Data

Chinen, Allan B., 1952–
Once upon a midlife: classic stories and mythic tales to
illuminate the middle years / Allan B. Chinen.
p.   cm.
Includes bibliographical references.
ISBN 0-87477-677-5
1. Middle age—Psychological aspects. 2. Fairy tales—
Psychological aspects. 3. Mythology—Psychological aspects.
4. Aging—Psychological aspects. I. Title.
BF724.6.C48   1992   91-5174
155.6 ' 6—dc20   CIP

Jeremy P. Tarcher, Inc.
5858 Wilshire Blvd., Suite 200
Los Angeles, CA 90036

Distributed by St. Martin's Press, New York

Manufactured in the United States of America
10   9   8   7   6   5   4   3   2   1
First Edition

*To Michael, Marshall, and Diane,
in our middle years.*

Contents

Acknowledgments

Like the branch of a tree, supported by a sturdy trunk and fed by deep roots, this book draws its life from many people, and their encouragement and wisdom. I particularly want to thank Jack Zipes and David Gutmann for their generous and helpful comments; Gloria Gregg, for her warmth and insights; the men and women with whom I have worked in therapy, who have been my teachers through the years; Florence Irvine, for illuminating the way home and the meaning of being human; and Michael Lidbetter, for making everything possible. Above all, I want to thank the storytellers who have preserved middle tales over the centuries, and the stroke of luck, fate, divinity, and magic that revealed those hidden treasures.

Foreword

Reading this book is a treat. Having read most of the research and books in this area over the last fifteen years, and having written my own book on the subject, I am often bored with the repetition of ideas about midlife. Frankly, I didn't anticipate a pleasurable read. I have been delightfully surprised.

Allan Chinen has forged his own modern midlife mentality with timeless "middle" tales, fairy tales for the second half of life. I had never heard of or thought about middle tales, which the author distinguishes from youth tales (live happily ever after) and "elder" tales. He may not have created the category, but he has certainly established it as a rich source of illustration for those phenomena that other researchers and writers in this field already have described. His own clear observations to this body of knowledge are a welcome contribution.

The midlife period is too important and too personal to be described solely by academics who must subscribe to the rigors of methodology. It is also too textured to be swept into large containers by those theorists looking for a principle or two to explain it all, as if coming to grips with mortality or emancipation from gender roles can subsume all that has been described.

What struck me most about this book is the way the middle tales from Japan, China, Egypt, Russia, India, Polynesia, and American Indian lore were used as illustrations of both large, sweeping concepts, such as Jung's anima/animus, and the nitty gritty specifics of Rorschach interpretations by contemporary men and women. In the hands of a skilled psychiatrist/writer, these tales are transformed into mental pictures. Concepts become frames for the pictures, while the research specifics become details highlighting different colors and shapes, and evoking different responses. Being an old pro in the midlife industry, I have never before been treated to such a visual-emotional display of the tapestry of midlife.

The gift of this book is to help us see and feel the essential phenomena of midlife. The book is filled with research descriptions, professional case histories, and quotes from scholars in the field that tie contemporary time to timeless formations of other cultures coming through the tales. The person tying it all together is himself in the midst of mid-life evolution, working with patients in the room and in these other worlds. Patients and characters in the middle tales are blended into a mythic reality that has a peculiar substantiality.

This kind of approach, without a specific, overly determined context, is the ideal vehicle for revealing the slippery, but solidly anchored phenomena of midlife, which are inner happenings, subtle shifts, awakenings, graspings of truths. Midlife is about being in touch with a self that always was there, except it was disguised, split, and disavowed. This book allows the reader to see these phenomena without being confused by American cultural norms, or prescriptions of behavior implicit in age normalizing. There is nothing in this book that one midlife spouse can throw at another, saying, "See, this is what you should be doing."

Yet there is something to learn for everyone. For there truly is wisdom buried in these simple middle tales from around the world.

Roger Gould, M.D.
author of *Transformations*

Introduction

The story is familiar, and from Cinderella to Snow White the plot is similar. The young hero and heroine meet, fall in love, defeat horrible enemies, marry, and then live happily ever after. We hear the tale in childhood, hope it is true in youth, but find out later that the story runs thin. By midlife, it usually runs out.

This book is about what happens next, when the Prince goes bald and the Princess has a midlife crisis. The fairy tales gathered here from around the world portray middle-aged men and women juggling the demands of family and work, grappling with self-doubt and disillusionment, and ultimately finding deep new meaning in life.

These *middle tales* differ dramatically from more familiar stories, like Sleeping Beauty or Tom Thumb. The latter are *youth tales,* which are focused on children or adolescents, and reflect the psychology of youth. Middle tales take up where youth tales end and contain astonishing insights for men and women struggling through the journey of midlife.

FAIRY TALES FOR ADULTS?

The idea that adults can learn from fairy tales may seem odd today. After all, fairy tales are only children's fare. Nothing could be further from the truth. Long ago—and this is not a fairy tale—fairy tales were told by adults for adults. The stories expressed the hopes, fears, and wisdom of grown-ups, not children. Fairy tales were serious business and played the role that newspapers and television play in today's society. The stories offered news, entertainment, and commentary, challenging listeners to reflect on their lives.[1]

Only in the last few centuries were fairy tales directed at children, as Jack Zipes points out in *The Brothers Grimm*. When literacy became more common and technology more complex, adults began to look down upon folktales. The stories seemed good enough for peasants and children, but not for educated grown-ups. Yet the tales are too important to remain forgotten. Even today, many adults read fairy tales only in secret, afraid of appearing foolish. Maria Tatar notes in *The Hard Facts of the Grimms' Fairy Tales* that illustrious writers like George Bernard Shaw and C. S. Lewis kept their love of fairy tales secret—until midlife.

The reason for the ageless appeal of fairy tales can be summed up in an old Hasidic proverb: give people a fact or an idea and you enlighten their minds; tell them a story and you touch their souls. Jerome Bruner, the eminent psychologist, puts this ancient insight in more modern terms in his book *Actual Minds, Possible Worlds*. There are two basic modes of thought, he argues. The first is *scientific*, logical and linear, the language of commerce, work, and problem-solving. The second is *narrative*, the medium of drama, myth, literature, and fairy tales—the stuff of the human soul. Gisela Labouvie-Vief, another cognitive psychologist, uses more poetic language. She describes the two modes of reasoning as *logos* and *mythos*. Both are Greek terms meaning "word," but *logos* refers to words used in explanation, calculation, and planning, while *mythos* refers to the language used in stories, drama, and dream. By any name, stories touch the human soul and unveil the unconscious psyche.

Fairy tales offer adults a clear conduit to the unconscious, which is particularly important at midlife, when practical worries prevent most people from introspection. Fairy tales create this direct access with their characteristic invocations which warn listeners to suspend belief and rational thinking.

European stories start with "Once upon a time," Arabic tales use "There was, there was not," while African storytellers say, "Ho!" which signifies, "We do not really mean what we say. . . ."[2] This allows unconscious material to emerge in a process analogous to the free association of psychoanalysis. Fairy tales are also typically told in relaxed settings, around a fire after a hard day's work or at bedtime. Storyteller and scholar John Boe observes that these settings contribute to an altered state of consciousness that activates unconscious images and symbols.

To paraphrase Freud and Jung, fairy tales are like dreams. But fairy tales have an important advantage over dreams. Dreams tend to be idiosyncratic and often have meaning only for the dreamer, while fairy tales are universal in scope and appeal. This is because fairy tales were passed from person to person. In the process, purely idiosyncratic elements are eliminated, leaving only the themes that appeal to many people. Traditional fairy tales thus address basic human issues. And middle tales focus on the fundamental tasks of midlife.

Surprisingly, middle tales do not reflect conventional social values. This is particularly important for women, because most cultures are patriarchal and denigrate the feminine. Yet middle tales are astonishingly feminist. The stories portray strong, independent women exercising their talents and overcoming tremendous social oppression. There are several reasons that feminist themes appear in middle tales. First, the stories were customarily told among friends and relatives, away from public view. The tales thus escaped the control of church and state. Since fairy tales also demand disbelief, storytellers could tell biting satire and still disclaim responsibility. "It's only a fairy story!" they could say. This playful, private nature distinguishes fairy tales from myths and legends. The latter represent the official, public ideology of a society, and are typically used to justify patriarchal authority. (Kings commonly claimed descent from gods or legendary heroes.) Middle tales are iconoclastic and represent something of a counterculture.

Finally, women traditionally tell fairy tales as often as men. Jack Zipes points out that the Grimm brothers obtained most of their stories from women informants. Classic fairy tales like the Arabian Thousand and One Nights also emphasize the importance of women storytellers, because it was the beautiful Scheherazade who told all the stories. Not surprisingly, then, fairy tales incorporate women's concerns.

Middle tales contrast sharply with youth tales like Cinderella, where heroines are beautiful, dutiful, helpless, and stereotypically feminine. Both Jack Zipes and Maria Tatar emphasize that indoctrinating children in traditional male and female roles is a major function of youth tales. Since middle tales deal with adults who have already been socialized, the stories do not reinforce tradition. Instead, they encourage men and women to question social conventions. Middle tales bring up truths that individuals and society would rather ignore. The stories are often disconcerting, but because they force men and women to reflect on themselves, middle tales are ultimately healing.

The healing power of fairy tales has been appreciated for centuries. In Navajo and Hindu traditions, telling tales was a crucial part of healing rites. And many psychotherapists today use fairy tales to inspire dramatic changes in people's lives.[3] Middle tales are equally therapeutic, and they specifically offer hope, wisdom, and practical advice for the conflicts and doubts of midlife.

THE QUEST FOR MIDDLE TALES

While these are the rational reasons for adults to heed middle tales, I confess that I approached the stories in a different way. Fairy tales erupted in my life quite unexpectedly. Like many others, as a child I was delighted by the world of fairy tales and myths. But as I grew older I put fairy tales aside for more practical pursuits. This was especially true during college and medical training, where intellectual rigor is demanded.

Then some years ago, vivid images began filling my mind when I was jogging, meditating, or walking alone on the beach—images of dragons and castles, kings and queens. These visions were archetypal in intensity and often moved me to tears. Although they were similar to dreams, they demanded something more than interpretation. I soon realized that the images were the endings to different stories. The tales cried out for elaboration, so I started writing them down. The results were fairy tales,[4] but with protagonists who were middle-aged or older. I thought this odd at the time, since the only fairy tales I knew featured young heroes and heroines, tales like Snow White and Jack and the Bean Stalk.

Sometime later, on a sunny spring day, as I walked to the university library to do some research, I paused beneath a cherry tree in full bloom. An inspiration hit me then, and it was as if a fairy godmother or a wise old man whispered a word of advice in my ear. The idea was simple. If I had written fairy tales about middle-aged and older people, others must have done so, too. Hence there must be traditional fairy tales about middle and later life somewhere. I began looking for such tales and was astonished at the treasures I uncovered.

Middle tales, I found, are neither common nor familiar. They constitute only about 10 percent of some five thousand fairy tales I read. The overwhelming majority of stories are youth tales, which specifically call their protagonists *young*. About 5 percent of stories say their protagonists are *old*, and qualify as *elder tales*, which I discussed in an earlier book, *In the Ever After*. Middle tales are distinguished by one feature: their protagonists typically are neither young nor old, are married, and earn a living. In real life, these are surely the defining characteristics of the middle years.

Middle tales grapple with personal failure, marital conflict, and tragedy. Although most prominent at midlife, these problems are not limited to the middle years, since younger individuals often divorce or face terminal illnesses. Middle-tale themes are really ageless.

INTERPRETING THE STORIES

Middle tales offer maps of the midlife passage, pictures of obstacles, oases, dangers, and delights, recorded by men and women who have survived the journey. Like all maps, middle tales must be interpreted, and I have included psychological commentary on the tales. I followed several simple rules in analyzing the stories, because fairy tales can be used to support any conclusion if interpreted wildly, just like statistics and horoscopes.

The first rule, which comes from Northrop Frye, the literary critic, and Robert Pelton, a folklorist-philosopher, is simply to listen to fairy tales and let them speak before trying to interpret them. Alan Dundes, a folklorist, notes that many psychological discussions of fairy tales do the reverse; that is, they try to force stories to fit pet theories. This is analogous to the scene in the original Grimms' version of Cinderella when the evil stepsisters cut off their toes to fit their feet into the glass slipper. In interpreting fairy tales, writers often take an issue that they have worked on for many years, find a story that illustrates it, generalize from personal experience, and then pontificate about human nature.

The second rule of interpretation I call the Noah's Ark principle. To be included in this anthology, a story had to have at least one partner—a tale with similar themes from another country. By means of this qualification we avoid overinterpreting the details of a particular story—an error that many psychoanalysts, like Bruno Bettelheim, commit. In his book *The Uses of Enchantment,* Bettelheim discusses Little Red Riding Hood, and emphasizes that the girl's cap is red. He associates the color with blood, menstruation, and the onset of puberty. Unfortunately, in other versions of the story, the cap is not red, the girl is often far from puberty, and sometimes she has no cap at all! Images that seem highly symbolic are often idiosyncratic, and are not archetypal or universal.

But when middle tales are placed side by side, striking cross-cultural parallels appear. These common themes reflect the archetypal tasks of midlife.

HOW THE BOOK IS ORGANIZED

Middle tales depict a common sequence of tasks, which reflect different stages of the middle years. For this reason, I have divided the book into four sections. Part I deals with stories that focus on what happens immediately after the young hero and heroine marry and set up a household together. These stories depict early midlife and the period of settling down in society. The tales in Parts II and III turn to the painful reversals that erupt several years later. These dramas illuminate the proverbial midlife crisis. Part II focuses on problems specific to men and to women, while Part III addresses issues facing both men and women. Finally, Part IV shifts to tales that depict reconciliation and renewal, portraying men and women resolving the doubts and conflicts of midlife.

A FEW CAVEATS

Middle tales do not specify ages for these phases, because people follow their own timetables. If any rule applies to adult development, it is that people become more and more unique over time.[5]

This leads to another caveat. Middle tales emphasize universal themes and ignore the specific problems that beset people in real life—for example, trouble with a boss, a parent, or a spouse. Many of these problems stem from childhood experiences, which middle tales skip over. The stories assume that their protagonists have completed the tasks of youth and come to terms with their childhood. This exclusion is an advantage. If middle tales sacrifice breadth, they gain clarity. By ignoring childhood issues, the stories focus more keenly on the tasks of maturity. Middle tales also remind us that the final destination in life is not merely the resolution of painful childhood traumas, but something far larger and more important—becoming fully human.

My interpretations of the stories are inevitably shaped by my biases, so a confession of my theoretical interests is in order. I began with a strong Jungian orientation and expected to find certain themes of which Jungians are fond. I was not disappointed. However, many themes are not discussed within Jungian thought or contemporary gerontology. To understand these unexpected motifs, I had to range far afield in mythology, folklore, adult cognitive development, and recent research about midlife.

The strong feminist motifs in middle tales also obliged me to read feminist literature, which I must admit, like many other men, I had avoided. My interpretations of the stories are therefore eclectic. But then no single theory or discipline is broad enough to encompass the complexities of middle tales—or of midlife. Fairy tales are far too rich to be exhausted by any single interpretation, as are the middle years themselves. I therefore include the middle tales in this book, so readers can interpret the stories for themselves.

A PERSONAL COMMENT

Middle tales became an unexpected source of guidance, delight, and inspiration for me over the last few years. I discovered that the fairy tales I wrote for myself repeated images in stories from around the world. I also noticed astonishing similarities between middle tales and my dreams from several years ago. Equally dramatic parallels appeared in the dreams and fantasies of middle-aged men and women with whom I worked in therapy. Middle tales mirror real life. More than that, middle tales edify everyday experience. These stories have helped many, including myself, to move through the issues of adult life.

Middle tales brought magic back into my own life, and the reason is not hard to guess, nor do I think my situation is unusual. Fairy tales awaken the inner child in us all, and that child is sorely needed in the middle years, when men and women are weighed down with responsibilities and endless chores. This is the promise of the stories. To every man or woman, pausing perplexed in the middle of life, magic and wisdom await in unexpected places. Without further ado, I turn now to the stories themselves.

PART I

SETTLING DOWN

ONE

The Loss of Magic

The Elves and the Shoemaker
from Germany

nce upon a time, a shoemaker and his wife fell upon hard times. No matter what they did, things went from bad to worse. One day, the cobbler found he had only a small piece of leather left in his shop. The cobbler did not despair, but sat down, cut the leather carefully, and started to sew a pair of shoes. When evening fell, the shoemaker left his work unfinished and returned home to have dinner with his wife.

The next day the cobbler found a pair of shoes in his shop! Someone had come in during the night and finished his work. The shoemaker sold the shoes and used the money to buy more leather. He spent the day cutting the new material. When evening arrived, he again put his work away and returned home to his wife.

The next morning, the cobbler found several more pairs of shoes in his shop. His mysterious helper had come again. And the new shoes were even prettier than the first ones. The shoemaker sold the shoes, bought more leather, cut it carefully, and left the pieces in his workshop overnight. The following day, the cobbler found a row of boots, sandals, and shoes set neatly on his table.

This went on for some time. Each night, the cobbler left pieces of leather out in his workshop. Each morning, he found beautiful shoes in his shop. The shoemaker soon prospered and his reputation for marvelous shoes spread far and wide.

One day, around Christmas, the cobbler said to his wife, "We must find out who is helping us, so we can thank them!" His wife agreed. That evening they hid in the workshop, and waited anxiously. Right around midnight, the shoemaker and his wife heard singing, and saw two elves leap through the window. The elves were as naked as the dawn, barefoot and carefree. They danced, did somersaults, and sang. Then they sat down, started making shoes and boots, and in no time at all they finished their work. They skipped around the room and vanished on a moonbeam.

The shoemaker and his wife could scarcely believe their eyes. "Two elves have been helping us!" they said. "We must give them a gift to thank them!" Since the elves were naked, and since it was winter, the shoemaker and his wife decided to give them clothes. The shoemaker stitched two tiny pairs of boots, lined with fur, while his wife sewed two jackets and two pairs of pants, warm and fleecy.

On Christmas Eve, they set out their presents in the workshop, hid and watched. At midnight, the two elves leaped through the window, and looked around in bewilderment. There was no leather for them to sew, and no tools to use! Then they saw the gifts.

"Ooh!" one elf exclaimed, as he picked up a tiny shoe and tried it on. "Ahh!" the other cried, as he squirmed into a shirt and coat. All the clothes fit perfectly. The elves admired each other as they danced with glee, then vanished into the moonlight. The shoemaker and his wife were delighted, and went to bed as happy as could be.

The next evening the elves did not return. Nor the night after, or ever again. "What have we done?" the shoemaker and his wife asked themselves. But they were practical people, so the cobbler started working once again. With a little practice, he made shoes as beautiful as the elves had made, so he and his wife lived happily for the rest of their days.

THE LOSS OF MAGIC

This German story makes an excellent introduction to middle tales. It is likely to be familiar to many readers since it comes from the Grimms' anthology, which is perhaps the most widely read collection of fairy tales. The shoemaker is someone who has learned a trade and married, unlike the protagonists of more familiar youth tales like Hansel and Gretel and Tom Thumb. This immediately tells us the story is a middle tale.

The cobbler falls on hard times, but then finds help from the elves. This is a typical theme in most youth tales, where a young man and woman find magic help and live happily ever after. So what happens in this story is unexpected. The shoemaker and his wife give the elves thank-you presents, and the elves never return.

The loss of magic turns out to be common in middle tales around the world, and the importance of the theme emerges if we compare The Elves and the Shoemaker with youth tales. In the latter, young characters lose a magic treasure only if they do something greedy or wicked. In this tale, the cobbler is *not* greedy. He and his wife are grateful and generous, but they lose the magic anyway. What might this loss symbolize?

The magic lies in the elves. Their most striking features are that they are naked and wholly uninhibited. Innocent and playful, they are not yet burdened by social conventions or self-consciousness. They personify the carefree spirit of youth and childhood. The disappearance of the magic elves symbolizes the inevitable experience of growing up, surrendering play for work and innocence for responsibility.

The story reinforces this theme with several small details. The elves vanish when the cobbler and his wife give them clothes. Clothing reflects social decorum and conventional behavior. In giving the elves clothes, the cobbler and his wife symbolically try to socialize them.

The story also says that the gifts are Christmas presents. It is relatively unusual for fairy tales to specify particular dates. (Part of the timeless quality of fairy tales comes from their vagueness.) This suggests that the date is symbolic. Here it is useful to remember the cultural background of the story.

In Germany, elves were pagan creatures—holdovers from what was thought of as the dark, barbaric period before Christianity. The elves leave when they receive Christmas presents, suggesting a conflict between an earlier, uninhibited, pagan order and a newer, disciplined, civilized one. This is analogous to the transition from youth to adulthood. The detail about Christmas does not appear in other fairy tales, but the symbolism parallels that of the clothes. Christmas and clothes reflect socialization and discipline. Like pieces in a mosaic, the details may seem insignificant in themselves, but when put together they form a coherent picture.

The present fairy tale does not explain why the elves leave, but other middle tales clarify the issue. In the Japanese tale The Stork Wife,[1] a man married a beautiful woman. After their wedding, the wife worked every day, weaving the most wondrous fabric anyone had ever seen. The husband sold the cloth for great profit, and the two lived happily with their children. The husband became curious because his wife always labored in secret. One day he spied on her and discovered that she was actually a stork fairy. While weaving, she became a stork and used her own feathers to make her cloth. The wife realized that her husband was watching her and sadly told him she could no longer stay. She flew off, leaving her children and husband behind.

The husband loses his magic wife when he spies on her and learns she is a fairy. His knowledge leads to the loss of magic. Analogously, in the shoemaker's story, the elves are magic creatures from nature, like the stork fairy. When the elves receive their Christmas gifts, they realize that they were seen and leave. A similar theme of self-awareness happens in the biblical story of Adam and Eve after they ate from the Tree of Knowledge. They became conscious of themselves and were banished from Eden, losing the magic of paradise.

Taken together, these tales show that the development of consciousness and knowledge destroys the magic of youth.

Although the story of Adam and Eve implies that this loss is punishment, The Elves and the Shoemaker emphasize the opposite. The cobbler and his wife acted generously and still lost the elves' magic. Other middle tales corroborate the point. The loss of magic is not an ethical issue, but a developmental one. It is not punishment, but simply the result of growing up.

When the elves leave, the cobbler is not ruined. He returns to making shoes himself and prospers. Here the story contains an important if unsavory truth: after the magic of youth comes work! The shoemaker does not lose the elves' magic so much as he transforms it into his own skill and discipline. The story elaborates on the motif in subtle ways. The cobbler's trade itself is symbolic. He makes *shoes*. These are mundane things, usually taken for granted and even more often dirty. But therein lies their importance: they represent grounding. Shoes appear in the same light in other middle tales, like Abu Kasem's Slippers,[2] Stubborn Husband, Stubborn Wife (chapter 4), and The Golden Tree (chapter 16). Youth tales, I might add, focus on magic shoes that can transport people to distant lands, like seven-league boots, or Dorothy's ruby slippers in *The Wizard of Oz*. (Dorothy, of course, is only a child, making hers a youth tale.) Shoes in middle tales relate to labor, not magic, and practical, everyday life rather than enchanted kingdoms.

Another Grimms' tale conveys the role of labor in the middle years. Called "The Duration of Life," the story is so charming and humorous that I cannot resist including it here. After creation, God granted all animals thirty years as their natural span of life. The ass, all too familiar with its destiny as a beast of burden, asked for a reprieve from so much labor. So God took back eighteen years. The dog, fearing old age, asked to have several of his thirty years removed. So God obliged. The monkey also feared old age and pleaded with God for a shorter life. God kindly deducted ten years. Finally humans appeared. Men and women felt dissatisfied with thirty years, and asked for more. So God gave human beings the eighteen surplus years from the ass. Still unhappy, people requested more life, and God offered the dog's extra years, and finally the monkey's excess ten.

Thus human beings live in health and happiness for the first thirty years, because that is their natural span of life. Then men and women live out the ass' eighteen years, working without stop, beaten and harried every day. The next dozen years are the dog's years, when people sit near the fireplace, grumbling and growling. Finally the monkey's years arrive, when people do whatever they feel like.

Most men and women at midlife can identify with the donkey's lot. Giving up the innocence, spontaneity, and freedom of youth to be a beast of burden is neither easy nor palatable. Inevitably, there is an element of mourning and sadness in growing up. Some people fail to make the transition, or refuse to do so, and this leads to a variety of difficulties. One such problem is the Peter Pan syndrome or, as the Jungians call it, the Puer complex (*puer* is Latin for "child"). Individuals suffering from this problem, like Peter Pan, want to enjoy the freedom and spontaneity of youth forever, so they avoid responsibilities in jobs or relationships, fleeing commitments from career or spouse.

The syndrome sometimes takes subtle forms. Some men and women marry and settle into a job—but only outwardly. Inside, they harbor dreams of writing the great American novel, becoming a millionaire, or finding the perfect lover. But they never do anything to make their dreams come true. Then around forty, they arrive at a shocking insight: they no longer have time to achieve their dreams.

Fortunately, most adults give up the magic of youth earlier, without undue difficulty. In my own experience, the loss of magic appeared in a series of dreams. I did not fully understand them at the time and rediscovered the dreams only when I went through my journals as part of writing this book. In these dreams, I flew around with a flock of magnificent birds. (I kept my human form, but somehow could fly with them.) The birds were the size of large storks or herons, but had iridescent plumage, sparkling like gold and jewels. Flying with the birds was a magic experience, and we glided over plains and fields, watching the world from a lofty height. All these dreams ended in great disappointment. The birds descended, heading for their nests, which were in mundane locations atop city buildings or telephone poles. As they flew lower, the birds lost their beautiful colors and became drab, brown, and nondescript. Worse, I lost the power of flight. Sometimes I tried to break away from the flock and fly back up into the sky, only to find myself gliding inexorably down to the earth. So I had to follow the birds to their nests.

Flying with magical birds reflects the freedom and enchantment of youth. Coming in for a landing and losing the power to fly, on the other hand, captures the loss of youthful magic. The birds also landed in nests, pointing to the reason for giving up the magic of youth—to settle down in life, and establish a home. Although my dreams did not involve elves, the underlying theme is the same as in The Elves and the Shoemaker. And Joseph Henderson, a Jungian analyst, observed that most adults have analogous dreams as they move from youth to maturity.

The cobbler's story contains another level of meaning about the loss of magic, which has to do with creativity. The elves arrive at night and do their work in the dark. They offer a charming symbol for unconscious creativity. When conscious thinking cannot find a solution, sleeping on a problem and turning it over to the "inner elves" often succeeds.

The fact that the elves leave after they receive their gifts suggests that consciousness hinders creativity. Various artists, scientists, and writers have noted precisely this problem, as Arthur Koestler discusses in *The Act of Creation*. Creativity typically requires a suspension of conscious judgment and intention, a particular brand of naïveté and playfulness reminiscent of children's innocence. If scrutinized, criticized, or forced to operate on command, this elfish creativity quickly flees.

When the elves leave, the shoemaker goes back to work. His labor replaces the elves' magic. This brings up the role of labor in creativity, which Thomas Edison summarized in his pithy comment about genius being 1 percent inspiration and 99 percent perspiration. This proportion changes over the years. Elliott Jaques, a psychoanalyst, studied creativity at midlife, examining the lives of several hundred highly successful artists, composers, and writers. Jaques noted two basic types of creativity. The first he described as "hot from the fire," where a creative work, whether a sculpture, a novel, or a musical composition, typically appears fully developed in the artist's mind. The youthful Mozart, for instance, apparently *heard* new compositions in his head and simply transcribed them on paper. This type of creativity involves frenzied inspirations, and tapers off after midlife. The second type of creativity then comes to the fore, and Jaques called it "sculpted" creativity. The artist begins with an incomplete inspiration and then works and reworks the idea. The fitful flashes of creativity characteristic of youth evolve into the consistent work habits and reliable skills of maturity. If youthful creativity is 99 percent inspiration, mature creativity is 99 percent perspiration. Magical elves become steady cobblers.[3]

Although most adults associate fairy tales with enchantment and happy endings, middle tales contain a surprisingly sober note—the loss of youthful magic. Middle tales warn us not to dismiss them as the stuff of fantasy and wish fulfillment. These stories contain important, often unpleasant, but always perceptive insights.

Youthful Ideals at Midlife

The Magic Purse
from Korea

nce upon a time, a husband and wife earned their living by cutting firewood in the forest. Although they worked hard, times were difficult and they were as poor as could be. One day the husband and wife worked longer than usual, and returned home with two loads of wood. It was too late to go to the market, so they left the firewood outside and retired for the night. The next morning, they discovered someone had stolen half their wood. The husband and wife cursed the unknown thief, gritted their teeth, and went back to the forest. By evening they gathered two more hefty loads. They returned home late and left the wood outside. "Who would steal from us again?" they asked themselves. But when they awoke the next day, someone had! The husband and wife fumed and swore, and then returned to the forest. But the same thing happened that night and the next: while they slept, exhausted from their labors, someone stole half their wood.

On the fifth day, the husband cried out, "Enough is enough!" So that evening, he concealed himself inside one bundle of wood and waited, swearing he would catch the thief. At midnight, a great rope descended from the sky, looped around the cord of wood in which the husband was hiding, and hoisted the whole load into the sky. Finally the wood came to rest in the clouds, and the poor man crept out.

An old man with a long white beard greeted the woodcutter. "So you are the man who cuts two loads of wood every day!" the sage exclaimed. "Why so much?"

"My wife and I use one bundle for ourselves, and we sell the rest," the husband explained. "It is the only way we can earn money for food."

The sage nodded. "I see," he said thoughtfully. "Your life is difficult." The old man paused and then said, "I know how I can help you." He waved his hand and seven beautiful maidens appeared. They led the husband to a storehouse, filled with money bags, overflowing with treasure. "Choose any purse you wish," the maidens told the husband.

"That one!" the man cried, pointing to a wallet full of gold and jewels.

"No, no," the old man interrupted, "this is the one for you." He gave the husband a small purse and said, "Once each day, and only once, you can take a silver coin from this purse. Use the money wisely, and you will not go wanting." The husband felt disappointed, but he remembered his manners and thanked the sage. Then the old man lowered the husband back to earth.

The man rushed to his wife and roused her from sleep. He told her what happened, showed her the magic purse, reached inside, and pulled out a silver coin. "Good heavens!" they both exclaimed, staring at the money.

"Let's buy some fish for dinner!" the husband suggested. "No," his wife said, "I prefer sausages!" "Well, then," the husband replied, "how about some pigs? We can raise them, and sell them later." "Right now," the wife countered, "we need new clothes." The husband and wife argued back and forth, louder and more forcefully. Finally they decided not to spend their money until they could agree on what to buy.

The next morning, the couple took out another coin from the magic purse. They quarreled over what to buy and ended up not spending the money. This went on for some time. Each morning they took out another coin, argued over how to use it, and so bought nothing. Soon they had a modest fortune saved up. Finally, they both had the same idea: "Let's build a new house!" They hired masons and carpenters, and soon a beautiful new house took shape. Then the husband and wife ran out of money.

The husband fetched the magic purse, and shook it. A silver coin rolled out. He paused a moment, remembering the old man's warning about taking only one coin each day. But the husband looked longingly at his unfinished home. Hesitantly, he reached in the wallet and found another coin! The husband grinned, shook the purse, and a third coin materialized. He jubilantly opened the bag again. This time thunder rolled over the land, and the new house vanished. The poor husband was horrified. But no matter what he did, no more money came from the purse.

The husband and wife bewailed their misfortune. They were right back at the beginning! But they were practical people, and so they returned to work, cutting wood in the forest. Their backs groaned and their arms ached, but when they carried their wood home, no one stole from them. So they sold the wood in the village, and earned a penny each day. The pennies became a silver coin, and the silver coin a flock of chickens, and the flock a cow, and the cow a new cottage. And that was enough for them.

MAGIC AND THE IDEALS OF YOUTH

The tale begins with a poor man and woman who obtain a magic treasure. But instead of living happily ever after, the husband and wife quarrel. And when the couple finally agree on building a house, they lose their magic treasure altogether. The story repeats the loss of youthful magic in The Elves and the Shoemaker and adds several new insights.

The husband and wife lose their fortune when the man takes more from the magic purse than he should. But he is not monstrously greedy. He takes only a few more silver coins than he is supposed to and for a relatively modest purpose—to build a new house. He does not seek something grandiose, wishing for a fabulous palace or asking to become king. Most readers today could probably identify with the poor man and woman, struggling hard to make ends meet and dreaming of a little comfort in life. It seems a bit harsh for the couple to lose everything. After all, the husband and wife suffered when the old man in the clouds stole their wood. Surely they deserve some compensation!

The man and wife lose the magic because of a small, human fault. The same theme resurfaces in other middle tales. In a Welsh story,[1] a young man marries a beautiful fairy, and she sets only one condition—that he never strike her in anger. They start a family and live happily together, until one day the husband becomes angry with an unruly horse and throws the bridle at it. The bit accidentally strikes his wife. She immediately vanishes, never to return. The poor man loses his wife, and his children lose their mother, because of an ordinary human vice—impatience. The husband was not even angry at his wife, but at the horse.

The Magic Purse helps explain how a small fault causes such a grievous loss of magic. The enchanted purse symbolizes the magic of youth and the husband obtains it from the old man in the sky. Living in heaven, the sage must be divine. This implies that the magic he gives the husband, the magic of youth, is also divine. The Welsh story about the impatient husband repeats the theme. His magic young wife is really a fairy, and so her beauty is supernatural or divine.

The divine magic symbolizes youthful idealism and visions. Such inspiration takes many forms, such as hope for world peace, romantic dreams of true love, and visions of becoming a champion athlete. Daniel Levinson and his colleagues stress the point that the dream's content differs for each person, but the numinous power of the dream does not. Behind the divine inspiration of youth lies an image of perfection—the hope of establishing a perfect society, playing a perfect game, finding a perfect love. Innocent and inspired, young men and women assume that perfection is possible. Experience with the real world eventually shatters that dream; that is why men and women in middle tales lose magic. Small human faults and inevitable human frailties eclipse the divine dream of perfection. Theologian Adrian Van Kaam calls this process *de-idolization.* Young men and women surrender the idols and ideals of youth, and settle for doing what is good enough. Donald Sandner, a Jungian analyst, rephrases the point: young men and women sacrifice their "godlikeness" in order to become adults.

Understandably, many problems arise along the way. Star athletes provide the most poignant example. Michael Messner observed that young champions live out a fairy-tale existence, enjoying triumph, fame, and honor. But in their early thirties, these champions discover they have passed their prime and cannot defeat younger challengers. Worse, the erstwhile victors are often disabled by sports injuries. Finding a satisfying second career is traumatic. Joseph Henderson found that a similar situation applies to war heroes.

The sacrifice of the divine magic of youth often takes the form of an early midlife crisis. A man or woman awakens one morning with a sinking realization: "I'm turning forty and I haven't done anything yet! I haven't made my mark on the world!" Yet these men and women, like most, have achieved much by thirty or forty years of age. They have taken a place in society, earn a reasonable living, and support the less fortunate with their taxes. Most have married and raise children reasonably well, and do not commit murders or go insane. These are all significant achievements. The problem is that they seem pedestrian compared with the glorious dreams of youth. True!

Giving up the idealism of youth came home to me in a humorous yet humbling way during my medical internship. I started out like most interns, starry-eyed and naive, eager to heal the sick, comfort the suffering, and be all things to all people. Then one day, while I was assigned to the emergency room, I walked to work earlier than usual, thinking I would help out the night staff before my shift started. A few blocks from the hospital, I came upon an ambulance just leaving a house, accompanied by a number of police cars. I knew something awful had happened there, probably a shooting or some other disaster. I also figured that the ambulance would be going to the nearest emergency room, where I would soon be on duty. So I began to walk slower and slower, pausing to read the headlines of the papers on the newsstand and admiring the flowers growing in window boxes. I arrived at the hospital just when my shift started and found the two things I had expected. First, the ambulance had arrived, bringing a patient who had been wounded by a shotgun. The emergency team had tried to save the man, in an exhausting and ultimately vain effort. And second, the team had finished everything, including cleaning up, so I had nothing to do as I started my shift. So much for youthful visions of helping the sick and alleviating suffering!

Most adults, I suspect, undergo a similar process of disillusionment. Whether we are teachers, businessmen, scientists, or writers, human frailties and practical realities eclipse the divine ideals of youth. Women, though, face an additional obstacle. Most cultures encourage young men to pursue their dreams, but actively prevent women from doing so. Women are told to marry, stay home, raise children, cook, and keep their mouths shut. While men deal with the loss of magic, women battle with a more deadly and difficult problem, the loss of identity and autonomy, of self and soul.

Middle tales like The Elves and the Shoemaker and The Magic Purse share a common theme, expressed in different ways. In moving from youth to adult life, men and women metaphorically eat from the Tree of Knowledge and are exiled from Eden. They lose the divine perfection, innocence, and idealism of youth, and instead learn to labor and suffer. Difficult though the transition is, the alternative is worse. Refusing to give up the magic of youth leads to disaster, as the next story illustrates.

THREE

Hoarding the Magic

The Fisherman and the Mermaid
from Wales

nce upon a time, a poor fisherman walked by the sea. A storm blew up and the man took shelter in a cave. To his surprise, he found a mermaid inside. She gave the fisherman a box, asked him to return early the next morning, and swam away.

The fisherman went home, opened the box, and found it full of gold and jewels. The next day he awoke late and hurried to the cavern, but the mermaid was nowhere to be seen. The fisherman returned sadly home. Later that night, he heard tapping on his window and saw the mermaid outside. She asked him to meet her at the cave the next day and warned him not to be late. Then she vanished.

The fisherman arose early the next morning and went to the grotto. He found the mermaid there, without her fishy tail. She was so beautiful, he fell in love with her. "Will you marry me?" he asked her.

"Yes," the mermaid agreed. "I heard you singing as you sail upon the ocean and fell in love with you. So I took on a human form to meet you."

The fisherman and the mermaid married and had five sets of twins—five sons and five daughters. The mermaid brought a great treasure from the sea with her, so she and her husband lived grandly. The two often journeyed together under the sea, leaving their family in the care of servants. Neither parent ever told their children about the mermaid's secret, but the neighbors suspected. "Your mother is a fish!" they taunted the mermaid's children.

One day, the eldest son overheard as his father made plans to leave on a long trip with his wife. The son secretly followed his parents and saw them leap into the ocean and swim off, like two fish. The son was shocked to discover that his mother was a mermaid, and died soon afterward. At his funeral, a merman appeared from the sea and carried the coffin into the ocean.

A year later, the fisherman returned without his wife, and the next day he died. The mermaid appeared at his funeral, but she was so distraught by her husband's death that she returned forever to the sea. She gave her children great treasure so they were never wanting. But they missed their parents dearly and often sat on the seashore, hoping to see their mother again. She never came back, but sometimes they heard her singing to them, from far across the water.

HOARDING THE MAGIC: A WARNING

The tale starts out with a fisherman and a mermaid who fall in love and live an enchanted life together. Unlike what happens in The Magic Purse or The Elves and the Shoemaker, however, the fisherman keeps the magic. This is an apparent exception to the loss of magic in middle tales. The story, however, quickly reveals its unique insights—and its stark warning.

Notice how the fisherman's children suffer greatly. The sons and daughters are taunted about their mother being a fish, and neither parent addresses the issue. Worse, the husband and wife often leave their children at home, relying on servants to take care of them. Although this was (and still is) a common practice for the wealthy in many cultures, the story says that the parents were gone for a whole year on their last journey. This is an excessive length of time, even with nannies and tutors! By indulging themselves with long, magical adventures, the fisherman and his wife hoard their magic, and their children suffer for it. To dramatize this destructive effect, the eldest child dies when he discovers his mother is a mermaid. Neither parent thought to tell him about her secret, which might have prevented the mortal shock to the boy.

The story clearly depicts a dysfunctional family, where the parents are absorbed in themselves and do not nurture their children emotionally. Children in such families end up taking care of their parents, as Alice Miller has pointed out in *The Drama of the Gifted Child*. Such children fail to develop psychologically and, in extreme cases, die in spirit, as the fisherman's tale suggests.

The fisherman and the mermaid do not consciously injure their children, but they do neglect them. Perhaps the most telling indictment is that the parents do not attend the funeral of their eldest son. The story foreshadows this irresponsibility in a small detail. When the fisherman first meets the mermaid, she gives him a treasure and tells him to return early the next morning, but he arrives late, and misses her. This is unusual. Most people would be prompt after receiving a wonderful treasure. So the fisherman is careless about important tasks, first with his wife and later with his children.

The fisherman also suffers from his carelessness. He dies after he returns from his last sojourn in the sea, suggesting that hoarding the magic was destructive to him. Unable to relinquish the magic of youth, the fisherman does not move beyond the first third of life. He cannot or will not embrace maturity. And so, in the melodramatic language of fairy tales, he perishes.

Other stories repeat the warning.[1] Fortunately, most middle tales show men and women successfully giving up the magic of youth. These positive examples reveal something important: the magic of youth is not so much given *up* as it is given *away*. The Elves and the Shoemaker offers a good example. The elves vanish after the cobbler and his wife give them gifts. Husband and wife lose their magic when they shift from *receiving* gifts to *giving* them—and this is a good measure of when youth ends and maturity begins.

Modern psychology corroborates these fairy-tale insights. Erik Erikson was one of the first psychoanalysts to explore adult development and delineated eight psychological tasks that individuals must master over the life span. The fundamental issue for the middle of life, he felt, was developing *generativity*. This is a nurturing attitude directed first toward one's children, and then toward the whole next generation— toward one's students, protégés, and junior colleagues. Failing to develop generativity, Erikson warned, leads to misery and psychological stagnation in later life. The Fisherman and the Mermaid dramatizes this negative outcome with the deaths of the fisherman and his eldest son.

A large body of research confirms the importance of generativity at midlife. In youth, men and women normally focus on personal achievement and gratification, but in the middle years they shift toward humanitarian concerns and donate more time and money to charitable causes. Successful men and women also care deeply about helping younger people advance at work.[2] Both Else Frenkel, a Viennese psychologist, and Carl Jung independently observed that *I want* dominates youth, while *I must* governs maturity. Responsible generativity replaces personal gratification.

Generativity also takes the form of dedication to one's own work. Freud notes that love and work are basic to adult life, and that devotion to work can be as generative as love. Artists make great personal sacrifices to pursue their creative calling, scientists work long hours for the sake of knowledge, and good managers feel responsible for those who work under them. The Fisherman and the Mermaid explores this generativity of work by offering an insightful metaphor about creativity. The beautiful mermaid arising from the sea symbolizes a creative insight emerging from the unconscious.

These inspirations are usually exciting and enchanting, just like the mermaid.

After the creative moment, a new task arises—translating lofty visions into concrete achievements. The story symbolizes this process by having the fisherman and the mermaid marry and start a family. Raising children is analogous to making a creative inspiration a reality: writers must transform their intuitions into novels, and scientists must test their theories. Long labor and dedication are required. The fisherman and the mermaid fail in this task—they do not nurture their children and their eldest son perishes. Analogously, if an individual does not work out the details of an inspiration, the creative flash dies.

True generativity is more than devotion to work, raising children, or doing charitable works, because there are many subtle, secret ways of clinging to the magic of youth. The medieval tale of Tristan and Isolde dramatizes this point. Tristan was a knight in the service of his uncle, King Mark. At the king's request, Tristan arranged for the monarch to marry the beautiful princess Isolde, known as Isolde the Fair. Tristan accompanied Isolde on her journey to King Mark, but on the way they accidentally drank a love potion meant for the king and Isolde. The two youths fell in love and pursued a passionate love affair, even after Isolde's wedding to the king. When the monarch discovered their treason, Tristan and Isolde fled and lived like wild animals in the forest. Many years later, the king found them and forgave them and Tristan and Isolde repented. She returned to the king and took up her duties as queen, although her life felt empty and meaningless to her. Tristan left the country and met another Isolde, called Isolde of the White Hands because she was so skillful at sewing, weaving, and other everyday activities. Tristan and Isolde of the White Hands married, but he could not forget his love for Isolde the Fair. Tristan's marriage to the practical Isolde remained emotionally barren, a matter of external form, with no inner love or joy. Tristan attempted to renew his affair with Isolde the Fair, but his effort failed, and he died shortly thereafter.

- Magic comes to young Tristan and Isolde the Fair in the form of a love potion. They fall passionately in love and, despite the risk and wrong of it, refuse to give up the magic. Years later, Tristan and Isolde are given a second chance to surrender the magic, when the king discovers them in the forest and forgives them. By this time the magic potion has mostly worn off, and so Tristan and Isolde the Fair seem to adapt to the world, and assume generative roles. Isolde returns to King Mark, and Tristan marries Isolde of the White Hands. But internally the two ex-lovers have not changed at all. They still secretly long for each other, and refuse to give up their magic romance. Isolde the Fair finds her life empty, while Tristan dies.

The same drama—an inner refusal to give up the magic of youth—occurs in real life, with equally tragic results. The story of a young man, whom I shall call Paul, brought this point home to me several years ago. Articulate and intelligent, Paul came to therapy in his mid-twenties. He had many dreams for his future and a talent for dealing with people. He was active with several idealistic causes and prided himself on helping friends in need. Yet he had difficulty embarking upon a career, which prompted him to seek therapy. Paul had passed through a succession of jobs, all of which he began with great enthusiasm, only to give up some time later. Over the course of therapy, the reason became clearer. He secretly fancied himself the hero of a fairy-tale drama—wealthy, powerful, generous, and altruistic. Paul's dreams were not unusual, since they simply reflected the normal aspirations of youth. But he refused to modify his dreams to fit practical realities. The thought of starting at the bottom of a corporation and gradually working his way to the top was discouraging. And so he left jobs whenever his initial enthusiasm subsided and the need for continued work became evident.

Paul wrestled in therapy with his youthful visions, trying to reconcile them with reality. At the height of his efforts, Paul died tragically. He skidded off the road on a rainy day while riding his motorcycle. The tragedy profoundly moved and disturbed me. I sensed that Paul's death, although apparently an accident, was on some level a suicide. He had joked several times at the beginning of therapy about preferring to die rather than give up his noble dreams.

Paul's death saddened me, but I was also angered by it—by the loss of his talents and his proud refusal to apply them in the real world, a refusal that bordered on arrogance. At the same time, Paul's tragedy forced me to reflect on my own life. I realized then that I, too, harbored secret pride in the dark corners of my soul. Part of me clung to glorious dreams of youth and spurned the realities of the world, no less than Paul. And I think this is true of most people. Embracing the world and giving up magic may seem to be common sense, but this is evident only in retrospect, from the vantage point of the middle years. There are many secret ways to delay or avoid the sacrifice. Realism is an achievement that costs dearly, and for some, like Tristan or Paul, the ransom is life itself.

Many details of The Fisherman and the Mermaid are symbolic, but I will pursue only two more points. First, the story is unusual in dealing explicitly with children, because most middle tales usually focus only on a husband and wife. This is surprising, given the significance of family life in the middle years. However, most adults focus consciously on child rearing and do a reasonable job. Middle tales do not belabor the issue; instead, they concentrate on tasks that parents tend to overlook or postpone, namely their own development as individuals and as married couples. Middle tales portray the psychological tasks of the postparental years, after children have been launched in the world, when parents can reflect on their lives and take up their own personal calling.

The second intriguing detail is the number five. Notice

that the fisherman and the mermaid have five sets of twins. The number appeared earlier in The Magic Purse, where the husband and wife gather wood five times before receiving the magic purse. As it turns out, the number five appears regularly in middle tales. This surprised and dismayed me. Although I had read a bit about number symbolism, I was generally skeptical about the topic, particularly since numerology is associated with astrology, divination, and other fields of uncertain repute. But the number five is so prominent in middle tales that I could not ignore it.

Various scholars have extensively discussed the symbolism of three and four.[3] Three has connotations of conflict and competition, which are particularly well-illustrated in love triangles: two rivals vie for the affections of a third person, like Tristan, King Mark, and Isolde the Fair. Such competition is common in youth, and so the number three appears prominently in youth tales.

Four is associated mythologically with wholeness, completion, and totality, as Jung pointed out. There are four corners of the earth—north, south, east, and west—which constitute the totality of the world. In many traditions, there are also four basic elements—earth, air, fire, and water—that make up the universe. As I discussed in *In the Ever After,* the search for wholeness and integration is a central task for later life. Not surprisingly, the number four appears frequently in elder tales.

Five is specific to middle tales. The number has several symbolic connotations. If four symbolizes wholeness and completion, by extension five connotes *excess*. It is one step beyond four. Excess is clearly a theme in The Magic Purse and The Fisherman and the Mermaid. In the first story, the husband takes an excessive amount of money from the magic purse. In the second, the fisherman and the mermaid are excessively self-indulgent. These excesses all have to do with material concerns, which brings up a second meaning of the number five—its association with materialism. In the Hindu and Buddhist traditions, the number five is associated with the five senses, and thus with the sensual, material order. There are also five fingers on the hand, linking the number to grasping, holding, and counting things. (The abacus is based on the number five.) The two themes of excess and materialism are summarized in the pentagram, which has long been associated in Europe with witchcraft, and the pursuit of money, power, and sex through illicit means.[4] Given this background, the reason that five appears prominently in middle tales becomes a little clearer. Material concerns are major issues at midlife—the need to earn a living, and the desire for comfort—while excess indulgence is a major danger.

Taken together, stories like The Fisherman and the Mermaid and Tristan and Isolde provide a sober warning. The loss of magic may be saddening, but it is a necessary development, and refusing it leads to tragedy. Yet the loss is not so much an outright disappearance of magic as a *transfer*—from oneself to one's family, to the next generation and, ultimately, to society.

PART II

REVERSALS

Role Reversals

Stubborn Husband, Stubborn Wife
a Persian tale

nce upon a time, a husband had the habit of sitting out-side his home every day, while his wife cooked their meals, swept the floor, and washed their clothes. The two quarreled constantly. "Why do you sit there doing nothing?" the wife would ask.

"I am thinking deep thoughts," the husband would reply.

"As deep as a pig's tail is long!" the wife would retort.

One morning, the calf lowed hungrily in the barn. "Go and tend the calf," the wife told her husband. "It is man's work."

"No," the man declared, "it is for men to speak and women to obey."

"Real men work!" the wife replied sharply.

"I inherited a flock of sheep from my father," the husband countered, "and a shepherd tends them and gives us wool and cheese. I provide for you, so you must feed the calf."

"Provide? Only with misery!" the woman shot back. The two argued all that morning and all that afternoon. Then, in the evening, the husband and wife both had the same idea at the same time.

"Whoever speaks first," they said simultaneously, "will feed the calf from now on!" The two nodded in agreement, and said nothing more. They went to bed in silence.

The next morning, the wife awoke, lit the fire, cooked break-fast, swept the floor, and washed the clothes. Meanwhile, her husband sat on his bench, smoking his pipe. The wife knew that if she stayed home watching her husband do nothing all day, she would say something. So she put on her veil, and went to visit a friend. Her husband saw her leave, and wondered what she was up to.

A short time later, a beggar came by the house and asked the husband for food and money. The husband was about to reply, when he stopped himself. This is my wife's trick! he thought. "She is trying to make me talk." So the husband kept silent. The beggar thought the husband was a deaf-mute, and went into the house. No one was inside, but the cupboards were full of bread and cheese. So the beggar ate everything and left. The husband started to yell at the beggar, but he remembered his wager with his wife and kept silent.

A traveling barber passed by and asked the husband if he wanted his beard trimmed. The husband said nothing. This is another one of my wife's tricks! the stubborn man fumed. The barber thought he was dealing with a deaf-mute, but he wanted to be helpful, so he trimmed the husband's beard. Then the barber motioned for money. The husband did not move. The barber demanded money again, and became angry. "I will shave off your beard and cut your hair so you look like a woman!" the barber threatened. The husband refused to stir, so the barber shaved off the husband's beard, cut his hair, and left in a huff.

An old woman came up next, peddling cosmetics and secrets of beauty. Her eyesight was poor, and she mistook the husband for a young woman. "Dear lady!" the old woman exclaimed, "you must not sit in public without a veil!" Especially, the old woman added to herself, when you are so ugly! The husband said nothing, so the old woman assumed he was a deaf-mute. "You poor thing," she murmured, "ugly as sin, and deaf to boot!"

The old woman had an idea, and took out her cosmetics. She put a wig on the husband's head, rouge on his cheeks, and lipstick on his mouth. "There," she declared, "you look better!" Then she motioned for payment. The husband refused to move or speak, so the old woman reached into his pocket, took all his money, and left. The husband fumed silently: I will avenge myself on my wife!

A thief then approached. He thought it odd for a young woman to be sitting outside alone. But strange situations were often profitable for him, so he went up to the woman. "Dear lady," he said, "you should not be out alone. Have you no husband or brother to look after you?"

The husband almost laughed aloud. My wife will not give up her tricks! he said to himself. The thief assumed the husband was a deafmute, went into the house, which was filled full of costly carpets, vases, and clothes, and packed everything in a bag. He left with his loot and waved merrily to the husband.

I will punish my wife for her tricks, the man swore to himself. By then it was midmorning, and the calf in the barn was thirsty. It broke out of its stall, and ran through the village. The wife heard the commotion, and came out from her friend's house. She caught the calf and returned home. Then she saw the strange woman sitting on her husband's bench.

"Who are you?" she demanded, "and where is my husband? I am gone only a few hours and he has taken another wife!"

"Aha!" the husband sprang up. "You spoke first, so you must tend the calf from now on!"

The wife was incredulous. "You shaved off your beard and put on rouge just to trick me!" She stormed into the house and saw that everything was gone. "What happened?" she demanded of her husband. "Who has taken all our things?"

"The man you hired to act like a thief," the husband chortled. "But I did not fall for your deception!"

"I hired nobody!" the wife declared.

"You cannot fool me," the man boasted. "You lost the wager, and so you must tend the calf from now on."

"Foolish man!" the wife exclaimed. "You sat watching a thief steal everything from our house!"

"I knew it was only an act!" the husband gloated.

The wife could barely speak, she was so angry. "You lost your face and your fortune, and all you can think of is our wager!" She glared at her husband, and then said, "You are right, I shall tend the calf from now on. But that is because I am leaving and taking the calf with me. I will not stay with a stubborn fool like you!"

The woman walked to the village square with the calf and asked a group of children if they had seen a man go by carrying a large bag. The children pointed to the desert. In the distance they could see a man hurrying away, carrying a satchel on his back. The woman stared grimly after the thief, fastened her veil securely, picked up the calf's halter, and struck out into the desert. She caught up with the thief at an oasis. She sat across from the man, sighing and batting her eyelashes at him.

The thief was flattered by the wife's attention. "Where are you going all by yourself?" he asked her. "Have you no husband or brother to protect you?"

The wife fluttered her eyelashes at the thief and sighed. "If I did," the wife said sweetly, "would I be walking in the desert with only a calf for company?"

The two started talking and resumed their journey together. The wife kept sighing and glancing at the thief, and he soon asked her to marry him. She agreed, and so they planned to stop at the next village and have the chief marry them. By then evening had fallen, and the wife knew it was too late for a marriage ceremony. When they arrived at the village, the chief said as much, and invited them to stay with him for the night.

After everyone fell asleep, the wife arose and looked in the thief's bag. Sure enough, there were all her valuables—carpets, clothes, vases, and money! She loaded the bag on her calf and started to leave. Then she had an idea. She tiptoed into the kitchen, cooked some flour and water over a candle, and poured the dough into the thief's shoes and the shoes of the village chief. Finally she hurried into the desert with her calf.

When dawn came, the thief awoke and found his bride-to-be missing. He looked out a window and saw the woman hurrying away with his sack of loot. He rushed to put on his shoes, but found his feet would not fit in them. The dough in the shoes had hardened like a brick! The thief grabbed the shoes of the village chief, but they, too, were ruined. Finally, the thief ran out barefoot. The sun had risen by then, heating the desert sand, and his feet were soon blistered and burned. The thief was forced to halt.

For her part, the woman went back home, thinking about her husband. When she arrived at their house, she saw that her husband was not on his bench as usual. She ran inside and found the floor swept, the water drawn, the fire lit, and dinner cooking. But her husband was nowhere inside! She rushed into the courtyard, and there she found him, hanging laundry to dry.

"Stubborn husband," the wife exclaimed, "what are you doing?"

"I lost my face, my fortune, and my wife," the husband replied, "because I was a stubborn fool!"

The wife took the clothes from her husband, and said, "This is woman's work!" At that moment, the calf lowed, demanding water.

"I shall tend to the calf," the husband said.

"No," the wife retorted, "I shall do it." Then the two of them looked at each other and laughed. They came to an agreement, and from that day on, the husband took care of the calf and worked like any other husband, while the wife tended the house and never complained. In the evenings, when they finished their chores, they *both* sat down on the bench and watched the world go by.

ROLE REVERSALS

This amusing story introduces us to the next themes of middle tales. The drama starts off with a couple who have long since lost the magic and romance of youth. Their domestic life is no happy-ever-after, but a series of endless disputes.

Perhaps the most striking feature of the story is the fact that the husband and wife switch traditional masculine and feminine roles. The husband begins as a stereotypical patriarch, sitting on his bench outside the house while his wife toils inside. He insists that it is his prerogative to tell his wife what to do. Then the husband loses everything—his dignity, his property, and his authority. His beard is shaved off, his face powdered and rouged, and his wife finally leaves him. By the end of the tale, the husband looks like a woman and does housework. He shifts from a traditional masculine role to a stereotypical feminine one.

At the same time, the wife defies her husband, rejects her role as housekeeper, and leaves home, pursuing the thief. She outwits the ruffian and returns triumphantly with her household treasures. Her journey across the desert mirrors the usual quest of the young male hero in fairy tales. The wife throws off feminine stereotypes and adopts a traditional masculine role. This reversal is especially amazing because the story comes from a Moslem culture, a highly patriarchal tradition. Yet similar dramas appear in middle tales from around the world,[1] suggesting that switching gender roles is a major task for men and women at midlife.

This is surprising. By middle age, most individuals have a clear masculine or feminine identity. If any fairy tales challenge customary ideas about gender, we might expect tales of youth to do so, since adolescents commonly reject conventional values. Oddly, youth tales rarely question traditional masculine or feminine roles. The contrary holds. In Sleeping Beauty, Snow White, Rapunzel, and other youth tales, the young man plays the gallant hero, battles evil enemies, and rescues the beautiful princess. The young woman waits demurely for the hero and is typically a paragon of altruism, kindness, and passivity. These roles are traditional in patriarchal society: men focus on power, action, independence, and prestige, while women emphasize intimacy, nurture, relationships, and feeling.[2]

Why would middle tales reverse gender roles? Carl Jung offers an explanation.[3] One of the first psychologists to study adult development, Jung noted that at midlife men begin to struggle with traditionally feminine interests and needs. Middle-aged men put aside the masculine competition for power and status that motivated them in youth. They turn to relationships and feelings, which men usually reject in youth as too feminine.

Conversely, women reclaim their self-assertiveness, autonomy, and sense of adventure—stereotypical masculine traits. Women shed the submissive, self-effacing roles that most societies impose on girls from an early age. As Jung put it, the noon of life involves "the reversal of all the ideals and values that were cherished in the morning."[4]

Systematic research confirms this midlife role reversal. Young men typically make success at work their primary source of personal fulfillment, but at midlife their emphasis shifts to marital happiness and relationships with coworkers. These changes occur in both middle-class and blue-collar individuals, and among the intellectually gifted. Older men even begin to do more chores around the house, and become increasingly concerned about their appearance. Stubborn Husband, Stubborn Wife illustrates this point when the husband is covered with lipstick and makeup. Women, on the other hand, give up traditional homemaker roles to focus on personal achievements, starting new careers or completing educational degrees. They become less concerned with adornment and more with independence.[5]

The reversal of masculine and feminine roles can be seen in dreams. Heroic dramas typically dominate young men's dreams at night, but become increasingly rare from middle age on. The opposite happens for women, who dream more often of vigorous, heroic action after midlife.[6]

Anthropology provides further examples of midlife role reversals. Among Native American tribes, older Hopi and Ponro men frequently perform traditionally feminine tasks, which young men never do. Middle-aged men in China become less aggressive and more contemplative, while older Fijian men express their feelings with greater ease. Similar shifts can be seen among the Samburu, Kikuyu, Galla, and Kipsigis tribes of Africa, as well as the Comanche of America and the Groot Eylandt aborigines of Australia. Men in these cultures are aggressive warriors in youth, but then become cautious, conciliatory tribal counselors at midlife.

Women become more assertive and exercise greater public authority after menopause. This dramatic change in women's roles can be seen among the Amazon tribes of Brazil, the Bemba and Kaliai of Africa, the New Guinea Papuans, and the North American Chippewas, as well as in Hindu India and Confucian China. The LoDagaa of northwest Ghana even use a term for middle-aged women that translates literally into "have turned into men." Among Southwest American Indians, mature women are also called "manly hearted women" and acquire much of the authority of men (not that the older women want such "privileges"—some refuse them!).[7]

A Moroccan folktale offers a dramatic image for midlife role reversals. Every boy is born with a hundred devils, the story goes, and every girl with a hundred angels. As each year passes, the boy and girl exchange a devil and an angel. If they live to be one hundred, therefore, the man will have a hundred angels, and the woman a hundred devils![8]

Stubborn Husband, Stubborn Wife offers detailed insights about the process of role reversals. Although the husband starts off as a patriarch, he is soon humiliated and cast down. His face is painted and rouged like a woman's, and he loses all his property. His midlife encounter with the feminine is a calamity. The same theme appears in other middle tales. Role reversals are traumatic for men. One reason comes from basic masculine psychology. Young men normally repudiate and fear the feminine as part of their development. Boys usually abhor anything "sissy," and would rather die than associate with girls. As teenagers, young men fear being wimpish or effeminate and strive to be macho. Psychoanalysts have explained why this rejection of the feminine is essential to male development. Boys and girls normally develop close attachments to their mothers, but boys must break away from this bond if they are to develop a clear sense of male identity. The relationship with the mother is difficult to give up because it satisfies deep feelings of dependence and the need for intimacy. To make the break boys usually resort to an extreme measure: they reject not only their mothers, but the whole realm of dependency and intimacy, which they equate with the feminine and regard as something shameful.[9]

The masculine rejection of the feminine takes dramatic form in male initiation rites. Among aboriginal societies boys are taught men's secrets, which usually involve an abhorrence of women. The young men of New Guinea are told to avoid "contamination" from their wives during intercourse, while tribes in South America and Africa teach initiates secret misogynist myths. According to these legends men originally worked as slaves under women, until the men rebelled and took over. Since then, the myths say, men must keep women under control. The male repudiation of the feminine runs across cultures, and lies deep in the male psyche.[10] Reversing the pattern is understandably difficult at midlife.

The male shift from rejecting the feminine to honoring it is well illustrated by a man I shall call Mark. As a youth, Mark was artistic and loved drawing, painting, and sculpting. He abandoned these pursuits when he joined the army during the Korean War. Mark later became an F.B.I. agent and lived in a traditional masculine world. His wife tended the house and raised the children, while he earned a paycheck and watched football games on TV with his buddies. In his fifties, Mark's forgotten artistic interests resurfaced. He began taking painting classes at a nearby college, initially in secret, for fear of being ridiculed as effeminate by his fellow law-enforcement agents. Mark gradually became more open about his art, until he had a showing of his work in a local gallery. He successfully reversed his youthful repudiation of the feminine, which he associated with his artistic side.[11]

One of my own encounters with the inner feminine came up in an amusing way as I worked on this book. After I finished writing the first few drafts, I sensed that something was missing in the manuscript. The book seemed too intellectual, distant, dry, and lifeless. I wrestled with the issue, writing and rewriting more drafts, to no avail. Then it hit me. What was lacking was a personal element—descriptions of my own experiences, feelings, and thoughts about the middle years. These, after all, constitute "the real stuff" behind intellectual comments. I needed to rewrite the book from the heart—once more, with feeling. That meant exploring the traditionally feminine domain of emotions, personal reactions, and relationships. The insight broke the impasse in my writing, but I had to laugh at myself. It took me months to figure out what was wrong with my work, although the middle tales I was writing about constantly repeated the solution! I had only to listen to the stories and take them to heart.

My initial reaction to this suggestion, I must confess, was one of horror. Reveal my private experiences? In public? And make my work *feminine*—filled with personal anecdotes and feelings, like the many books I had read over the years that were written by women? (This was the voice of the unconscious, which usually says crude and embarrassing things.) I abhorred the specter of sentimental writing and much preferred the traditional, safe, masculine voice, always magisterial and authoritative, declaiming about objective facts, eternal truths, *deep thoughts*—like the stubborn husband's. So I tried various ruses to make the book come to life without having to reveal my personal experiences. One ploy I tried is particularly common for male writers. This is simply to describe case examples, emphasizing that they are about patients, colleagues, neighbors, friends—everybody except oneself. Of course, the examples are really autobiographical.[12] I tried this subterfuge, but an annoying inner voice kept saying the book was still not right. Finally, I started over. I went through the journals I had kept over the years and re-wrote this book, drawing on my personal experiences. (But my case examples are really about other people!) Fortunately, the annoying inner voice shut up. I satisfied the inner feminine—for the moment.

Stubborn Husband, Stubborn Wife has equally percep-tive insights about women's development at midlife. The wife voluntarily leaves home and starts out into the desert. She ac-tively seeks change, in contrast to her husband, who suffers it passively. The story reflects reality here. At midlife, it is fre-quently the wife who takes the lead, breaking out of familiar habits and developing rapidly. Her changes then force her hus-band to develop.

The wife's quest to catch the thief is a traditionally mas-culine, heroic venture. Yet she does not lose her feminine na-ture. She does not try to defeat the thief by force, which would be a stereotypical masculine strategy. Instead, she tricks him, using a uniquely feminine brand of wisdom. She entices the thief into a marriage proposal in order to steal her belongings back. Since the thief stole her property, she steals his heart! The wife does not rely on strength, but the power of persua-sion and relationship.

The wife's feminine wisdom is dramatized by a clever de-tail in the story—she makes dough and pours it into the thief's shoes. By preventing him from using shoes on the burning des-ert sands, she stops him from pursuing her. This detail under-scores an important point. Although the wife becomes adven-turous, independent, and assertive, she does not become a man. She simply becomes herself—a strong, resourceful woman.

The incident with the shoes also returns us to a theme from The Elves and the Shoemaker. In both middle tales, shoes represent grounding and pragmatism. They symbolize the importance of ordinary, everyday reality.

The wife apparently suffers no qualms or fears when she

leaves home and embarks on her heroic journey. In real life, women's reclamation of their masculine qualities is typically anxious and tentative at first. Women fear that they will alienate those close to them if they become assertive. This is a realistic fear. At work there are subtle, unconscious prejudices against outspoken women, and at home husbands often feel threatened when their wives assert themselves. Consciously or not, many husbands initially undermine their wives' development at midlife.

After outwitting the thief, the wife returns to her husband. This might seem odd. Why should she go back to her foolish, chauvinistic mate? Partly, the story reflects cultural realities. Because of patriarchal restrictions on women in Islamic society, it is difficult for them to live independently. Yet there is more here. The story implies that the wife *chooses* to return to her husband after thinking about the matter on the way home. She returns voluntarily, not by necessity, and in triumph, not resignation. From her new position of strength, she affirms her relationship to her husband. If the wife reclaims her aggressive, heroic, masculine side, she does not neglect her feminine strengths—attention to relationship, communion, and intimacy. The story reinforces this point in a small detail. Throughout her heroic journey, the wife keeps her calf with her. Because the calf needs care, it makes a good symbol for the wife's traditional feminine role as someone who nurtures others.

The wife's return is important for another reason. She discovers that her husband has changed his ways. His reformation is astonishing. In youth tales, odious characters—and the lazy, arrogant husband would qualify as one—are usually punished in cruel ways. In Cinderella, for instance, the stepsisters and the stepmother are haughty and lazy, just like the stubborn husband. And in the original Grimms' version, Cinderella's stepsisters and stepmothers are punished by having their eyes plucked out by doves. In middle tales, by contrast, proud, nasty, and otherwise unsavory characters see the error of their ways and reform. Without such self-reformation, middle tales would simply be tragedies, where imperfect human beings meet sad endings, and all-too-human foibles are summarily punished.

Fairy stories are deeply perceptive here. Youth tales sharply distinguish virtuous young heroes from villains. And young men and women really do see themselves as the good guys, the heroes and heroines, blaming other people for causing problems—usually parents, teachers, and bosses. In psychological terms, youths project their faults and difficulties onto others, and fairy tales reflect the process. This projection is adaptive. If young men and women dwelled on their own shortcomings, they might never take risks and make their way in the world. By blaming others, youth can defy the world and thus engage with life.

By midlife most individuals stop blaming external villains for problems. They accept their shortcomings more readily and change their ways. This willingness to reform is a major difference between those who age well and those who do not.[13]

If flexibility is a virtue at midlife, it is not necessarily so in youth. The young hero or heroine needs perseverance to succeed, rather than flexibility. In many youth tales, heroes and heroines search for a magic object, like a ring or cup. On the way, they are tempted by other magic treasures. If they are distracted, hero and heroine are destroyed. Such a single-minded sense of purpose is essential to young men and women making their way in the real world. But the resoluteness of youth easily becomes pigheadedness at midlife, so middle tales reverse course and emphasize flexibility.

Before leaving Stubborn Husband, Stubborn Wife, there are several details that deserve a closer look. The story begins with the wife complaining constantly about her husband. From a modern viewpoint, she has reason to grumble, but she is sharp-tongued and aggressive. She starts with a negative expression of assertiveness. Her masculine side emerges at first as nagging. Meanwhile, her husband is proud and refuses to work, expecting everything to be done for him. He starts off with an unsavory way of showing his feminine side. This is typical of the first phase of role reversals. Since the man's feminine side is unconscious and has been suppressed so long, it emerges first in distorted and unpleasant ways. The same applies to the woman's masculine side. After being repressed for so long, women's assertiveness initially takes distressing forms. At this stage, many women fear that they will become nasty or sadistic, and thus try to repress their assertiveness more. The reverse is usually the case. Liberating the assertiveness tames it, while repressing it makes it more troubling.

Stubborn Husband, Stubborn Wife is amusing, a farce sure to elicit laughter from most people. As other stories will demonstrate, humor plays a prominent role in middle tales, but is much less common in youth stories. The latter are more likely to take an exalted, inspirational, or moralistic tone, in line with the divine inspirations of youth.

Unlike most fairy tales, Stubborn Husband, Stubborn Wife lacks any magic. There are no elves, enchanted purses, or mermaids. This confirms the importance of the loss of magic. Even more significantly, there is no need for wizardry. The protagonists of youth tales typically require supernatural help to solve their problems. In middle tales, human wisdom suffices. And learning such wisdom is one of the main challenges of midlife. On a deeper level, magic assumes a different form in adulthood. Middle tales do not portray enchanted rings that change people into animals or transform huts into palaces. The stories focus on a more mysterious magic—the transformation of the human heart.

The people who approach the husband include a beggar, a barber, an old woman, and a thief. Their occupations are telling. Husbands and wives eventually beg, bluster, bargain, and steal from each other. Moreover, the husband remains silent when the four people approach him, but he speaks when the fifth person appears—his wife. This brings up the symbolism of the number five again. And the number in this tale, as in previous stories, conveys implications of excess—particularly the husband's excessive stubbornness.

Stubborn Husband, Stubborn Wife offers an amusing overview of the different paths that men and women take at midlife. The next two chapters take a closer look at those journeys.

Women's Emancipation at Midlife

The Wife Who Became King
a tale from the Uighar culture in China

Long ago, there lived a beautiful, clever young woman. Her family was very poor, but she was cheerful and worked very hard, embroidering clothes for sale. She fell in love with a young man who lived in her village. Like her, he was very poor, but he was a good man, so the two married. They lived in a tiny hut, and were happy together.

One day, the King's ministers bought a cloth the wife had sewn. The minister gave it to the King, and the King was astonished at its beauty. "The woman who made this must be even more lovely," the King exclaimed.

"Aye," the minister replied, because he had seen the wife.

"Well, then," the King declared, "I want to marry her." The King already had many wives, but he sent his minister to bring the beautiful woman to the palace.

When the minister told the wife about the King's proposal, she replied, "How can I marry the King? I am married already."

"Then leave your husband!" the minister said.

"No," the wife replied, "I love my husband and I am happy with him." The minister was shocked. No woman had ever refused the King.

When the King heard about the rejection, the monarch was furious. "I am King. I will make her one of my wives, sooner or later!" he vowed.

One day the beautiful woman turned to her husband. "I have an idea that will make us rich," she said. "Buy some silk, and I will sew a bedspread that we can sell for a good sum."

The husband bought the thread, and his wife worked day after day. When she finished the quilt, it was so beautiful it shone like the sun and the moon. "Take this cloth," the wife told her husband, "and sell it for twenty silver coins. Go to any street to find a buyer, but do not go into the forty-first street."

The husband took the bedspread to the city, and immediately a crowd gathered round. No one had ever seen anything so beautiful. But no one could afford the price, either. The husband was loath to return home without selling the quilt, because his wife had worked so hard on it. So he forgot her warning and stepped into the forty-first street, looking for a buyer. The homes were magnificent, and the husband realized that the street led to the King's palace.

At that moment, the King appeared with his retinue. "Who are you?" the King asked the husband. "Don't you know no one may come here without my permission?"

The husband apologized, and started to leave, but the King saw the bedspread. "Show me what you have," the King commanded, and when the husband opened the cloth, the King was amazed. Nothing in his palace was as beautiful. But the King also recognized the style of the work. "It is from the woman who refused to marry me!" the King muttered to himself.

"I want the bedspread," the King declared, taking the cloth. Then the King told the husband, "Tomorrow I am going hunting, and I will stop at your house for a rest. Have your wife prepare for my visit."

The husband knew there would be trouble. When he returned home, his wife asked what was wrong, and he explained the problem.

His wife consoled him. "Don't worry," she said. "I will hide tomorrow when the King comes, and he will soon give up and leave."

The next day, the King arrived at their home, eager to meet the beautiful woman. When he did not find her waiting for him, he grew angry.

"My wife had to visit some relatives," the husband explained lamely.

The King was cunning, so he figured the wife must be hiding somewhere in the house. "Never mind her," the King said, and he plied the husband with wine. The King's wine was extraordinarily strong, and the husband soon fell asleep. The monarch and his men searched the house and found the wife.

"Marry me," the King commanded her.

"I cannot," she said. "I am married already."

The King ordered his men to tie her up, throw her on a horse, and take her back to his palace.

"Wait," the woman said. "If you insist that I marry you, you must do me a favor."

"Anything you desire," the King replied, hoping she had changed her mind.

"Among my people," the woman explained, "when a wife leaves her husband, she puts out cakes by the roadside as offerings for the spirits. Otherwise, something bad will happen."

"That's fine," the King replied, and ordered his ministers to buy cakes. The wife put some in the house, and then departed with the King. But she had the monarch stop periodically, so she could set out more cakes by the roadside. And each time she left one behind, she made a secret mark on the pastry, which her husband would understand.

When the King arrived at the palace, he told the wife, "Let us be married now."

"No," the woman declared, "if we are to marry, it must be done properly. You must prepare a wedding feast, and I must sew a wedding gown." Then the woman looked at the King and smiled enticingly. The King trembled with eagerness and hastened to order the preparations.

Meanwhile, back at home, the husband awoke. He found his wife missing and saw the cakes she had set out. So he followed the trail straight to the palace. "The King has kidnapped my wife!" the man exclaimed. "I must rescue her." But the palace was guarded night and day, and the husband could not enter. He paced beneath the walls for several days, until an old woman came up and asked what troubled him.

The man explained his problem, and the old woman thought a moment. Then she said, "Buy mirrors, combs, threads, needles, lipstick, and rouge." She nodded knowingly. "Then go to the palace saying you are selling things for women. Your wife will come out and you can talk with her."

A few days later, when the King went out hunting, the husband called on the palace, saying he was selling women's wares. The wife recognized her husband's voice, and met him at the palace gate. The two were overjoyed to see each other, but they dared not embrace. Instead, the wife took out two silver coins and gave them to her husband, whispering, "Use these to buy two horses at the market tomorrow. Then in three days, meet me here at midnight. We shall escape together."

When the King returned from his hunt, the beautiful woman scowled at him. "What is wrong?" the King asked. "Are you not happy?"

"No," she pouted. "I sit alone in this palace and have no authority. Nobody obeys me here."

The King smiled. "That is easily remedied." He took out all the keys to the palace and gave them to her. "Now you are in charge."

The wife sighed and gave the King a look that made him shiver with desire. "When will we be married?" the King asked.

"Three days," she replied, "and you will wait no more."

The next day, the wife unlocked the stables, chose the two best horses, and told a servant to take them to the market. "Sell them only to a man with two silver coins," she said. The servant obeyed and the husband bought the two horses at the market.

Three days later, when night fell, the husband went to the palace with the horses and waited for his wife. He had not slept for several days, worrying about their escape. As the night wore on, he became tired and fell asleep.

A bald-headed man walked by. He was a murderer by trade, and he thought it odd that a man would be sleeping with two horses next to the palace. In the next moment, two bags fell from a window and a woman climbed down. The brigand recognized her as the King's bride-to-be.

"Quickly," the wife whispered, "load the bags on the horses, and let's be off." She was in such a rush, she did not look at the brigand.

"This is my chance," the bald felon told himself. So without saying anything, he rode off behind the beautiful woman.

After a long while, the woman paused for a rest. Then she saw who had been riding behind her! She recognized him as a murderer. "Oh what have I done?" the woman thought to herself. She said nothing aloud, went on riding, and by dawn she had come up with a plan. "I mistook you for my husband," she told the bald villain. "But that does not matter to me. As long as I escape from the evil King, any man is good enough for me. We can marry if you like, but only if we do something about your bald head. You are too ugly as you are now. Fortunately, I know a cure for baldness."

The brigand was overjoyed. Marry the beautiful woman? And regain his hair? The woman explained that in her village, bald people used hot oil to make their hair grow again. So the brigand heated a vat of oil. When it was boiling hot, he turned to the woman. "What do I do with the oil?"

"This!" the wife exclaimed, pushing the murderer into the pot. He died in an instant, and the wife rode on alone. She soon came upon four hunters. They saw how beautiful she was and seized her. "I will marry her," each hunter declared. Then they argued over who saw her first.

"I'll tell you who will marry me," the wife declared. "I will shoot four arrows in four directions. The one who retrieves an arrow first will marry me." The men eagerly agreed, and the woman shot the arrows into the distance. When the men ran off to fetch them, the woman escaped.

The wife rode on until she came to four gamblers. They also saw how beautiful she was, and seized her. Then they argued over who would marry her. "I'll tell you who can marry me," the woman offered. "The one who can drink the most wine without falling asleep will be my husband." The gamblers readily agreed to the contest, and the woman took out a bottle of the King's wine. The gamblers started drinking, but they were not accustomed to such strong wine. They all fell asleep and the wife promptly rode away.

"It is not safe for a woman to travel alone," the wife muttered to herself. So she stopped, opened one of her bags, and put on a man's outfit. Then she continued her journey to the next city.

When she arrived, everyone was staring at the sky and running to and fro, with great excitement. The woman asked what was going on, and the people explained that their king had just died. So they were choosing a new monarch, according to an ancient custom. The Bird of Happiness had been released from the palace, and when the sacred bird landed upon a man, that man would become the next king.

"How odd," the wife thought, and she stopped to watch the ceremony. The Bird of Happiness flew over the city, and all the men held their breath, hoping the bird would choose him to be king. Finally the Bird of Happiness landed—right on the wife's shoulder! Because she was dressed like a man, the city immediately acclaimed her king. Before should could say anything, the people put the crown on her head.

The wife quickly learned how to be a king. She was fair and wise, and soon all the people loved their new monarch. Only one thing troubled them: their king was alone. They wanted the King to be happy, so everyone encouraged "him" to find a bride and marry. But the King always put the question aside. In private, she pined for her husband.

One day, a minister came to the King, and told her that four hunters asked for an audience. "The hunters say they are searching for a women who promised to marry one of them, but then ran away," the minister explained. "They want to know if she might have come here."

The King smiled. "Put them in prison until we find this lady." The minister thought the command was odd, but he obeyed, since the King was so wise in every other matter.

A few days later, the minister approached the King again. "Four gamblers have come for your aid. They say that a beautiful lady agreed to marry one of them, but then she ran off. They want to know if she might have come here."

"We must find this lady," the King replied. "But until then, put the four men in prison."

Several days afterward, the evil king arrived in the country—the very man who had kidnapped the wife. "A beautiful woman promised to marry me, but then ran off," the tyrant explained to the wife who was king. "I heard she came to your country, and I ask your help in finding her."

The wife turned to her minister. "Put this man in prison until we find this lady." The minister was horrified. Throw a neighboring monarch into prison? But he figured his king must have reasons, and so the minister obeyed.

A few days later, the minister approached the wife. "A lone man has come calling," the minister explained, "and says he is looking for his wife. Does he go to prison, too?"

"No," the King replied, "bring him to me." When the man appeared, she recognized him at once. It was her husband. Because she was dressed like a monarch, the husband did not recognize her. So the King sent away all her ministers and talked to the man privately.

"You are looking for your wife," the King said. "But how will you know her? Does she have any marks on her body?"

"Yes," the man replied. "She has a small black spot on her breast."

The King opened her shirt. "Is it like this?"

"Goodness, it is you!" the husband cried out with joy. His wife quieted him.

"I cannot reveal my identity, but I know how we can be together. Tomorrow," she went on, "you must wear women's clothing and eat lunch at such-and-such café." She told him where the place was and explained her plan.

The next day, when the King went riding in the city with all her ministers, she suddenly stopped in front of a restaurant. Her husband was there, dressed as a lady. "That is the person I want to marry," the King exclaimed. She sent her ministers to arrange the matter, and soon the wedding was celebrated.

The King and her husband lived happily in the palace. She taught him all she had learned about being a king. And then one day she turned and said to him, "We cannot keep up this pretense. I will tell my story to the people." So she gathered all the citizens together, and told them her tale—how she was kidnapped by the evil tyrant, and then pursued by the murderer, the hunters, and the gamblers, until she finally became king of their country. When the wife finished her story, she ordered the hunters and gamblers released from prison. "Their time in jail is sufficient punishment," she declared. But the evil tyrant she refused to release. "He is a menace to his people," she declared, and her people roared their approval.

The citizens of the country were moved by the wife's great suffering, courage, and justice. They consulted among themselves and came to a decision. "You ruled us wisely as king," they told the wife, "and we want you to stay and govern us as queen." So they acclaimed the wife queen, and made her husband king to help her rule the country. And the two reigned over the great land in peace, wisdom, and happiness for the rest of their days.

OPPRESSION AND LIBERATION

This story is extraordinarily rich, so I will take the tale a step at a time. The drama starts with a man and woman who fall in love and marry. Instead of living happily ever after, the wife is kidnapped by an evil king. This calamity is due to small lapses by both the husband and wife, like those that occur in The Magic Purse. Because she wants money, the beautiful wife makes a quilt so beautiful that it draws the King's unwanted attention to her. The husband compounds the problem when he ignores his wife's warning about the forty-first street, shows the evil king the bedspread, and reminds the tyrant about his beautiful wife. Husband and wife lose each other and the magic of youth because of small human failings.

The wife suffers much more than the loss of magic. She is abducted, imprisoned in the palace, and pressured into becoming one of the King's many concubines. She loses her freedom and is threatened with losing her identity as well. Later, when she manages to escape the King, she falls into the hands of a murderer, hunters, and gamblers. They insist on marrying her, against her wishes. The wife is oppressed on all sides.

The oppression of women is clearly portrayed in middle tales around the world. Indeed, the wife's story is mild. Other middle tales equate marriage with exile, imprisonment, oppression, or even death for the women. (For men in youth tales, marriage usually means triumph, happiness, power, and honor.) In the French story Bluebeard (which has variations around the world), the villainous Bluebeard marries young women, murders them, and piles their bodies in a closet. The same thing happens in the main story of The Thousand and One Arabian Nights, where a deranged king marries a new wife each day and then kills her the next morning. Similarly, in Greek myth, Persephone was abducted, raped, and then forced to marry Hades. Other mythic marriages begin more auspiciously, but also end tragically for the woman. Princess Ariadne rescued Theseus from the monstrous Minotaur and married him. In gratitude, Theseus took her with him on his ship, only to abandon her later on an island.

In highlighting women's oppression, middle tales are deeply feminist. This is particularly compelling since the stories come from patriarchal cultures. I am not overemphasizing feminism, or reinterpreting old tales in the light of new social and political theories. Women's oppression is as evident in tales published long ago as in newer ones.

The oppression of women depicted in middle tales reflects grim realities across most cultures. Virtually every known society puts women at a disadvantage in some way, especially after marriage.[1] In modern America, married women are more dissatisfied than single women, while the reverse holds for men. And single women live longer than married women: marriage is rewarding for men, but stressful and even unhealthy for women. In highly patriarchal cultures, like that of Mexico, single women enjoy some degree of freedom and autonomy, but lose it when they marry. Not surprisingly, many newly wed women unconsciously associate marriage with death and think of death more often than middle-aged or older adults. (Newly wed men think of death the least!) And newly wed women express despair and entertain suicidal fantasies more often than do older individuals.

Women's dreams also reflect oppression. More commonly than men, women dream of being attacked, robbed, or victimized in some way, and the assailants are almost invariably men. Annis Pratt found the same theme in literary works written by women.[2] In her book *Archetypal Patterns in Women's Fiction,* Pratt analyzed the work of British and American women writers in the last few centuries and found that they repeatedly portray marriage as humiliation, imprisonment, or torture for the wife. The dramas typically end in tragedy. Women protagonists go insane or die, or if they rebel and escape an unjust situation, they must live alone, apart from society. As Pratt notes, women writers could not imagine happy endings, given the cultural realities they lived in.

This is where middle tales like The Wife Who Became King offer priceless insight and encouragement. They depict women who *are* successful in liberating themselves and who find a place in a new world. The stories are utopian in the best sense: they remind us of what individuals and society can be, rather than what usually happens.

When the wife is kidnapped by the King, she does not give up. She invents a story about offering cakes for the spirits and leaves clues for her husband to follow. Imprisoned in the palace, she later manages to stall the King in his plans to marry her. She does not outright refuse the King, which would presumably be dangerous since he could resort to force. Instead, she leads him to think she will marry him gladly and maneuvers the King into giving her the keys to the palace. The wife's cunning echoes that of the woman in Stubborn Husband, Stubborn Wife. In the Persian story, the wife sighed and batted her eyelashes at the thief in order to trick him. While many fairy stories portray female wiles as something negative, middle tales laud women's cleverness. In fact, women have no alternative but to be cunning if they are to defend their identity and integrity in patriarchal society.

In the story, an old woman advises the husband on how to make contact with his wife, repeating the theme of feminine cleverness. The husband manages to talk to his wife, and she comes up with a plan of escape. Significantly enough, the wife orchestrates everything. Unlike Cinderella and other heroines of youth tales, who sit around and wait for a man to rescue them, the wife takes an active role here. Unfortunately, the husband falls asleep at the appointed time and foils his wife's plan. This is the husband's second lapse in the story. (The first was his wandering into the forty-first street.) The husband's failure is understandable. He worried himself to exhaustion about his wife and fell asleep. The lapse is poignant, because it reverses the theme of Sleeping Beauty. Here the man sleeps, not the woman! Throughout the drama, the husband plays a passive role, which dramatically contrasts with the activity and cunning of his wife. This underscores the role reversals of midlife, so prominent in Stubborn Husband, Stubborn Wife.

In her haste, the wife rides off with the bald-headed murderer. Here the wife makes a mistake, so the story remains evenhanded. Both husband and wife err. (Notice that his lapse is passive, namely sleeping, while hers is overactive, rushing ahead. This is one more example of role reversals.) The wife recognizes her danger and escapes the murderer by pushing him into a vat of boiling oil. The original version of the story carefully emphasizes that the brigand had murdered many men before, and so he deserved to die himself. But in killing him, the wife becomes a murderer herself. She is not punished in any way, and is later rewarded when she becomes king of a great country. The story thus implies that killing the brigand was necessary and even desirable. Other middle tales reiterate this point:[3] women often must kill their oppressors to escape.

Women do not really become murderers at midlife. But the motif dramatizes a major issue women struggle with in the middle years—aggressiveness. In youth, women are taught to suppress their assertiveness, ignore their own needs, and nurture other people. This is the psychological equivalent of binding women's feet. Most women end up feeling guilty about being assertive, even in self-defense. Several women brought this point home to me when they described their experiences in learning self-defense techniques. They discovered that they instinctively and unconsciously pulled their punches, holding back from using their full strength, even when their practice partners were safely padded. Taken to an extreme, this reluctance to injure other people traps women in abusive relationships. Wives of alcoholic men frequently say they cannot leave their husbands because that would destroy the men. The Wife Who Became King rejects such self-sacrificing behavior. To make sure we get the message, the tale has the wife kill the brigand.

The wife next falls into the hands of robbers and gamblers. Like the evil king, they treat her as a sex object and try to force her to marry one of them. The wife, however, outwits them. The story is particularly charming here, because the wife beats the men at their own games. She tells the hunters to retrieve an arrow and since hunters routinely use arrows, they probably thought they would have no problem with the task, or that the woman could not shoot very far. Similarly, the wife tells the gamblers that whoever drinks the most will marry her. Because gamblers usually drink, they probably assumed the drinking contest would be child's play.

After escaping the hunters and gamblers, the wife puts on

men's clothes to disguise herself. The act is symbolic in two ways. First, it reinforces the theme of women's oppression. Women are always vulnerable to attack. Second, aggressiveness, autonomy, and heroic journeys are usually considered masculine in most societies. As part of her midlife development, the wife reclaims these virtues in herself. Symbolically, she dons men's clothes. Other middle tales reiterate the theme, and portray women wearing male clothes as they embark upon heroic journeys.[4]

Today, middle-aged women resume careers or start new ones, particularly after launching their children into the world. And despite multiple obstacles put up by society, many women succeed admirably. This is not simply a result of modern feminism; the process is archetypal. In the Victorian era, many women made names for themselves after midlife. Typically these wives took over the family business after their husbands died, and then built larger and more profitable enterprises. In Africa and Asia, similarly, middle-aged women are freed from the social and sexual taboos that restrict young wives to the home; they travel freely and run the major trading networks. In Malaysia, this midlife liberation has an amusing spin-off. Finally able to travel where they wish, middle-aged women have become the principal smugglers! Women also take political roles in midlife. In New Zealand, middle-aged Maori women recently led a revival of native spiritual traditions, which sparked a general renaissance of Maori culture. This reclamation of power occurs even in highly patriarchal cultures, like that of China. Although women have few rights and less opportunities there, they exercise increasing authority in their extended families after midlife, and their husbands often become figureheads.[5]

These precedents should not be taken to mean that women must wait until midlife before becoming assertive and exercising their strengths. The examples show that even when obstructed by patriarchal traditions, women still develop their native talents and strengths. In more favorable situations, women regain their personal resources much earlier, or never hide them in the first place.

In the story, the wife becomes king of a great country, symbolically reclaiming her authority and independence. Similar dramas come from around the world, emphasizing the archetypal nature of the theme.[6] The wife also becomes king through an odd procedure: the Bird of Happiness alights on her and chooses her to be king. Like strange details in dreams, odd events in fairy tales are often symbolic. Here, some knowledge of the story's cultural context is helpful. The story comes from the Uighar people, who are not ethnically Chinese but who have long been part of the Chinese Empire. In the latter, the emperor rules by the mandate of Heaven and is chosen by the gods. This official doctrine was spread throughout the Chinese Empire to legitimize government authority and so presumably was familiar to the Uighars. In the tale, the Bird of Happiness acts as a divine agent, choosing the next monarch. The bird thus bestows the mandate of heaven on the new sovereign. This divine approval is unusual because patriarchal traditions usually portray strong women as witches and attribute their power to demonic sources. In youth tales independent, strong-willed girls are usually punished. The present story and other middle tales decisively reject this patriarchal bias.

There are deeper meanings to the wife's divine election. Jungian psychology offers one interpretation, related to the notion of the Self. The Self in Jungian thought is the center of an individual's being, conscious and unconscious. The Self is thus distinct from the ego, which is the center only of conscious life. The Self is also distinct from the social roles an individual plays—for example, being a mother or a business executive. The Self thus represents the individual's truest nature. Jung noted that the Self is typically symbolized in dreams by divine or magical figures, like the Bird of Happiness. The divine bird symbolizes the wife's true Self—her deepest being.

Despite external oppression, she remains true to herself and defends her integrity. So a symbol of her inner Self emerges.

The connection to the inner Self is vital. Many women unconsciously fear that they will become overly aggressive if they assert themselves. But the connection to the true Self prevents such excess. When the wife becomes king, she does not go mad with power. She acts from her own center and proves to be fair and just.

The Bird of Happiness is symbolic in another way. When the wife becomes king, she learns about the heights of power and glory. Metaphorically, she flies. Flying, however, is usually associated with men—as are royal power and glory. Not surprisingly, women in real life often feel that they do not know how to fly, or dare not do so. They fear the heights. This changes as women reclaim their authority, and flying images become more prominent in the dreams and fantasies of middle-aged women.

Ann Mankowitz, a Jungian analyst, reports a dramatic example in *Change of Life,* with the case of Rachel, a fifty-one-year-old woman. After struggling with many issues in therapy, a particularly inspiring image came to Rachel. This involved a phoenix rising out of a fire, flying to Rachel, laying a golden egg, and then teaching Rachel how to fly. Initially afraid of the bird, Rachel soon began imitating the phoenix, flapping her arms like wings. She slowly ascended into the sky. At the time of this image, Rachel began reclaiming her own authority and independence in real life, breaking out of traditional feminine roles. She learned to fly psychologically and exercise her power, just like the wife who became king.

To return to our tale: the hunters, the gamblers, and the evil tyrant come to the wife for help after she becomes king. She throws all of them into prison, but eventually releases the hunters and the gamblers. The point may seem small, but it is significant. The wife does not act simply out of personal vengeance and anger. She maintains a sense of justice and fits the punishment to the crimes. Again, she acts from her inner center.

At the end of the tale, the wife is reunited with her husband. The way in which she engineers this is worthy of note. She tells her husband to dress like a woman, so she can marry him. The story echoes Stubborn Husband, Stubborn Wife, where the husband was rouged and powdered like a woman, and both tales focus on midlife role reversals. The wife eventually reveals her identity to the people, and her husband becomes king and rules with her. This ending may seem unsatisfactory, since the husband has done little to deserve being king, except being married to his wife. The unsettling note here is reminiscent of the conclusion to Stubborn Husband, Stubborn Wife, where the heroic wife returns to her obstinate husband. But the wife who became king does not lose anything. She gains much, because she now has public and private happiness. She rules a great country, lives with the man she loves, and no longer has to pretend to be somebody she is not. Indeed, she establishes a new order. Up to this point in the story, the only rulers mentioned have been kings, and this reflects patriarchal society, where only men can wield power. The wife changes that as a sovereign queen. On the other hand, the wife who is now queen does not subjugate her husband. She raises him up, and makes him her equal, as co-ruler. So she does not replace patriarchal rule with matriarchal government. She institutes a new, egalitarian system.

The story ends with the reconciliation of the masculine and the feminine. The wife overthrows social oppression and reclaims her masculine powers. But she ultimately remains true to her identity as a woman and relates to her husband with fairness, equality, and love. This theme also appeared in Stubborn Husband, Stubborn Wife, where the wife and husband come to a more equal, loving relationship.

Although The Wife Who Became King is optimistic and has a happy ending, it is not merely the stuff of fantasy. I have had the privilege of witnessing the same drama while working with women in therapy. For women raised in today's relatively more feminist climate, the process often begins earlier than midlife. Kate, for instance, came to therapy in her late twenties, as a graduate student. Married to a man she felt little affection for, but of whom her parents approved, Kate felt depressed and unsure of her direction in life. The reasons soon became evident. As a child, whenever she had pursued an interest of her own, Kate was scolded for being selfish or willful. She was told directly and indirectly that she should take care of other people, rather than herself. This is the stereotype of feminine altruism, which was forced on Kate. As a result, Kate wilted spiritually and hibernated, like Sleeping Beauty.

In therapy Kate gradually woke up. At first hesitantly, and then with greater certainty, she began insisting on what she wanted, instead of deferring to her husband's and parents' wishes. "I *do* know what I want!" she exclaimed one day. "It's just that I never said it to myself!" As Kate reclaimed her autonomy, her research work flowered. She came up with highly creative and original ideas, and her work soon attracted the attention of prominent scholars in her field. She was invited to numerous conferences to present her research, and for the first time she enjoyed the attention and felt it was well deserved. Psychologically, she reclaimed her true Self and experienced a burst of creative energy. Like the woman who became king, Kate found her rightful place in the world. She also remained with her husband, who was fortunately able to encourage her independence. Middle tales are not fantasy, but the truest magic possible—the drama of hope and transformation, drawn from the depths of the psyche.

There are an unusually large number of characters in the story of the wife who became king. Besides the wife and husband, there are the evil tyrant, the murderer, the hunters, and the gamblers. The latter all play the role of villains, but they also force the wife to develop. To escape them, the wife rides onward, until she finally comes to the country with the Bird of Happiness and becomes king. If she had not been kidnapped by the petty tyrant, or attacked by the hunters and gamblers, she might have stayed home all her life, comfortably ensconced in a traditional role. Although frightening and threatening at first, the male villains ultimately help the wife individuate. The men represent the essential enemy. The same theme appears in other middle tales,[7] and crops up frequently in real life. Many women reclaim their power only when they are forced to leave a neglectful or abusive spouse. Finally abandoning the hope that a man can fulfill their needs, women strike out on their own and discover dormant strengths and talents.

Sometimes the essential enemy takes the form of inner figures, appearing in dreams and fantasies. Jung called these mysterious, fascinating males *animus* figures. (The term *animus* is the masculine form of the Latin word for "soul.") He argued that the animus symbolized a woman's masculine side—her assertiveness, independence, and forcefulness. Jung suggested that the animus usually plays the role of a helpful, spiritual guide for women, leading them on a voyage of self-discovery. Middle tales do not reflect this positive view of the animus. In The Wife Who Became King, the evil tyrant, the bald brigand, the hunters, and the gamblers all represent animus figures, but they are frightening. Case reports indicate that the animus usually appears first as a villainous, intimidating character.[8] Annis Pratt found the same pattern in her study of women's literature, and Estella Lauter confirmed the theme in her examination of paintings by women. Male characters, or animus figures, are usually hostile to female protagonists.

Dangerous animus figures reflect the realities of patriarchal cultures, where men often attack women—as rapists, abusive spouses, or bosses who favor men over women. Because of social pressures, women are also taught to fear being assertive. Since the animus symbolizes assertiveness, he appears threatening at first.

The Wife Who Became King specifically says that there were four hunters, and then later four gamblers. In each encounter, the wife constituted the fifth person. At the end of the story, the wife must also deal with four male factions—the evil king, the hunters, the gamblers, and her husband. Again, she is the fifth person. This brings up the number five again. The present story reiterates the connotations of excess that we discussed earlier. The hunters and gamblers are excessively lustful toward the wife, as is the evil king.

Chinese tradition adds to the symbolism of the number five. In Chinese mythology, like many others, there are four basic directions in the world: north, south, east, west. Chinese folklore also distinguishes a fifth element, the center point, which unites all four corners of the earth. This fifth element was associated with the emperor, who represented the center of the universe. Five thus symbolizes an integrating focus, and the same meaning appears in other traditions. In ancient Babylonia five was the symbol of the ziggurat tower, which stood in the middle of the four earthly directions and represented a fifth one, linking heaven and earth. In Buddhism, the heart is thought to have four directions, with the fifth as its center—the quiet, still point. In many cosmologies five also symbolizes the creative force, from which all else derives, including the four cardinal points and the four fundamental elements. And in Navajo folklore there are usually four brothers who are great warriors with a fifth brother playing the role of medicine man, and acting as the agent of change; he represents a center of power for the other four.[9]

The same symbolism emerges in this chapter's tale. The wife becomes a monarch and the center of her new realm. Four factions come to her for help—the evil king, the hunters, the gamblers, and her husband. She represents the fifth element, tying them all together. In psychological terms, when the wife becomes king, she reaches the center of her being and integrates the different aspects of her life. She makes contact with the inner Self.

The story also links the themes of excess and integration associated with the number five. The tyrant's unbounded desire for the wife starts the drama; the husband's excessive laxity in wandering into the forty-first street leads to his wife's kidnapping;[10] the wife's unwise haste in riding away from the palace lands her in further difficulty; and the abusive demands of the hunters and the gamblers force the wife into her new country. Ultimately, these excesses prompt the wife to reclaim her strength, autonomy, and individuality. Paradoxically, excess leads to integration and individuation. The number five thus sums up a major task of midlife—transforming imbalance and error into harmony and identity.

SIX

Crossing Paths

The Lute Player
from Russia

nce upon a time, a king and queen lived happily together. One day, the King felt restless, and decided to
wage war on a heathen lord, infamous for cruelty and
evil. The King gathered a great army, took leave from
his wife, and set sail. When the King landed in the foreign realm, his
troops conquered all they saw. The King exulted, but the heathen
ruler massed his troops elsewhere, and in a few days they rushed forward. A ferocious battle ensued. The King's men were routed, and
the King himself was captured and thrown into a dungeon.

From that day on, the King was driven out every morning with
the other prisoners, and forced to plough the fields like an ox. Every
night, the King returned to the damp dungeon, exhausted and humiliated. After three years, the King finally befriended a guard, and
smuggled a letter to the Queen. In the letter, the King told his wife to
sell everything in the kingdom and give the money to the evil lord as
ransom for the King's freedom.

When the Queen read the letter, she wept with sorrow. She had
not heard from the King and she feared for his life. But now that she
knew his fate, she was even more distraught. She pondered the situation. "I cannot go in person to this heathen king," she reflected, "because then he will make me one of his many wives. And I dare not
send a great ransom with anyone else!" The Queen paced in her

room. "What shall I do?" Suddenly the Queen had an idea. She cut off her beautiful, long hair, removed her royal gowns, and donned the simple clothes of a minstrel. Then she took up a lute and secretly left the palace.

The Queen traveled far and wide, disguised as a boy, playing her lute and singing as she went. She traded her songs for passage on ships and journeyed to the foreign lord. She sat outside his castle and began playing her lute. Her songs were so beautiful that even the birds stopped to listen. The heathen king heard the Queen and sent for her.

"Boy," the lord told the disguised Queen, "your music soothes me. Play your lute and sing for me. Stay for three days, and I shall give you your heart's desire." The Queen bowed, and strummed her lute, filling the dark castle with songs of war and love. All that day the heathen ruler listened, so entranced by the Queen's music that he forgot to eat. The next day, the Queen played even more beautifully, and on the third day, too. Then the Queen stopped.

"My lord," she said, "I must take my leave. I am a traveler, and the road is my home."

"Alas!" the dark lord sighed. "But you stayed for three days, so tell me your heart's desire and I shall give it to you."

The Queen bowed graciously. "I travel alone, and the solitude often wears on me. Give me one of your prisoners for company, and I shall be grateful."

"That is easily done," the heathen monarch declared, and he took the Queen to his dungeon. Among the prisoners, she picked out her husband immediately, although he was thin and scarred from his ordeal. The King did not recognize his wife, dressed as a minstrel, and she said nothing to him. The dark lord released the King, and the Queen set off with her husband. They traveled together for many miles, and still the King did not recognize his wife. Nor did she reveal herself. Finally they came to their own country.

"I am the King of this land," the King told his companion, "and if you release me, I shall reward you greatly."

"Go in peace," the Queen said. "I need no reward."

The King protested. "Let me honor you with a feast," he said. But the Queen declined.

The two parted company, and the King walked eagerly to his castle. But the Queen knew a shortcut, and she returned before him. She took off her minstrel's clothes, and put on her royal gowns.

All the people acclaimed the King's return, but when the Queen went to meet him, he turned away from her. "Who is this woman," the King asked angrily, "who left me to die in prison?" The King's ministers explained that the Queen vanished the day she received his letter. "Faithless wife!" the King fumed.

The Queen returned to her room, put on her minstrel's cloak, picked up her lute, and went outside and began playing. The King immediately ran out of the castle. "He is the one who freed me!" he exclaimed. Then he took the minstrel's hand. "Now you cannot refuse me," the King declared. "You must tell me your heart's desire, and I shall give it to you."

"I desire only you," the Queen said. She shook off her minstrel's disguise and revealed herself. For a minute, the King was speechless. Then he embraced the Queen, and begged her forgiveness for doubting her. He thanked her for rescuing him, and ordered a double celebration—one for his rescue, and one more for the Queen's wisdom.

MEN AND WOMEN AT MIDLIFE

This charming story summarizes the different tasks men and women face at midlife. The drama begins with a married couple who happen to be a king and queen. This turns out to be a common theme in middle tales, and the symbolism is straightforward. Middle-aged individuals constitute the generation in charge of society. Men and women at this time head households, run businesses, and lead governments. The power and responsibility of midlife are aptly symbolized by protagonists who are kings and queens. The story does not deal with the settling-down phase of adult life, but with what comes next, when the middle-aged man or woman makes it in society.

The Queen's drama begins when she learns of her husband's defeat and imprisonment. She embarks upon a heroic journey to rescue him, and her action parallels the adventures of the women in The Wife Who Became King and Stubborn Husband, Stubborn Wife. All three tales portray women reclaiming their inner power and strength at midlife.

The details of the Queen's story are instructive. First, the Queen rejects a traditionally feminine path. When she receives the King's letter, commanding her to sell everything in the kingdom as ransom for him, she refuses. She realizes that if she went to plead with the heathen lord, he might seize her and make her one of his many concubines. And if she sent the ransom with others, they might run off with the fortune. In disobeying the King, the Queen rejects a traditional wifely role. On the other hand, she does not simply raise an army and try to rescue the King by force—a stereotypical masculine reaction.

Instead, the Queen comes up with a creative alternative. She disguises herself as a minstrel and journeys to the foreign lord. Then she sings to him. Here she integrates the masculine and the feminine. She displays great courage in facing the heathen lord, while she appeals to music, emotion, beauty, and gentle persuasion. The Queen's heroism is uniquely feminine.

The story of Scheherazade, from the main drama of The Thousand and One Arabian Nights, provides another example of feminine heroism. In the tale, a deranged king marries a young maiden each night, and then executes her the next morning. To stop his atrocities, the beautiful Scheherazade came up with a plan. She married the King, and on their first night together she told him delightful fairy tales, but, at dawn, stopped in the middle of a story. The King wanted to hear the ending, so he postponed Scheherazade's execution until the next day. The second night, Scheherazade finished her tale and started another story, which she also left unfinished at sunrise. The King spared her life another time, and this went on for a thousand and one nights. Finally, the King came to his senses and stopped murdering women. Scheherazade reformed him with her courage and grace, strength and gentleness. She appealed to fairy tales rather than music, but like the Queen in The Lute Player, Scheherazade relied on the power of relationship, persuasion, emotion, and beauty, rather than challenge, force, or battle.

The story specifically says that the Queen cuts her hair and dresses in boy's clothing before going on her heroic journey. We saw the same theme in The Wife Who Became King, when the wife dresses like a man. There are several levels of meaning to the motif. Wearing men's clothing provides a concrete symbol of women reclaiming inner strengths and powers that are usually considered masculine. The Queen, though, specifically masquerades as a *boy*. The point can be taken almost literally. The Queen becomes boylike. Psychologically, women return to their youth at midlife, to the period before they adopted restrictive feminine stereotypes, when girls are uninhibited about being assertive, independent, or adventurous, just like boys. Girls know what they want and go after it. By adolescence, however, most girls have been forced to suppress this side of themselves by social pressures—unlike boys, who are encouraged to remain assertive and independent. To survive, girls hide their true selves and, like Sleeping Beauty, hibernate psychologically. At midlife women wake up. They reach back into their past to a time relatively free of constricting gender roles, and reclaim their youthful wholeness, energy, assertiveness, and vitality. This is a crucial task, because women who fail at it suffer from emotional problems and unhappiness later in life.[1]

Because they have not yet adopted strict gender roles, boys and girls are relatively androgynous. This brings up another important theme of middle tales: the balancing of masculine and feminine traits in an individual. A large body of research demonstrates that psychological androgyny increases at midlife. More important, this androgyny correlates with successful aging and greater happiness. Married couples who are satisfied with their marriage have less traditional gender roles compared with younger individuals or with unhappy couples. When middle-aged men and women are given the Rorschach inkblot test, they respond with unique, individualized answers that do not conform to gender stereotypes. Young adults, by contrast, gravitate toward strict, conventional male and female roles. (Interestingly enough, so do older individuals who suffer from dementia.) Flexible notions of the masculine and feminine—that is, androgyny—correlate with successful aging.[2]

The Queen's androgyny also brings up the issue of menopause. For most cultures, femininity is closely identified with menstruation, fertility, and childbearing. Menopause ends this traditional identity. In modern Western culture, menopause usually has been viewed negatively, and many women become depressed in the climacteric. Originally attributed to physiological changes, these depressions were thought to be inevitable and were often treated with hormone injections. But recent research reveals that only a few women become depressed at menopause, and specifically those who invested their whole lives in being mothers. When their children grow up and leave home, these women have no other source of personal fulfillment and suffer the proverbial empty-nest syndrome. Women who have pursued personal interests or careers usually find menopause liberating. This is true even of women who have no children. Menopause is depressing mainly for women bound to a single, narrow stereotyped role—mother. Most non-Western societies regard menopause as emancipation. Postmenopausal women are exempt from social taboos that are strictly enforced on young women. With pregnancy no longer a risk, women become sexually free, and middle-aged women in many cultures make ribald jokes with men. The same behavior from a younger woman would be intolerable.[3]

When menopause causes depression, it is often because women do not overthrow constricting feminine roles. In a fascinating study, David Gutmann found that depressed middle-aged women tend to elaborate highly aggressive themes on Rorschach tests—images of bulls battling, for instance. This reflects repressed aggressiveness, rather than loss or depleted energies. Unable to express their assertiveness in real life, these women turn their energy inward and become depressed. Women's reclamation of assertiveness at midlife is not merely a matter of personal fulfillment, but a vital necessity.

From this discussion of women's psychology, I turn now to the King's part in this tale, and what it reveals about men's midlife transitions. The King's drama begins when he becomes restless with his life and seeks adventure in a foreign land. Such restlessness troubles many men in the middle years. The Viennese psychologist Else Frenkel-Brunswick studied the biographies of several hundred prominent individuals, including artists, scientists, business tycoons, and statesmen. They were mostly men, and they began traveling more frequently in middle age. Many men also change jobs at midlife, responding to an inner restlessness. Although our tale does not specifically say so, we might guess that the King wants one more chance at glory, and that is the reason he embarks upon his heroic journey. In our society, of course, men do not go off on grand crusades, but they do rush into exercise programs or experiment with love affairs. The activity varies, but the underlying motivation remains similar—to keep the glory of the hero.

Yet heroism will not do. The King is defeated, captured, and thrown into prison. This reiterates the theme of men's humiliation and suffering at midlife, introduced in Stubborn Husband, Stubborn Wife. The theme reappears in other middle tales[4] like the *Odyssey*. The saga begins with Odysseus at the height of honor and fame. After years of fruitless efforts by the greatest heroes of Greece, Odysseus finally engineered the Greek victory over Troy with his famous wooden horse. But Odysseus had no chance to enjoy his honor, because he was persecuted by angry gods who forced him to wander for many years before returning home. Odysseus suffered greatly, losing his ship and all his men before reaching home. He was cast down from the pinnacle of success, like the King in The Lute Player.

Dante offers a more recent literary example of the theme. In his *Divine Comedy,* Dante describes his descent at midlife into Purgatory and Hell. Dante's writing drew directly from his own midlife experiences, because he was forced to flee from his native Florence after a political upheaval. Dante lost all his power and prestige and, in miserable exile, turned to writing. Hell and Purgatory were personal realities for him, as Helen Luke points out in *Dark Wood to White Rose.*

The drama of a powerful man thrown down at midlife symbolizes the proverbial male midlife crisis. Today, an unexpected heart attack may shock a man into facing his own mortality, while being passed over for promotion may force another to admit personal failure. And a divorce or serious problems with teenage children may shatter a man's family life. Statistics show that men's depression and psychosomatic problems gradually rise during midlife, until they finally equal those of women. Alcohol and drug abuse also proliferate among men, and suicide becomes progressively more common, even with apparently successful individuals. Other, more subtle signs of distress appear. When asked to draw themselves men create bigger and bigger pictures through early adulthood, reflecting their increasing self-confidence and self-esteem. From midlife onward, men draw smaller and smaller portraits, revealing their greater sense of vulnerability and humility.[5]

Midlife crises are particularly prominent among creative men. As mentioned in chapter 1, Elliot Jaques studied the lives of great artists, composers, and writers. Most of these individuals were men, and they typically experienced a crisis in their thirties or forties, when they stopped creating. Some actually died then, like Mozart. Fortunately, most emerged from the crisis with deepened creativity. John McLeish reports a similar pattern in his study of creative older adults, *The Ulyssean Adult.* Gerald O'Collins called this painful midlife experience "the second journey." The first journey is that of youth, when men voluntarily embark upon a quest for fame and fortune through adventure and action. The second journey at midlife is involuntary, full of suffering, and ultimately leads to wisdom rather than glory or wealth.

By now the notion of a male midlife crisis is common knowledge. Surprisingly, only a quarter of middle-aged men experience a full-blown crisis. This statistical finding does not overthrow the concept of a male crisis. Men are socialized to conceal vulnerability and distress, so many hide their turmoil and doubt at midlife. Men often function well outwardly, while suffering inside. Middle tales focus on inner truth, rather than external appearances. Most men also deal with the issues of midlife gradually. Men usually reduce the grand ambitions of their youth through a series of small disappointments and compromises over many years, and not in a single, dramatic crisis. Middle tales speed up this slow, gradual process like time-lapse photography. A dramatic picture of crisis results, exaggerated to make a point.

Men's painful odyssey at midlife is like purgatory, and the crises are purging. The suffering burns up old ways of thinking and acting, and clears the way for the new. First and foremost of the new elements is the feminine. The story demonstrates this well. The King begins as the leader of a crusading army, epitomizing masculine concerns with power and glory. He is defeated and ends up in the role that youth tales usually assign to women: helpless and waiting for someone to rescue him. He is forced to acknowledge his dependence on other people and the importance of relationships in his life—the traditional domain of the feminine. The task is a basic one for men at midlife: to give up the hero's power, and come to terms with the vulnerability that men usually project onto women.

The King is defeated specifically by the heathen lord, a powerful male figure that wounds and humiliates the King. The story is deeply perceptive here. As Robert Bly eloquently describes in *Iron John,* men discover in the middle years that they are injured most deeply not by women, as they thought in youth, but by other men, and particularly by their fathers. A host of male writers, from San Osherman in *Finding Our Fathers* to Guy Corneau in *Absent Fathers, Lost Sons,* describe how mature men return to childhood memories and realize how much they longed for more contact with their fathers and how hurt, lonely, and vulnerable they felt without that connection. The heathen lord in the tale symbolizes the encounter with the dark, wounding side of the father. Working through these painful early experiences with the father helps men understand and heal their wounded manhood. Paradoxically, in confronting their "feminine" vulnerability and neediness, men also come to terms with their masculinity.

The defeated King is eventually freed by his wife. This introduces another major masculine theme in middle tales: the men are rescued by women. In the *Divine Comedy,* Dante is aided by the beautiful Beatrice on his odyssey through Hell and Purgatory—she personally leads him up to Paradise. In the *Odyssey,* Odysseus is rescued from many a mishap by Athena, the goddess of wisdom. The nymph Kalypso and the goddess Circe also aid him, and the beautiful Nausikaa gives him the ship that finally takes him home. An even older example of the motif comes from the myth of Osiris, which qualifies as a middle tale. Osiris was married to Isis and had a job being Lord of the Earth. At the height of his power, Osiris was murdered by his evil brother Set, struck down just as the King was defeated in The Lute Player. The evil Set cut up the body of Osiris and scattered the pieces over the earth. Isis collected the parts, put them back together, and raised Osiris up from the dead. Osiris was rescued and literally given new life by his wife.

Today men can meet such helpful women in dreams and

fantasies. Jung called these magical women anima figures. (The term *anima* comes from the feminine form of the Latin word for "soul.") The anima personifies a man's long-neglected feminine side and is the complement of the animus, discussed in chapter 5.

Near the end of the story when the King returns to his palace, he is furious at his wife, thinking she did nothing to save him. Remarkably, he never recognized her during their long journey home. The point is small, but reappears in other middle tales, like The Golden Tree (chapter 16) and the Grimms' tale The Handless Maiden. Husbands often do not recognize their wives playing different roles. Men often see only public facades, not the individual behind them. This reflects men's difficulty in mastering interpersonal interactions and relationships.

In having the Queen rescue the King, the story reverses the drama of youth tales, and other middle stories reiterate the theme. The youthful Hero becomes the middle-aged Martyr, as Carol Pearson observes in her book *The Hero Within*. Conversely, the woman who played the Martyr in youth becomes the Hero in the middle years. Male rescuer and female victim switch places.

Robert May found that these contrasting dramas resonate deep within the human psyche. In his studies of men's and women's fantasies, described in *Sex and Fantasy*, young girls and grown women consistently elaborate stories that begin with victimization, suffering, toil, and torment and end with victory and happiness. Males use the complementary plot. Their stories start with triumph and glory but end in disaster and victimization, a pattern also visible from early childhood. Like Icarus, boys expect to fly high and then crash. Boys sense on some level that the youthful, masculine focus on power, glory, achievement, and independence is one-sided and ultimately leads to catastrophe. Analogously, girls realize, whether consciously or not, that they are entitled to more in life than sacrifice and suffering. They deserve the proverbial happy ending. Middle tales are important because they pick up where these archetypal fantasies of youth end. Middle tales show women reclaiming their power at midlife, and men learning wisdom through suffering.

Two caveats are in order here. First, we cannot assume that these traditional masculine and feminine patterns are innate. Why they exist and whether they are immutable are questions that I leave for others. And cultural changes do affect archetypal themes. Young men today dream less about heroic themes, and more about vulnerability, compared with their counterparts from several decades ago.[6] Conversely, contemporary women do not wait until midlife to use their talents. Many young women are assertive, independent, extroverted, and creative, and at midlife shift into a more introspective, nurturing spirit. However, the basic tasks remain the same for men and women, no matter what the starting point: individuals must come to terms with power and intimacy at midlife, confronting whichever half they neglected in youth.

The second caveat is that not everybody reverses roles in the middle years. Many individuals remain happy with tradition and do not change. There are several reasons for these exceptions. As mentioned before, the one rule that holds in aging is that everybody becomes more individual with time. No single pattern applies to everybody. Second, role reversals often take subtle forms that are easily missed. David Gutmann found that older men often retain their traditional masculine roles in public behavior, while becoming more "feminine" in their private lives, and particularly in their spiritual experiences. Naturally these inward changes are harder to detect. Psychological tests that specifically measure unconscious attitudes, like the Thematic Apperception Test and Rorschach cards, however, pick up hidden changes. Even when middle-aged men and women want to escape traditional roles, social pressures and obligations also prevent many of them from doing so. Still, mature individuals *aspire* to flexibility in gender roles,[7] and middle tales reflect those ideals and hopes.

Before closing this chapter, I would like to emphasize one last point. The King's imprisonment forces the Queen to embark on her heroic journey to rescue him, while her success frees the King from the prison of his traditional concepts about the masculine and feminine. The same interaction occurs in Stubborn Husband, Stubborn Wife. The husband's obstinacy and pride prompt his wife to leave him, and force her to develop her assertive side, whereas her departure compels the husband to give up his foolish pride, affirm the importance of his marriage, and start doing household chores.

This dialectic process of development is reflected in more commonplace situations. A wife may go back to school or resume a career once the children leave home. The husband must learn to cook, wash the clothes, and do more of the emotional work in the relationship. Or a husband may turn toward his family and away from his career, paying more attention to his children. This frees his wife to pursue her own personal goals. To be sure, most marriages do not change so smoothly. Sometimes one partner is unable or unwilling to develop along with the other, or a spouse may develop quite rapidly, and the other may feel threatened and envious. A woman's new career may take off just when her husband is grappling with the realization that he will not advance much further in his. Today, many women also embrace feminism, and their discovery frequently throws their husbands into a painful period of self-reflection. Roger Gould in his book *Transformations* notes that many couples simply do not recognize the need for continued development in adulthood. Middle tales like The Lute Player offer hopeful reminders that the challenge is shared by all, and successfully accomplished by many.

If men and women face divergent tasks at midlife, reversing traditional masculine and feminine roles, the stories in the next section address the common crises shared by both sexes.

PART III

COMMON CRISES

SEVEN

Death at Midlife

The Mortal King
from China

nce upon a time, a king went riding with his friends. They stopped atop a mountain to rest. The King surveyed the countryside and then smiled with pleasure. His land was rich, his people prospered, and he felt justifiably proud of his realm. Then a terrible thought struck him. "I will die one day, and lose all this!" the monarch declared.

His companions paused and then echoed the King's lament. "Aye, dying is cruel," they murmured, thinking of what they would lose—families, wealth, and honor. Only one lord among them said nothing.

"I wish we could live forever!" the King exclaimed. "That would be wonderful!"

His nobles nodded in agreement, but the silent lord laughed softly. The other nobles glanced curiously at their companion.

The King went on. "Think of all the hunting and feasts we could enjoy! We would never have to worry about growing old." The nobles sighed, picturing the delights of immortality. The bold lord laughed again.

His companions turned to him. "What is amusing about death? Do you spurn the wish for immortality?" they demanded, but the laughing lord said nothing.

The King ignored the interruption. "To live forever as we are now, in the prime of life—what greater boon could a man enjoy? An eternity of happiness!" he exclaimed.

The lords nodded again, and murmured approval, but the other noble chuckled once more. This time the King turned to the laughing lord. "What is the reason for your humor?" the King demanded. "I see nothing comical about death or immortality!"

The noble bowed to his monarch and said, "I do not mean to offend you, Sire. But I thought of what life would be like if we all lived forever as you suggested." The lord paused. "Why, then, all the heroes of history would still live among us—the king who first unified the land, the law-giver who brought peace, the great sages with all their wisdom, and the holy prophets of our people." Again, he paused. "Compared to them, we would be peasants, fit only to plough the fields! And you, my lord," he turned to the King, "would no doubt be a clerk in the provinces!"

The King stared at the impertinent lord, and all the other peers held their breaths. Then the King laughed long and hard. "You are wise and brave, my friend," the King said. "But you speak the truth."

The King turned to the other nobles and said, "For encouraging me in my vanity, I penalize you two draughts of wine each!"

The King embraced the laughing lord. "As for you, my friend," the monarch decreed, "whenever I lament the thought of my own death, you must cry out, 'A clerk! A clerk!'"

DEATH AT MIDLIFE

The chapters in Part II focused on the different paths that men and women take at midlife, and the many role reversals with which they struggle. This story introduces issues that *both* men and women must face. The first of these common crises is the ultimate reversal in life—death.

The issue of mortality is specific to middle tales. Youth tales treat death lightly, and young heroes and heroines regularly escape or cheat the grim reaper. Stories about elderly protagonists do not dwell on death, either. Elder tales simply treat death as a fact of life, not as a problem. In middle tales like The Mortal King, death is a central issue, and middle-aged protagonists wrestle painfully with their mortality. Fear of death often triggers the proverbial midlife crisis in real life, and the greater the fear of death, the more intense the turmoil.[1] Midlife begins when a person measures his or her age in years until death, not years from birth.

Men and women usually do not confront mortality in one dramatic moment, but over many years. A Grimms' fairy tale, Death's Messengers, makes the point. One day, as Death traveled on his business, he was attacked by a giant, severely beaten, and left by the roadside. Unable to move, Death fretted about humanity. "If I cannot do my job, the world will become too crowded with people!" A young man came up, saw Death, took pity on the ailing figure, and helped him revive. When Death recovered, he turned to the youth and said, "I am Death, and I thank you for saving me. Even so, I cannot spare you when your time comes. But because you helped me, I promise I will send messengers to warn you before I come, so you can prepare yourself." Fair enough, the young man thought. The two parted and the young man went merrily on his way.

One day, the man fell ill with fever. Doctors feared for his life, but the man was undaunted. "I will not die from this. Death promised to warn me before my time is up." Sure enough, the man recovered and lived happily again. Then another illness struck him with dizziness and weakness. "This is misery!" the man exclaimed. "But at least I know I won't die from it! Death has not sent me a messenger." The man recovered, and went about his business only to fall ill again and recover later. This happened several times, until one day someone tapped the man on the shoulder. It was Death. "I have come for you," the grim figure said. "But you gave me no warning," the man protested, "and you promised!" "No warning?" Death exclaimed. "Did you not shiver with fever and chills? Were you not plagued by weakness and pain? I sent many messengers to you! And now I have come for you myself." The man realized Death had kept his promise and went away with him.

If personal illness is not enough warning, the deaths of friends and relatives at midlife highlight the issue of mortality. Bereavements become more common and ominous. In the queue that ends in death, as parents and older friends move on, middle-aged men and women become the next to go.

The way in which the mortal king accepts his death is instructive. He begins with an egocentric view, concerned only with what he will lose when he dies. Then he glimpses the larger picture—the succession of generations throughout history and his small place in it. He realizes that he must yield to the next generation, just as his predecessors gave way to him. It is this spirit of generativity, which we discussed in chapter 3, that resolves the King's fears of death.

Modern psychology confirms this fairy-tale insight. Generative individuals suffer less anxiety over their own deaths, and the reason is simple. As long as an individual is wrapped up in egocentric concerns, death can only be a catastrophe, because death obliterates the ego. If an individual transcends private interests and is committed to something beyond personal gain—to one's children, for instance, or to a social movement—death becomes less of a threat. The individual must die, but the children or the cause lives on.[2]

As a task for midlife, developing generativity or self-transcendence is supremely ironic. In youth, men and women spend most of their efforts establishing themselves in the world. They are naturally preoccupied with their projects and ambitions. At midlife, individuals are asked to reverse course and transcend their personal dreams, seeing themselves as a small part of the "big picture." The tale of The Mortal King sums up this paradox. Its protagonist is a monarch at the summit of power and prestige, surveying his domain from an appropriately lofty place—a mountaintop. Yet it is there that the thought of death humbles him.

The secular context of the tale is significant. The monarch accepts his death because he recognizes that he received his power and wealth from his predecessors and must pass it on to his successors. He focuses on worldly matters, not religious or spiritual ones. The larger picture that the King sees involves human history and the cycle of generations, rather than spiritual revelation or metaphysical insight. This secular treatment of death constitutes an important theme of middle tales, which an Arab folktale dramatizes.[3]

One day a man went hunting with his son, only to have the child killed by an ogre. The father carried his dead son home, wrapped in a cloth, and told his wife that he brought home a gazelle that was so special it could be cooked only in a pot that had never been used for a "meal of sorrow." So his wife went to all their neighbors and relatives to borrow such a pot. No one had anything like it. One friend explained that she had used her pots at her husband's funeral, another for her son's, still a third for a daughter's. Finally the wife returned home and told her husband that there was no home that had not suffered sorrow. The father then unwrapped the cloth from their son's body and said that it was now their turn.

The bereaved father and mother have only one consolation for losing their son—the fact that everyone else has suffered comparable grief. The parents accept their son's death, not through sublime spiritual insights but by recognizing death as a part of life.

The Mortal King illustrates another aspect of coping with death—the importance of a legacy. The monarch recognizes that his throne is a gift from the past to him, and that he must leave it as an inheritance to those who will succeed him. Daniel Levinson found that the legacy theme becomes increasingly important from the middle years onward. If an individual cannot live forever, he or she can create something that will last and so attain a symbolic form of immortality. The form of the legacy varies from one person to another. It may involve a large sum of money, a scientific discovery, or a literary work. Or it may simply be raising one's children and giving them the wisdom and strength needed for happiness. Sometimes there are purely selfish motives behind legacies, like a desire to live on through one's children, or to glorify oneself through an institution. But for most people, the ego-centric element is a minor motif, and generativity the major one—the desire to enrich the next generation and leave the world a better place.[4]

If generativity helps resolve fears of death, death also fosters generativity. As the King demonstrates, the shock of mortality forces individuals to transcend their egocentricity.

The case of Mike offers a real-life example. A well-to-do business executive, Mike divorced his wife in his late forties after some twenty years of marriage. He had felt trapped and frustrated in his marriage and, like many other middle-aged men, started an affair with a younger woman. In his divorce, Mike, caught up in his new romance, felt little concern for the emotional and financial crisis he inflicted on his wife. Some years later, Mike was diagnosed with leukemia. The shock of that news, reinforced by the noxious effects of chemotherapy, precipitated a full-blown midlife crisis. He started psycho-therapy for the first time and continued after his leukemia went into remission.

Mike then realized how insensitive he had been toward his wife and family during his divorce. He made strenuous ef-forts to improve relations with them. At the same time he reas-sessed his career ambitions. He had fought many years to climb the corporate ladder, intent on personal success. Fearful he might die in a short time, he rearranged his priorities. He left the large corporation he worked for and opened his own office as a business consultant. His particular interest was helping young men and women move ahead in their business careers, and Mike became active as a mentor. He explained his career change quite simply: it was a way of returning some of the benefits he had received from society. Mike's confrontation with death and his transformation are not unusual. His example can be multiplied many times.[5] Death is often the best teacher of generativity.

Before concluding this chapter, several subtle but important points in the tale deserve discussion. First of all, while most people wrestle with death at midlife, there is no strict timetable. Young adults and children afflicted with fatal illnesses must also struggle with self-transcendence, generativity, and the issue of leaving a legacy. Indeed, Elisabeth Kübler-Ross observed that many youths arrive precociously at the same secular wisdom of the King—seeing their place in the larger scheme of things.

The Mortal King makes clear that the monarch's acceptance of his own death is humbling. His insight contrasts sharply with the reaction that young men and women have to death. To youth, death is dramatic, heroic, or romantic, and young men and women willingly die for Love, Truth, or Justice. But death is only an abstraction to youth. At midlife, men and women give up this illusion. Death becomes a sobering reality, stark and inevitable, no longer a matter of glory, but of limitation.

Shakespeare illustrates this shift in perspective. In *Romeo and Juliet,* one of his earlier plays, death is romantic, melodramatic, bittersweet, and glorious. In Shakespeare's later, historical plays, written at midlife, death becomes a simple tragedy, denuded of golden frills. Karl Kerenyi observed the same evolution in Homer's two classics, the *Iliad* and its sequel, the *Odyssey.* The *Iliad* lionizes young heroes like Achilles and emphasizes the glory of death in battle. The *Odyssey* focuses on the middle-aged Odysseus and presents death in a decidedly more somber light—often devoid of meaning, occurring by accident, and without glory or honor.

Despite the grim subject, The Mortal King is humorous. And the laughing lord enlightens his egocentric King through a joke, saying the King would only be a clerk if all the ancient heroes and sages were alive. The impudent comment helps the King step outside of himself for a moment, and see his vanity and egocentricity. Humor fosters self-transcendence.

The present story is short and simple. Accepting death is rarely so easy, and the process is often long and difficult, as the next story illustrates.

EIGHT

Death and the Inner Journey

The Man Who Did Not Wish to Die
from Japan

L ong ago, there lived a wealthy man who inherited a fortune and lived a life of ease. He was known as the millionaire. One day, a terrible thought struck him. "I shall die someday! But I want to live forever!" From that moment, he grew troubled in spirit.

Eventually, the millionaire heard tales about the Elixir of Life, possessed by hermits in the mountains. So he left his home, seeking the sages. He climbed the highest peaks and searched all the valleys, but try as he might, he found nobody with the magic elixir. One day, the millionaire met a hunter, and asked the man if he knew of any hermits nearby.

"No," the hunter replied, "but there is a band of robbers who live in this forest."

The millionaire felt discouraged. He went to a temple, and prayed to the god of hermits for six days and nights. On the seventh night, the door to the sanctuary flew open. A great light shone from within and the god of hermits stepped out.

"Foolish man!" the god scolded the millionaire. "How do you expect to find the Elixir of Life, when you have lived a life of ease, pleasing only yourself?"

The millionaire trembled, but could not say anything. The god went on. "You know nothing of spiritual discipline, and only those who do can drink the Elixir of Life!"

"But I do not wish to die!" the millionaire pleaded.

The deity paused, took out a small crane made of paper, and gave it to the millionaire. "You lack the wisdom to drink the Elixir of Life, but this crane will take you to the land where no one dies." The god vanished.

In the next moment, the crane grew larger and larger. The millionaire climbed on its back and the bird leaped into the air. They flew for many miles over a great ocean, until they came to a distant shore. The crane landed upon a beach, and the man hastened to the nearest habitation.

"What land is this?" the millionaire asked the first person he met.

"It is the land of perpetual life!" the man replied, and the millionaire rejoiced. The stranger was friendly and helped the millionaire find a home and a job in the town. The millionaire settled down and then noticed how strange his neighbors were. They collected poisonous mushrooms and ate them; they caught venomous snakes and played with them; and they bleached their hair white, so as to look older.

The millionaire asked the people to explain their odd behavior. They said, "We want to die! We are tired of living forever, and we have heard of a place called Paradise, where only the dead can go!"

The millionaire shook his head. "I never want to die!"

The years rolled by and became centuries, and the millionaire became bored with life. Every day was the same as the next. One afternoon, the millionaire walked by the beach. "I hate this life!" he muttered to himself. "If only I could return to my own land and live like an ordinary person, dying in my own time!" Then he had an idea. "If the god of hermits brought me here, perhaps he will let me return home to die." The millionaire said a prayer, and in the next moment something fell from his pocket. It was the old paper crane from the god of hermits, and before his very eyes, the bird grew larger and larger. The millionaire climbed on the crane, and the bird took flight.

As they flew over the sea, a storm struck. The paper wings of the crane crumpled in the rain, and the bird fell into the sea. "Help! Help! I will drown!" the millionaire cried out, floundering in the ocean. The millionaire saw a shark circling. "Help! Help! I don't want to die!" the poor man pleaded with the god of hermits.

In the next instant, the millionaire found himself sprawled on the floor of the mountain temple, screaming for help. The door to the sanctuary opened, a great light filled the hall, and a divine being emerged from the shrine.

"I am a messenger from the god of hermits," the luminous figure said. "He sent you to the land of perpetual life in a dream, because you yearned for immortality. Then you asked for death, so the god sent the storm and the shark to test you. But you only pleaded for your life once more." The messenger looked sadly at the millionaire. "You have no perseverance or faith. Immortality and the secrets of eternity are not for you." The celestial figure then brought out a book. "Go back to your home and family," the shining messenger said, "and be content with your lot. The god gives you this book of wisdom. Follow its advice—work hard, raise your children well, provide for their future, and help your neighbors. Then you will fear death no more." With those words, the messenger vanished.

The millionaire returned home with his book of wisdom. And from then on, he followed its counsel. He lived a good, honest life, and when his day finally came, he died with a smile on his lips.

DEATH AND THE INNER JOURNEY

This story is complicated, with many puzzling details. It recapitulates the motifs of The Mortal King in the last chapter, but in greater detail. The story features a millionaire rather than a monarch. But the millionaire's wealth serves the same symbolic function. His fortune represents the good life and the zenith of worldly prosperity that men and women anticipate from middle age. But in the midst of plenty, the millionaire is troubled by a dreadful thought. He will die someday. This is exactly analogous to the monarch's distress in The Mortal King. The King relished his success and power, only to think of his own mortality.

The millionaire searches for immortality, and his effort, metaphorically speaking, is a common response at midlife. Men and women throw themselves into work, exercise furiously, or diet fanatically, attempting to deny the inevitability of death. Others have affairs with younger lovers to bolster their own sense of youthfulness. Unfortunately, as the fairy tales indicates, none of these efforts succeeds. The millionaire cannot find the Elixir of Life.

What the millionaire does learn is that immortality is not everything he expected it to be. Given a chance to go to the land of perpetual life, the millionaire becomes bored with his unending, unchanging existence and craves a normal death. He discovers a paradox—death makes life valuable and exciting. And death offers the promise of rest, an escape from the burdens of life. As the inhabitants of the land of perpetual life exclaim, only the dead can go to the place called Paradise, which they imagine is more wondrous than their own land.

Other fairy tales emphasize the importance of death in human life. In one amusing tale,[1] a man trapped Death in a magic bottle. Because no one died anymore, problems multiplied throughout the world. The sick suffered interminably, and the number of infirm, old people soon became unmanageable. Finally Christ and Saint Peter came down from Heaven and asked the man to release Death. Death was too important to be imprisoned.

The millionaire eventually discovers that his trip to the land of perpetual life was a dream. The god of hermits tested the millionaire and found the man wanting. The god still tries to help the millionaire and gives the man a book of wisdom. One would expect profound advice from a divine document, so what the book says is unexpected. It simply tells the millionaire to work hard, raise his family well, provide for his children's future, and honor his neighbors.

Two themes immediately emerge here. The first is generativity. The god tells the man to provide for his children and help his neighbors instead of seeking his own immortality. Generativity—not immortality—is the millionaire's task. Several subtle but instructive details reinforce the message. When the millionaire searched through the mountains for the Elixir of Life, he met a hunter and asked the man about any hermits nearby. The hunter said only that there was a band of robbers in the forest. The answer seems out of place, but like strange details in dreams, the oddness indicates that the comment is symbolic. Robbers steal what is not rightly theirs, and the millionaire was trying to do the same thing. In seeking immortality, he wanted something he did not deserve, as the god of hermits later declares. The millionaire begins with egocentricity and must learn generativity.

A second detail corroborates the theme—the paper crane. In Japanese tradition, paper cranes figure prominently at wedding ceremonies and special birthdays. The cranes symbolize marital fidelity, because the birds, according to folklore, take only one mate for life. But paper cranes are usually associated with another magic animal—the turtle, symbolizing longevity. Turtles, of course, really do live a long time. So it would make more sense for the millionaire to travel to the land of perpetual life on a turtle. The fact that he travels on a crane is significant. As a symbol of marital fidelity and caring for another person, the crane personifies love and generativity. And this is exactly what the millionaire needs to attain, not immortality. The symbolism of the only other animal in the story, the shark, now becomes clearer. The shark is a ravenous creature, knowing only its own needs, and thus represents one more symbol of selfishness.

The second major theme conveyed by the god's book of wisdom is simple pragmatism. The god does not offer lofty philosophical insight or spiritual revelation. The god tells the man simply to work hard, raise his family well, and honor his neighbors. We saw the same practical tone in The Mortal King, and both tales are insightful. An encounter with death often forces indviduals to affirm ordinary, everyday life. Instead of turning to sublime spiritual practices and forsaking the world, mortality prompts men and women in the middle years to affirm the secular order. This process can be poignant and often heartrending, as the case of Guy, a thirty-seven-year-old gay man, taught me.

Guy led a carefree life in his youth, changing relationships and jobs almost at whim, and making few commitments. Then he discovered he had AIDS. Guy knew the grim statistics about the disease, became depressed and angry over his situation, and sought psychotherapy. As his health gradually deteriorated over several years, Guy worked hard psychologically. He settled into a stable relationship for the first time, gave up his recreational use of drugs, sought more responsibility at work, and was promoted to higher positions.

At the same time, Guy addressed painful issues in his past, stemming from abuse he suffered as a child. Traumatic memories resurfaced, of being beaten by his stepfather and periodically abandoned by his mother. Instead of using alcohol or drugs to deaden his feelings as he had before, Guy gradually mastered his painful emotions and began enjoying life in a new way. Simply awakening in the morning, he said, and watching the sun rise as he prepared for work gave him a deep sense of wonder and delight. Guy also started donating time and effort to helping other persons with AIDS. Like the millionaire, Guy learned to work hard, help others, and affirm the simple, everyday order of life. Both Guy and the millionaire read from the same book of wisdom. And Guy's case is not unique.[2] Paradoxically, death offers practical wisdom about living.

⁊ The Mortal King and The Man Who Did Not Wish to Die focus on men, and middle tales dealing explicitly with death usually have male protagonists. This is partly because fairy tales portray men as protagonists more often than women, reflecting patriarchal tradition. However, the preponderance of men in fairy tales about death also suggests that mortality is more an issue for men than for women. Research shows something more complicated. Women express more fears of death and score higher on tests of death anxiety than men, something true across cultures. But women, in general, are more open about their fears, since men habitually deny or minimize their anxieties, including fears of death.[3] This suggests why middle tales about death focus on men. The stories bring up an issue that men avoid and repress in conscious life.

Women tend to be more aware of death and do not need fairy tales to remind them of mortality. In historical times, women risked death with every childbirth and thus confronted mortality in youth. Men faced death mainly in war, and during peace could deny their mortality, at least until disease claimed its toll in middle age. Today, modern medicine greatly reduces the risk of women dying in childbirth, so that women live much longer than men. This produces a new situation, but with similar effects: men confront death at midlife, when they succumb to diseases like heart attacks and lung cancer, while women can postpone the issue until old age. Several factors also help women deal with death. Women experience many forms of social oppression in youth. Having faced suffering and vulnerability, the specter of death is less frightening to them. For men accustomed to power and glory, on the other hand, personal mortality is shocking and humbling. Women can also bear children, providing them a powerful compensation for the inevitability of death. In fact, when women think of motherhood, their fear of death declines.[4] Men must deal with death in other ways. Finally, women are socialized from early in life to take generative roles toward other people, while men are encouraged to seek what they want. Generativity is therefore usually more difficult for men to learn at midlife. Since generativity is crucial in resolving fears of death, men have more problems with mortality.

Men and women approach death from opposite sides in the middle years. For men, confronting death is humbling, as is most of midlife. For women, the encounter with death is often liberating. When women realize their time is running out, many break free from feminine stereotypes and reclaim their strength. Death warns them that they cannot wait for Prince Charming!

The case of Emily illustrates the point. A housewife, she devoted most of her life to her family and, to outward appearances, she was content with her role. In her late fifties, however, Emily discovered a lump in her breast, which turned out to be malignant. The cancer was removed before it spread, but Emily's close call with death prompted her to reflect on her life. She discovered that she was not satisfied with being a mother, wife, and homemaker. She realized that she had many other unfulfilled talents and dreams. Much to her surprise, and to her husband's, Emily returned to school and started a career as a psychologist. Her brush with death inspired her to reclaim her dormant abilities.

Death forces women to realize that they have a part in a larger drama, one much larger and more important than they thought. Death imposes the same insight on men—except men recognize that their part is smaller than they assumed.

In addition to focusing on death, our tale contains another vital motif—the importance of dreams. The millionaire does not actually go to the land of perpetual life, but reaches it in a dream. Middle tales use dreams quite frequently, and two other stories reveal the meaning of the theme.

In the Chinese tale Dreams,[5] a wealthy man forced his servants to labor all day, so he could make ever greater sums of money. But every night, the mogul dreamed of being a lowly servant, rushing around on endless tasks, berated and beaten. Meanwhile, one of the rich man's servants toiled all day without rest. But each night, the laborer dreamed of being a great lord, ordering everybody to work! When the wealthy man heard about his servant's dreams, he pondered their meaning and the significance of his own nightmares. He divined what his dreams meant, lightened the load on all his workers, cut back on his business ventures, and slept well afterward.

The Jewish tale The King's Dream[6] repeats the drama. A monarch once promulgated a series of cruel edicts, persecuting his people. One day he awoke and found himself a prisoner in a foreign country, humiliated and tormented. With the help of a wise rabbi, the King escaped, only to awaken and realize his suffering was all a dream. Fortunately, he guessed the meaning of his nightmares and rescinded his cruel edicts. His people prospered, and he slept well ever after.

In both stories, dreams bring up the issue that individuals ignore or deny. The rich mogul learns about poverty and labor in his dreams, while his servant enjoys wealth and ease. And the powerful King learns humility and compassion. Jung emphasized this function of dreams. They compensate for the limits of conscious thinking, bringing up issues that are repressed and ignored. Here Jung differed from Freud, and their dispute is relevant to the psychology of midlife. Freud held that dreams *conceal* forbidden wishes and disguise or exclude unacceptable impulses from emerging into consciousness. Jung disagreed and argued that dreams *reveal* the unconscious, counteracting repression and bringing up issues that individuals avoid. Freud worked mostly with young adults and drew his theory from them. But young men and women typically deny and avoid painful issues, and their dreams reflect this repression. Jung, on the other hand, worked with older adults, when issues represssed in youth normally reemerge from the unconscious. So Jung's and Freud's theories of dreams do not conflict so much as apply to different stages of life. Dreams shift from repression to revelation in the middle years.

The compensatory function of dreams came home to me in an amusing way as I was writing this book. After finishing the rough draft, I felt pleased with myself, thinking how clever I was to interpret so many different fairy tales. My work with the stories also gave me more confidence in interpreting dreams. Give me any symbolic drama, I thought, and I will give you a profoundly wise interpretation. Then I had the following dream.

I was a student in a large university chemistry class, and we were each given a different unknown chemical compound. Our assignment was to identify the substance, using a complex series of chemical tests. I was able to complete some of the simpler procedures, but could not figure out how to do the other tests. The instructions were written on the blackboard, but in strange symbols I had never seen before, like Egyptian hieroglyphics or alchemical formulas. I began to feel anxious, fearing that I would fail to complete the task. Worse, when I looked around, everybody else seemed to be breezing through their work! I worried that I had missed something important in class, and I awoke in perplexity.

The dream was disturbing and humbling. But it also made me laugh. In my conscious life I imagined I could interpret any fairy tale. My dream told me otherwise. Analyzing fairy tales, like identifying unknown chemical compounds, involves many complex steps and arcane symbols. And I knew only the simplest ones!

The dream motif in middle tales brings up an important insight. In chapter 6, we discussed how middle-aged individuals frequently embark upon a *second journey*. The king and queen in The Lute Player both go on heroic adventures, the king to conquer the heathen lord and the queen to rescue the king. The millionaire in the present story goes on a similar voyage, but in a dream. His odyssey is an *inner* one, an adventure in the psyche rather than in the material world. The midlife odyssey is fundamentally an inner exploration, a pilgrimage into the unconscious. The journey is introverted and psychological and differs sharply from the heroic quest of youth, which is devoted to seeking material reward through adventures in the world.

The millionaire in the present tale begins his midlife journey by searching for hermits who possess the Elixir of Life. He starts off with an external odyssey, and even assumes that his journey to the land of perpetual life is real. Only later does he learn that his journey was a dream. Something similar happens in real life. When men and women become restless at midlife, they often travel, change jobs, move their residences, or divorce spouses. They take concrete actions in the world and only later discover that what they seek can be found only within themselves. The midlife odyssey is an inner one, and an introverted attitude at this time correlates with better mental health and happiness.[7]

By using dreams as the agent of change, middle tales retain their realistic tone. The Man Who Did Not Wish to Die could be a true story. A man or woman today can encounter the god of hermits or some similar figure and then go on a journey to the land of perpetual life, all in a dream. Middle tales involve no magic, except perhaps the deepest type of all, that of personal transformation.

Important as death is in middle tales and in real life, it is not the only nemesis with which men and women must come to terms. There is another force, equally powerful, and perhaps more difficult to accept: fate.

NINE

Fortune and Midlife

Destiny
from Dalmatia

 nce upon a time, two brothers lived together. The elder toiled all day, plowing the fields and tending the animals, and the farm prospered greatly. The younger spent his time eating, drinking, and making merry. At length, the older brother had enough. "It is not fair that I do all the work," he told his younger brother. "We must divide our property, and go our separate ways."

"You have charge of everything, and we enjoy good fortune," the younger man pleaded. "Why make a change?" But the older brother insisted, and so the two divided their fields and flocks. The younger brother hired men to tend his herds and fields, and then spent his time as he always had, enjoying himself. The older brother, meanwhile, worked hard in his fields, and tended his own animals. But one thing after another happened to the older brother. Wolves devoured his herds, fire destroyed his home, and wild beasts trampled his wheat. Soon he was so poor that he could barely feed himself, and he walked barefoot on the ground.

At last the poor man resolved to visit his younger brother and ask for some help. On his way, the older brother came upon a large herd of sheep, watched by a beautiful woman. The maiden sat on a stool and spun golden thread. The older brother went up to her, doffed his cap, and asked to whom the sheep belonged.

"Your brother," the maiden said.

The man was astonished, and then asked, "And who are you?"

"I am your brother's Luck," she replied.

The poor man felt amazed. He asked, "And what of my Luck?"

"She is a hag who lives in that forest," the maiden pointed to the hills.

The poor man thanked the woman and then went to his brother's home. When the younger man saw his elder brother dressed in rags, the rich man wept with grief and brought out clothes, shoes, food, and money. The older brother stayed for a few days and then returned to his own home. There he picked up his walking staff, put a loaf of bread in a bag, and set off to look for his Luck.

The elder brother searched for some time in the forest. At last he came upon a hideous old woman, sleeping beneath a tree. The man struck her on the back to awaken her, and when she saw him, she eyed his new shoes and clothes and said, "Lucky for you I was asleep. Otherwise, I would have taken away the gifts from your brother, just like I took away everything else you had."

"So you are my rotten Luck!" the poor man exclaimed. "Cursed woman! You are the cause of all my troubles! Who sent you to me?"

"It was Destiny," the old woman said.

"Where can I find this wretch?" the man demanded angrily. "I have something to tell him!"

The old woman shrugged. "Go and look for Destiny yourself." She settled back down and then fell asleep.

The man went searching for Destiny and traveled far and wide. At last he came upon a hermit who knew where Destiny lived. "His home is on top of that mountain," the hermit said, pointing in the distance. "But when you see him, take care not to say anything until he speaks to you. Just do whatever he does."

The poor man thanked the hermit and walked up to the castle of Destiny. It was a magnificent place, full of servants, gardens, and rich tapestries. When the poor man went in, he found Destiny eating a splendid supper. Remembering the advice of the hermit, the man said nothing, sat near Destiny, and began to eat also. A little later, Destiny went to bed, and the poor fellow followed him and slept on the floor.

In the middle of the night, a great commotion shook the castle, and a voice cried out, "Many souls have come into the world tonight, Destiny. They await your gifts."

Destiny arose, went to a beautiful chest, took out gold and jewels, and threw them to the right and left. "I give those new souls the bounty I enjoy today. As I am now, so shall they be!" The poor man watched everything in silence.

The next day, when the elder brother awoke, he found that the beautiful castle had disappeared. In its place was an ordinary home, and when Destiny sat down to dinner that evening, there were no golden plates like the night before. Still there was meat and bread in abundance. Destiny and the poor man ate in silence, and then went to sleep.

At midnight, a commotion shook the house, and a dreadful voice cried out again, "Many souls have come into the world tonight, Destiny. They await your gifts."

Destiny arose, went to a small wooden box, and took out piles of silver coins. "I give those new souls the bounty I enjoy today," Destiny cried out, strewing the coins right and left. Destiny closed the box, returned to bed, and fell asleep. The poor man watched everything, but said nothing.

In the morning, when the older brother opened his eyes, he found himself in a smaller house. His supper that night was plainer, too. And when the terrible voice called out at midnight, Destiny gave out copper coins to the souls born that day. This went on each day, until one morning, the older brother awoke to find himself in a tiny hovel. Destiny was outside, digging in the ground for food, and the poor man followed his example. That evening, they had only one small loaf of bread for supper. Destiny broke it in two, giving half to the poor man. At midnight, when the terrible voice cried out, Destiny opened a small wooden chest and scattered pebbles and pennies.

"I give those new souls the bounty I enjoy today," Destiny proclaimed. "As I am now, so shall they be!"

In the morning, the poor man awoke and found himself once again in a magnificent castle. At this point, Destiny turned to the poor man and asked, "Why have you traveled so far to see me?"

"I labor long and hard and yet suffer only bad luck," the poor man explained. "So I have come to ask you why."

Destiny nodded. "You have seen the gifts I give to mortals each night. Those born when I cast out gold and jewels are rich all their days. But those who receive only pebbles and pennies suffer poverty and want. You were born on a day of pebbles and pennies, your brother on a day of gold and jewels."

"Is there nothing you can do for me, then?" the older brother pleaded.

Destiny thought a moment. "Your brother has a daughter named Miliza who was born, like her father, on a day of gold and jewels. Marry her, and she will be your good luck. But remember that everything you own will be hers."

The poor man thanked Destiny, hurried home, went to his brother's house, and asked to marry Miliza. The younger brother agreed, and the wedding was celebrated. Miliza went to live with the older brother, and his fortune quickly changed. He soon found himself a rich man.

One day, a stranger passed by as the older brother worked in the fields. The stranger stopped to admire the bountiful harvest, and he asked the older brother, "Is this wheat yours?"

"Yes," the older brother answered proudly. The moment he uttered the words, a fire started in the fields and spread throughout the farm, threatening to destroy everything. The older brother ran after the stranger, crying out, "Excuse me, sir, I meant to say that the wheat belongs to my wife, Miliza. Everything I have is hers!" Instantly, the fire vanished, and everything was restored. So from then on, whenever anyone asked, the older brother always said, "Everything I have is from my wife!" And so he and his wife prospered for the rest of their days.

MIDLIFE AND FATE

Unlike most fairy tales, which leave listeners and readers with a warm, cuddly feeling, this story may be disquieting. The tale deals with an unpleasant but important task of the middle years—coming to terms with fate, destiny, chance, or luck. The motif appears in middle tales around the world,[1] emphasizing the archetypal nature of the task.

Today the notion of fate or predestination may seem quaint and antiquated. It might be tempting to dismiss middle tales like Destiny as the product of a superstitious past. Enlightened modern cultures insist that personal effort and talent count, and that individuals are free to determine their own destinies. Destiny rejects this modern myth. Despite all his hard work, good intentions, discipline, and initiative, the elder brother descends into poverty. His younger brother, however, loafs through life and is richly rewarded. The story reverses the modern work ethic and favors sloth and fatalism! What is the meaning of this shocking reversal?

Destiny notes that the younger brother was born on a day of good fortune, and the elder on a day of poor fortune. In modern terms, we might say that the younger brother received the good genes and had greater native ability than his older brother. Alternatively, the younger man simply had more good luck. In either case, chance is involved—a contemporary version of fate. If most people today reject destiny as something planned by God or gods, we still accept chance and luck. And by midlife, most people realize that success is often a matter of being at the right place at the right time, rather than a reward for hard work, while failure is often just plain bad luck.[2]

Fate and luck are simply forces beyond an individual's control. Death is a prime example of such a power. But social convention often has the same effect as fate because tradition and family pressure often coerce people into unwanted careers and marriages. Fate also can be internal or psychological. Psychoanalysts emphasize that unconscious emotions and patterns control much of human action. The most dramatic examples come from mental disorders like alcoholism and other addictions, where internal compulsions control the individual. These are inner forms of fate.

In middle tales destiny is humbling, and individuals are forced to accept limits to their independence and power. The opposite holds for youth tales. Fate lifts young heroes and heroines into glory, aiding them at crucial moments. And young men and women really do assume, if only unconsciously, that fate favors them and that destiny will help them attain greatness. Paradoxically, youths also believe that they control their future. Young men and women rely on the power of chance or destiny at the same time they deny it. At midlife, these conflicting, heroic illusions collapse. Men and women confront powers beyond their control and accept limits in their lives. They submit to fate.

The story focuses on a man struggling with destiny, but the issue is not solely men's. Other middle tales present strong women trying to escape fate—and being defeated.[3] Fate is neither masculine nor feminine, but involves the psychology of power and mastery. Destiny is a problem for anyone experienced in life, confident of his or her skills, accustomed to success—and forced at midlife to confront impotence and vulnerability.

The poor man accepts fate by learning more about how it works. Destiny explains that individuals born on the nights he throws out gold and jewels are blessed with great fortune. Those born on the nights of pebbles and pennies are dogged by bad luck. The older brother sees his small place in the greater drama. He realizes that his misfortune is not unusual, and many others share his plight. The poor man's sobering lesson here is analogous to that of the monarch in The Mortal King, where the King was humbled by seeing his small place in the great scheme of things. A Japanese tale, The Stonecutter,[4] emphasizes the point in a poetic way.

Once upon a time, a stonecutter bemoaned his miserable life and wished he could be a rich man. A benevolent spirit granted him his wish, and the stonecutter found he had everything money could buy. On a particularly hot day, the man noticed how powerful the sun was. "I wish I were the sun!" he exclaimed jealously. The spirit granted him his second wish, and the man exulted in shining on the earth and making everybody hot. Then the man noticed how easily clouds covered him up. "They are stronger than I am!" the man declared enviously and wished he could be a cloud. His third wish was fulfilled. The man rained prodigiously on the earth and delighted in his power to wash everything away. Then he noticed the mountain was unmoved. "The mountain is stronger than me!" the man cried out, and asked to be the mountain. The spirit granted his fourth wish. The man rejoiced in being eternal and unchanging, until he noticed someone chipping away at his feet. It was a stonecutter, removing great blocks from the mountain. "How could this be?" the man exclaimed. "I am the mountain, but that man is stronger than me! I wish I were him!" His fifth wish was granted, and the stonecutter found himself back at the beginning, except now he was content with his lot.

The stonecutter begins from a position of envy and deprivation, just like the older brother in Destiny. Each time the stonecutter is granted his wish for a better situation, he remains dissatisfied. Eventually, the stonecutter asks for his old position back, affirming his original situation with all its limitations. (Notice that happens on his fifth wish, emphasizing the importance of the number five in middle tales.) The stonecutter returns to his old job with a new, wider perspective—a glimpse of the larger picture and an understanding of his small place within a greater drama. Middle tales suggest that it is this wider understanding that resolves the issue of fate and luck. The insight is wisdom.[5]

Research confirms that most people develop a reflective, philosophical attitude in the middle years. Maturity fosters the ability to see "the big picture," and this frequently involves a shift toward intuition, and away from logical, linear reasoning.[6] Here we come to one interpretation for a puzzling detail in the story. A helpful hermit tells the poor man where to find Destiny, and advises the man not to speak until Destiny addresses him first and to do everything Destiny does. The advice is symbolic. In remaining silent, the poor man suspends normal rationality, which is based heavily on verbal reasoning and dialogue with other people. He then sees the big picture and the nature of Destiny. Although not explicitly stated, the story implies that if the poor man talked or asked questions prematurely, he would interrupt Destiny's work and miss observing the full cycle of fate. The poor man needs an intuitive, experiential experience to fully understand the big picture— not an intellectual one.

After the poor man understands fate, he asks Destiny how to escape his bad fortune. Destiny suggests that the poor man marry his brother's daughter. So Destiny does not change the man's fortune; the poor brother is apparently stuck with wretched luck. But Destiny tells the man how to compensate for bad fortune. Similarly, men and women learn to accommodate fate in the middle years and give up their youthful efforts at defying fate or trying to change it.

The poor man escapes his plight specifically by marrying Miliza. So we have the familiar theme of a man being rescued by the feminine. Miliza plays the role of the anima here, and the tale emphasizes her importance in a dramatic way. As soon as the man claims the wheat field is his own, he almost loses it. Only by acknowledging that his good fortune comes from his wife can he keep it. Psychologically, he must honor the feminine.

Accepting the power of fate or luck yields a *tragic* vision of the world, in the original Greek sense of the term. Tragedy does not mean an unhappy ending, but rather insight into uncontrollable forces that shape one's life. This tragic view contrasts sharply with the heroic spirit of youth, where everything seems possible, given enough personal effort, wit, and work. Compared with the youthful spirit, the tragic perspective of midlife might seem depressive or dismal. But an acceptance of fate or luck in the middle years is actually liberating.

The case of Pat taught me this lesson in a moving way. Pat came to psychotherapy for anxiety and depression in her late thirties. A lawyer, she had been diagnosed some years before with lymphoma, but medical treatment induced a remission of her disease. Unfortunately, the lymphoma had reappeared. Pat started chemotherapy and radiation treatments again, optimistic that they would bring about another remission. She refused to cut back on her usual activities, and kept bicycling long distances, hiking in the wilderness, and pursuing a full caseload at her office. Pat tried to ignore the nausea and exhaustion from radiation, and her oncologist referred her for psychotherapy, concerned that she was pushing herself to the verge of collapse.

The reason for Pat's overexertion quickly became clear. She believed, like many, that a positive mental attitude was crucial to recovering from cancer. So she tried to keep active and cheerful. She had done exactly that the first time around with lymphoma, and she credited her remission partly to her positive attitude. She also subscribed to the view, common among New Age philosophies, that individuals cause their own illnesses—that stress, negative thoughts, and bad habits produce disease. Basically, she adhered to the heroic creed, characteristic of youth: "I can do whatever I set out to do!"

Pat had succeeded in life with much heroism, putting herself through law school, and steadily moving ahead in her law firm. She also "beat" lymphoma the first time by fighting it. When the lymphoma reappeared, the situation was different. Having looked up the medical literature, Pat knew that recurrent lymphoma is much less likely to go into remission. That, unfortunately, proved to be the case. The chemotherapy, which worked the first time, no longer helped. Additional agents had to be used, with increased side effects. To compound Pat's suffering, she felt that she was to blame because she had failed to maintain a positive attitude. It was painful for me to see her suffering three times from her situation—once from the lymphoma, again from the chemotherapy and radiation, and finally from blaming herself for her illness.

The reason Pat blamed herself gradually became evident. If she was not responsible for her problems, she felt deep down, she was not in control of her life at all. She believed she could be only heroic or helpless. She preferred to blame herself rather than admit she could not control her life. She denied the power of fate or luck, as heroes and heroines instinctively do. Pat gradually came to a middle ground. She relinquished her heroic efforts to stay in control, but also recognized that she did not thereby become helpless. Pat came to terms with her vulnerability and the limitations of her will. She made peace with fate or luck, in perhaps its darkest form—as the threat of an untimely death.

An extraordinary thing then happened in Pat's life. She experienced moments of peace and joy, mystical in intensity. They happened at different times—when she walked by the seashore, or paused in a forest, or ate breakfast with her cat in the morning. She noted the irony of these new experiences. She could no longer bicycle for miles or hike long distances, as she had before. But she no longer needed to. Her acceptance of fate or luck was liberating and inaugurated a joyful, contemplative phase in her life.

Pat's story is dramatic, dealing as it does with a life-and-death struggle early in the middle years. But the same issue—fate, luck, and the struggle with forces beyond one's control—confronts most men and women at midlife. Fate also takes many forms—being laid off at work in a recession, wrestling with a son's or daughters' drug problem, or caring for a parent with dementia. By whatever name and however explained, fate or luck demands its due in the middle years. The next story elaborates on the theme, and describes in detail a means of resolving the issue.

TEN

Wisdom and Luck

The King Who Would Be Stronger Than Fate
from India

nce upon a time, a queen gave birth to a beautiful baby girl. The King rejoiced greatly and doted on his daughter. One day, the King went hunting and pursued a magnificent white stag. The animal eluded him deep into the forest, and the King found himself lost in the wilderness. Night fell, and the King stumbled about, seeking his way home. At length he saw a faint light and made his way there. He found an old man sitting by a river.

"God be with you," the King said.

"And to you," the old man replied. But the hermit did not look up. He only stared at the river and cast leaves upon its surface, watching intently as they rushed downstream.

"What are you doing?" the King asked.

"I am reading the fates of men," the hermit replied.

The King paused thoughtfully. Then he said, "I do not need to know my fate, but I am curious about my newborn daughter. Can you tell me her destiny?"

The old man said nothing, took up more leaves, and cast them upon the stream.

"What do you see?" the King asked.

The hermit stirred. "Sometimes ignorance is wisdom."

"But I wish to know my daughter's fate!" the King persisted, until the old man finally yielded.

"Your daughter will marry the newborn son of a woman named Puruna," the hermit said. "She is the slave of the King of the North."

"Impossible!" the King declared. "I would never let that happen! Such humiliation!"

"No one escapes fate," the hermit said softly.

For a moment the King felt outraged; then he calmed himself. But that night, he tossed and turned. "I will never let my daughter marry the son of a slave!" the King vowed.

The next morning, the hermit showed the King the way out of the forest, and the monarch returned to his palace. He immediately wrote to the King of the North, and asked to buy the slave woman named Puruna and her son. For five days the King waited anxiously and then a messenger brought a reply, saying the monarch of the north would give the slave woman and her infant to the King as a gift.

The King rejoiced, disguised himself as a messenger, and rode off to receive the slave and the child. He took them both into a cave in the desert, drew his sword, and killed the mother. But he could not bring himself to murder the child. So he left the baby to die and returned to his palace, congratulating himself for outwitting fate.

The years passed, and the Queen died after a long illness. The King entrusted his beloved daughter to the wife of his closest friend, the governor of the eastern provinces. The governor's wife became a second mother to the Princess, and the King's daughter grew lovelier and more gracious with each year.

One day, the King disguised himself as a peddler and went traveling on a donkey. He frequently went about incognito to understand his people better, and to ensure that his officials were honest. The King stopped at an inn, tied his donkey to a fence, and went in to eat. Soon afterward, there was a commotion outside. The King saw his donkey being beaten by a young man. "Stop!" the King yelled. "How dare you attack my animal!"

"Your donkey was eating up my garden!" the young man replied hotly. "If he eats my cabbages again," the youth threatened, "I'll beat you instead!"

"We'll see about that!" the King exclaimed. The monarch returned to his palace and sent soldiers to arrest the young man. The King decided to make an example of the youth and was about to pass a harsh sentence when an old woman approached, weeping and wailing.

"Spare my son, my only son!" the old woman cried out.

"Your son?" the King asked incredulously. "Surely you are too old to be his mother!"

The old woman hesitated and then nodded. "You are right," she admitted. "I am too old to be his real mother, but this young man is like a son to me." She explained, "I am a widow and herd goats for a living. One day my nanny goat gave no milk. Since she was healthy, I thought someone was stealing her milk, so I followed her the next day. I saw her enter a cave in the desert, and when I looked in, I found a baby boy suckling my nanny goat! And beside the poor child lay his mother, dead as could be. So I buried the poor woman, took the child home, and raised him as my own. I named him Nur Mohammed, and if you take him away, I will die of grief!"

The King stood up in horror, remembering the slave woman he had killed years before and the prophecy of the hermit. Was the young man before him destined to marry his daughter? "Never!" the King vowed to himself. The monarch wanted to have Nur Mohammed beheaded on the spot, but an execution would have been too severe a punishment for beating a donkey. So the King thought quickly and came up with a plan.

"This young man needs discipline," the King declared. "If he will join my army, I will let him off." The old woman was grateful, and Nur Mohammed felt delighted. The young man now had a chance to move up in the world.

Once in the army, Nur Mohammed noticed that he was always given the most dangerous missions. But he succeeded with courage and strength, so his officers promoted him. The King was furious that his secret plans to kill the young man failed, and resorted to more desperate measures.

One day, bandits attacked Nur Mohammed as he traveled alone, but he outfought them and survived. Another time, a wall fell into the street just as the young man walked by, narrowly missing him. Later, the King made Nur Mohammed one of his personal guards, and shortly afterward a man attacked the King. Nur Mohammed stepped forward to protect the monarch, as was his duty, and the assailant stabbed the young man. But the wound was minor, Nur Mohammed survived, and the King was forced to reward the young soldier. On another occasion, Nur Mohammed sat down to eat his dinner when a dog came begging at the door. Nur Mohammed tossed the animal a piece of meat; the dog ate it and suddenly died. So Nur Mohammed threw his poisoned food away.

Meanwhile, the King fumed inside. All his plans went astray! But he came up with another strategy. He summoned Nur Mohammed and handed the young man a letter. "Take this message to the governor of the eastern provinces," the King said, "and give it only to him." The King smiled. The governor was his most trusted friend and would do what the King commanded.

So Nur Mohammed set out. The journey normally took five days, but he arrived in three. When he reached the governor's palace, it was noon and everyone slept, resting from the heat of the day. Nur Mohammed would not give the King's letter to anyone but the governor, so the young man went into the garden to wait. There he fell asleep under a tree.

A few minutes later, the Princess walked into the garden. She was staying with the governor and felt restless that day. As she wandered among the roses, she saw Nur Mohammed sleeping quietly in the shade. "Ah!" the Princess exclaimed, "it is Nur Mohammed." The Princess noticed the letter from her father. "I wonder what's in it!" She glanced mischievously around and then carefully drew the letter from the young man's hands.

When the Princess read the note, her heart stopped. "Kill this messenger at once! Keep it secret and ask no questions," the letter said. The note was signed by the King himself.

The Princess frowned. "How can my father kill Nur Mohammed! He is the best soldier in the army! And he is brave, kind, and handsome!" The Princess paused. "There must be a mistake! I must save Nur Mohammed!" she exclaimed. So she ran to her room, threw away her father's note, wrote another one, and resealed the envelope. Then she sped to Nur Mohammed, and slipped the letter into his hands.

A short while later, Nur Mohammed awoke and called on the governor. The official read the letter from the King, rubbed his eyes, and reread the note. Finally he called his wife and showed her the letter. It said, "Marry this messenger to the Princess at once. Make it public and ask no questions."

"We must obey the King," the governor said, and gave orders for a wedding. So that very evening, the Princess and Nur Mohammed were married, to his surprise and to her delight.

The next day, the governor sent the Princess and her new husband back to the King. When the King learned what happened, he flew into a fury. "How could this be!" he shrieked. "I will personally behead the governor and Nur Mohammed!" But the governor was a wise man, and he had sent back the original letter commanding the marriage to take place, so the King could see it himself. When the King read the letter, he recognized his daughter's handwriting. There was nothing he could do!

Outside, all the people acclaimed the marriage, for they loved both the Princess and Nur Mohammed. Finally, the King calmed himself. He remembered the hermit's prophecy and resigned himself to making the best of the situation. "No one escapes fate," the King murmured softly. Then the King ordered festivities throughout the land and made Nur Mohammed his heir. The young man proved himself to be as fair and wise as he was brave and strong, and when the old king died, Nur Mohammed and his wife became king and queen. And they ruled together in peace and prosperity for the rest of their lives.

EGO AND DESTINY

This tale is long, complex, and symbolic. Rather than plunge into the story and risk becoming confused in a thicket of symbols, the way the King raced into the forest and then lost his way, I will focus on the story's two major themes and then later turn to its details.

The first motif appears quickly. While wandering in the forest, the King chances upon a hermit who says he can read the fates of men. The story brings up the theme of destiny, fate, or luck, which we discussed in the last chapter. The King asks about his daughter's fate, and the sage reveals that the Princess will marry the son of a slave. Such a humiliating match is intolerable to the proud monarch, so he tries to defeat fate. He attempts to kill off Nur Mohammed, and this brings up the second theme of the story—the deadly competition between the King and the young man.

The basic drama involves a father figure trying to murder a son figure. This mortal rivalry appears prominently in middle tales around the world.[1] Psychoanalysts interpret such rivalry in terms of the Oedipal drama. In fact, The King Who Would Be Stronger Than Fate closely resembles the myth of Oedipus. According to the Greek tale, the Delphic oracle told Laius, the King of Thebes, that his newborn son Oedipus would grow up to kill him, and then marry Laius's wife, Jocasta. To protect himself, Laius left the infant Oedipus to die in the wilderness. Oedipus was luckily saved and raised in another land, ignorant of his royal heritage. Years later, Oedipus unknowingly returned to his homeland and killed a man in a fight, not realizing the victim was Laius, his father. Oedipus later married the Queen of Thebes, never dreaming that she was his mother. He thus fulfilled the prophecy, despite his father's efforts to thwart it.

In the King Who Would Be Stronger Than Fate a similar drama unfolds, although the characters are displaced outside the King's immediate family. The King hears a prophecy, not about his son, but about the son of a slave. And the young man is destined to marry the King's daughter, rather than his wife. But the tension remains similar—the battle between a father figure and a son figure over a woman.

Most discussions of Oedipal rivalry dwell on the son and

ignore the father. The very term *Oedipal complex,* rather than Laius complex, reveals the emphasis on the young man. The present tale reverses this traditional focus, taking the side of the King, the father figure, and not Nur Mohammed, the son figure.

The way in which the King comes to terms with his pride, rivalry, and envy is the second major focus of the tale, and constitutes a developmental challenge for midlife. The story portrays the King struggling with conflicting feelings. On one hand, he cruelly murders Puruna the slave woman to thwart the prophecy. Yet the King spares the infant boy out of compassion. And if the King is a murderer, he is also a conscientious and caring monarch, traveling incognito among his people to know their needs. Moreover, when the King has a chance to learn about the future from the hermit, he asks about his daughter's destiny rather than his own. Despite his egocentric pride, he is generative.

The story highlights similar paradoxes throughout the drama. The King is often impulsive and rash, and at the beginning of the story he pursues a stag recklessly. Later he wants to punish Nur Mohammed severely for beating a donkey. On the other hand, the King does have principles and can control himself. The King refrains from executing Nur Mohammed when he first learns the identity of the young man, but instead admits him into the army. And if the monarch constantly plots to murder the young man, he also promotes him, acknowledging the soldier's courage and skill. The King is torn between pride and justice, anger and honor, the desire to have his way and his concern for other people.

The story reflects the realities of midlife. Fathers usually feel pride and affection for their sons, but also envy and rivalry. This Oedipal conflict becomes intense at midlife. Just when the father notices the first signs of aging in his body, perhaps a decline in stamina and speed, his sons may reach the peak of their physical power. Similar problems occur with mentors. The mentor wants to help his or her protégé succeed, yet the senior also fears being displaced by the junior. Explosive conflicts often result.

The midlife Oedipal drama is not limited to men. The same conflict occurs between mothers and daughters or, more generally, between mother figures and daughter figures. Fairy tales like Sleeping Beauty and Cinderella make the point clear. In those dramas, an "evil" stepmother feels jealous of her stepdaughter's beauty and persecutes the younger woman. If many youth tales displace the conflict from mother and daughter to stepmother and stepdaughter, some fairy tales explicitly portray a mother and daughter battling to the death. Most mothers and daughters in real life enjoy relatively nurturing relationships with each other. But muted rivalry remains and breaks open periodically—often when the mother enters her middle years. As the mother grapples with the loss of youthful beauty, so important to stereotypes of the feminine, her daughters begin to blossom. The mother must deal with jealousy and envy. Older women who grew up in a restrictive era also have reason to envy their daughters' greater freedom and opportunities. Similarly, Oedipal rivalry often fuels the proverbial battle between the mother-in-law and her daughter-in-law. Such competition is particularly ferocious in patriarchal cultures, where women can exercise authority only within the confines of the family. Mother-in-law and daughter-in-law battle for control over the household.

Oedipal conflict at midlife is not a matter of masculine or feminine psychology. It deals rather with the psychology of parents and leaders, with people in charge, who feel threatened in some way by the next generation. Psychologists and psychoanalysts emphasize that envy of youth—jealousy and hatred—are central issues at midlife. If individuals do not come to terms with this dark, shadowy side of the human heart, problems arise. When parents cannot resist competing with their children, the children grow up wounded and resentful. But the parents' victory is short-lived, because children become adults, and parents decline in old age. Without a spirit of generativity, misery results for both generations.[2]

Many middle tales depict such a sad outcome, like the Grimms' story The Devil with Three Golden Hairs, the Serbian tale Three Wonderful Beggars, and the French drama the Wizard King.[3] These tales all end tragically, because the middle-aged protagonists refuse to deal with their envy toward youth. The warning is clear: individuals who do not transcend Oedipal jealousy at midlife and who fail to develop generativity are consumed by their own bitterness and rage.

A little envy and competition can nevertheless be helpful. Without the King's attacks on him, Nur Mohammed might not have learned to be brave, strong, and resourceful. In competing with the young man, the King plays the role of the essential enemy, forcing Nur Mohammed to develop.

The same applies to the Princess. When she reads her father's letter ordering Nur Mohammed's death, she takes matters into her own hands and decides to marry Nur Mohammed. This is contrary to Muslim custom, according to which marriages are arranged by parents. The King's cruelty toward Nur Mohammed thus provokes the Princess into defying tradition and claiming her independence.

Despite the King's efforts, his daughter marries the son of a slave. Confronted with the marriage, the King rants and raves, but finally calms down and accepts the power of fate. He echoes the words of the old hermit: "Nobody can escape fate!" The story shifts back to its original theme, the issue of fate and destiny. In presenting fate together with Oedipal rivalry, the story reveals a remarkably deep insight: what resolves one problem resolves the other. A proud man, the King initially competes with Nur Mohammed. But fate cuts the King down, and he recognizes there are powers beyond his control. With newfound humility, the King sees Nur Mohammed's virtues and names him his heir. The shock of fate teaches the King generativity, and this resolves the Oedipal battle.

Something similar frequently happens in the middle years, as the case of Karl illustrates. Karl played the role of a tyrant in his family, intimidating his wife and children into submission by the force of his personality. They had to follow his rules and agree with his beliefs, even when he was wrong. Of his three sons only one dared defy Karl, and Karl disowned the rebel. Karl dominated his family because he felt envious of his sons' youth and potential. Lording it over them bolstered Karl's shaky self-esteem, and his Oedipal envy wreaked havoc in his family.

In his late fifties, Karl was fired from his job as a corporate vice president when his company was bought out by a larger one. Karl had assumed he was too important to be fired and was devastated to find out otherwise. The result, many months later, was a humbler, more open-minded man, most evident in his family. Karl made a concerted effort to listen to the opinions and needs of his wife and children for the first time. He even reached out to the son he had disowned, welcoming the young man back home for the first time in years. The shock of fate—losing his job—forced Karl to come to terms with his rivalry toward his sons, and taught him the meaning of generativity.

Destiny per se does not resolve the jealousy of midlife. It is rather the *tragic* philosophical viewpoint that fate imposes—an acceptance of forces beyond one's control. The development of tragic insight in the middle years helps men and women cope with the dark side of life. The literary works of Shakespeare and Charles Dickens reflect this process. Both men wrote their most profound tragedies after midlife, and their tragedies reflect an acceptance of suffering, evil, and vulnerability.

The link between fate, tragic insight, and the Oedipal drama is also present in Sophocles' plays about Oedipus.

Oedipus Rex, in fact, is only the first of three dramas about Oedipus. The other two are often overlooked by psycho-analysts, but contain profound insights about the psychology of midlife and beyond, something Nancy Datan and Judith Schavrien independently observed. In *Oedipus Rex,* when Oedipus discovers that he unknowingly killed his father and married his mother, he is overcome by horror, guilt, and disgust. He puts out his eyes and flees from his land. *Antigone* and *Oedipus at Colonnus* portray what happens next. Oedipus gradually comes to terms with his horrifying deeds, so that by the last play he resolves his torment. Oedipus recognizes that he acted in ignorance when he killed his father and married his mother, and that the power of destiny ruled his life. As a pawn of fate, Oedipus was ultimately innocent of his crimes. The gods affirm Oedipus' tragic insight and take him bodily into the next world, appointing his spirit to be the divine guardian of Athens.

In recognizing the power of fate in his life, Oedipus emancipates himself from overwhelming guilt. He understands his life in terms of fate and tragedy, rather than guilt and sin.[4] Adopting this tragic vision of life marks a decisive turn from the psychology of youth to that of maturity. This is because guilt and blame inevitably accompany the heroism of youth. Young men and women usually assume, consciously or not, that they are in control of life. So when things go awry, it must be their fault, or somebody else's.

At midlife, men and women recognize the power of fate or destiny and admit that they have only limited control over events. But without control, there can be no responsibility, and thus no guilt or blame. Though sobering, the insight is ultimately liberating and helps men and women resolve regrets over the past. Individuals learn to forgive themselves for misfortunes and mistakes.

Ideally, they also learn to forgive other people, particularly their parents. Most individuals feel frustrated by their mothers and fathers at some time, and assume their parents could do better but refuse to. Young men and women feel their parents' lapses are willful, rather than the result of inability or limitation, because youth thinks in terms of blame and guilt. When men and women become parents in their turn, they discover their own limits. They realize that their own parents did not refuse love or support, but simply could not give more. The issue is not failure and guilt, but limitation and tragedy. The anger of youth thus yields to mourning, grief, and forgiveness. Humility and compassion flow from tragic insight.

Erik Erikson called this self-acceptance *ego-integrity*. It is the affirmation of one's life as "something that had to be and that by necessity permitted no substitutions."[5] The individual accepts his or her decisions over the years, right and wrong, and acknowledges the forces that shaped his or her life, from childhood experiences to cultural influences and chance events. Ego-integrity is an affirmation of one's fate, understood in a modern, psychological way.

Before ending this discussion on destiny, there are several details in the story worth mentioning. The drama starts off when the King loses his way while hunting, and the scenario sums up the situation of powerful men and women at midlife. Intent on personal projects and ambitions, these individuals rush ahead at full tilt, only to find themselves in unexpected and unfamiliar situations, confused and hesitant. This image of being lost in a forest at midlife appears frequently in literature and folklore. The *Divine Comedy* begins when Dante loses his way in a dark woods during the middle of life. And a number of Arthurian legends portray the middle-aged Arthur stranded in a forest.[6]

Another symbolic detail is the number five, which appears several times in the story. After the King asks his neighbor, the King of the North, to buy Puruna the slave woman, the story specifically says that the King waited five days for a response. Later, when Nur Mohammed takes his fateful message to the governor of the eastern provinces, the tale observes that the journey normally required five days, but the young man rode so swiftly he took only three. As discussed in chapter 3, the number three appears prominently in youth tales, usually in the context of an Oedipal competition, where two people vie for the attentions of a third. The theme is clear when the King and Nur Mohammed compete for the Princess. The number five, on the other hand, has connotations of excess and transformation, which are also evident in the King's actions.

Although fate is usually considered a metaphysical and philosophical issue, the story presents it in terms of an ordinary family conflict—the competition between a father figure and a son figure. Fate takes a concrete, mundane, human form. Conversely, the Oedipal conflict turns out to be far more than a private family issue. It is also a matter of fate and destiny. By linking fate with family rivalry, middle tales unite the abstract and the concrete, the sublime and the mundane. This is characteristic of the wisdom of midlife.

With The Man Who Would Be Stronger Than Fate, I conclude my discussion of the reversals that occur at midlife—reversals of gender roles and of fortune. The stories we have discussed are about opposites: male and female, life and death, power and fate. In the next and final section, I turn to tales that portray how these opposites are reconciled. Thus the stories move from reversal to renewal.

PART IV

RECONCILIATION AND RENEWAL

ELEVEN

Practical Wisdom

Clever Answers
from Russia

Once upon a time a soldier retired from the army. When he returned home, his family and friends asked him if he had ever seen the Tsar. He confessed he had not, so everyone teased him. "You served the Tsar for so long and never saw him once?" Finally the soldier packed his bags and made his way to the monarch.

"Why have you come to see me?" the Tsar asked the soldier.

"Great Majesty," the man replied, "I served you for five and twenty years, and never once did I see you. So I came to take a look."

"Well, then," the Tsar smiled, "look all you like." The soldier walked around the throne staring at the monarch. Then the Tsar asked him, "Good man, what do you think? Am I handsome?"

"Yes, my lord," the soldier replied, "indeed you are."

The Tsar nodded. "Then tell me, soldier, how far is it from heaven to earth?"

The soldier paused a moment and then replied, "It is just so far that when they make a noise there, we can hear it here."

"And how wide is the earth?" the Tsar continued.

"The sun rises over there," the soldier pointed east, "and it sets there," he pointed west. "That is the width of the earth."

The Tsar smiled. "And how deep is the earth, good fellow?" the monarch asked.

"Many years ago," the soldier reflected, "my grandfather died and we buried him in the earth. He has never come home again, so that must be the depth of the earth."

The Tsar laughed. Then he said, "I am going to put you in prison, but keep your eyes open. I will send you thirty geese, and you must pluck a feather from each of them." And so the monarch sent the soldier to the dungeon.

The Tsar summoned thirty rich men and asked them how far heaven is from earth, and how deep and wide the earth is. The merchants hemmed and hawed, but had no answers. So the Tsar sent them to the dungeon.

"Why are you in prison?" the soldier asked the thirty men.

"The Tsar asked us three riddles," they lamented, "and we did not know the answers." They repeated the Tsar's questions, and the soldier laughed.

"Well," he said, "I know the solutions, and if you will each give me a thousand rubles, I will tell you the answers." Every merchant took out his purse and counted out a thousand rubles, so the soldier told them how far heaven is from earth, and how deep and wide the earth is.

Two days later the Tsar summoned the merchants and the soldier. The monarch asked the rich men the same three riddles and they promptly gave him the soldier's answers. So the Tsar let them go. Then he turned to the soldier. "Now tell me, good man, did you manage to pluck a feather from each goose?"

"Aye, Your Majesty," he replied. "And it was a golden feather, too!" the soldier said, showing the Tsar the purse filled with money.

"Good," the Tsar said. "And how far is your home, soldier?"

"I cannot see it from here," the man answered, "so it must be far." The Tsar smiled, gave the soldier another thousand rubles, and sent him on his way. And so the soldier returned home and lived the rest of his life in ease.

PRACTICAL WISDOM

This tale is short and apparently simple. Yet the story contains important insights about the wisdom that men and women gain at midlife.

The story features a soldier who has served for twenty-five years in the army, putting him well into midlife. Soldiers appear frequently in middle tales and symbolize several tasks of the middle years for both men and women. Consider first the life of ordinary soldiers. They slog through mud, polish shoes, and stand guard for hours on end. Like beasts of burden, soldiers are expected to work without complaint. They offer a poignant metaphor for the toil of the middle years, applicable to men and women alike. Women, in fact, may feel even more like soldiers than men, since women have more drudgery forced on them, at home or at work.

Soldiers are also closely tied to the archetypal image of the Hero, and many youths join armies seeking glory. The soldier in the present tale, though, is not heroic at all. He has not even met the Tsar—the center of honor, fame, and loyalty. The soldier represents a *post-heroic* figure. Having presumably spent his youth trying to become a hero, he now finds himself left in the lurch at midlife. This is a familiar feeling to most people in the middle years as they reflect on their lives. After years of pursuing a career, men and women question whether the reward is worth the time and energy. And after all their efforts to be good mothers and fathers, middle-aged parents wonder about their children.

Fortunately the soldier does not give in to despair or self-pity. He goes brazenly to see the Tsar. The monarch asks the soldier a series of abstract, philosophical questions, such as "How far is heaven from earth?" The soldier's responses seem almost stupid and simpleminded at first, but here lies the major insight of the story.

Psychologists have long considered abstract thinking and logic to be the most advanced type of reasoning. So researchers were shocked to find that middle-aged adults use less abstract reasoning than young adults. When young men and women are presented with abstract problems, such as hypothetical moral dilemmas, they typically appeal to sophisticated ethical principles. By contrast, older men and women are more likely to cite personal experiences and concrete examples, using simpler types of arguments more typical of children than college students. Mathematicians and theoretical physicists also do their best work before thirty years of age, suggesting that the peak of abstract thought comes in youth. Men and women at midlife thus seem to regress in their reasoning abilities, and this was attributed to aging. From the middle years, people seem to become slightly stupid, like the soldier in the story.[1]

Fortunately, more detailed research reveals an entirely different picture. When presented with real-life problems, middle-aged adults come up with more effective, workable solutions than young adults. Middle-aged individuals know how to use abstract reasoning but consciously choose not to do so because pure logic is impractical for real-life problems. Mature adults distinguish between book learning and life learning, and the latter is pragmatic.[2]

The soldier's pragmatism appears immediately, when he answers the Tsar's first question, "Am I handsome?" Whether or not the monarch is, the soldier is wise enough to say yes, presumably because he knows the danger of insulting an autocrat to his face. Later, when asked how far his home is, the soldier simply says that he cannot see it, so it must be far. Unlike scientists, philosophers, and youths, who favor abstract or metaphysical answers, the soldier is more concerned with practical issues, such as how far he has to walk home.

Yet the story also emphasizes that the soldier can reason abstractly. The Tsar sends the man to prison with a comment about plucking thirty geese. The soldier quickly deduces that the remark is a metaphor when the thirty rich men are imprisoned with him. But understanding metaphors requires fairly sophisticated, abstract reasoning, which is beyond the capacity of young children. So the story makes clear that the soldier is no simpleton.

Once we know that the soldier understands metaphors,

his cryptic replies take on profound meaning. The soldier's comment about the earth being deep enough to hold his dead grandfather can be construed to be a metaphor about the finality of death. And the soldier's answer about heaven being far away, but near enough so that noises made there are heard on earth, appears to be a comment about the effect of fate on people's fortunes, and how external forces govern people's lives. As we discussed in the last four chapters, death and fate loom large in middle tales.

Research demonstrates that individuals evolve in their use of metaphors over the years, paralleling the development of practical wisdom. When young adults are asked to interpret a metaphor, like "A stitch in time saves nine," they typically answer with relatively brief, abstract responses, like "Preventing a problem is better than solving it." Middle-aged adults offer the same abstract comments, but with more practical, personal associations,[3] like "Prevention is better than cure, but also harder. It's easier to ignore small problems, like when I started having my first mild angina attacks. One-stitch problems are easier to deny, too. You have to be alert and willing to see bad things."

In youth, metaphors are generally used for poetic, aesthetic, or inspirational purposes, like writing "My love is a red, red rose." By middle age, metaphors become tools rather than ornaments. Fairy tales, I might add, are inherently metaphorical. And the whole point of this book is to show that fairy tales are not merely entertaining or poetic. They are thoroughly practical, offering important insights about midlife.

This is a long interpretation of a short fairy tale, but the practical wisdom of midlife appears in many other middle tales. The Japanese story How to Fool a Cat[4] is a charming example.

One day, two master artisans argued over who was better. So the lord of the land set up a contest between them, offering a reward to the man who could carve the most lifelike mouse. Both men labored night and day and at the appointed time presented their work to the lord. The first artisan's mouse was beautiful, wonderfully realistic, and so well carved that it looked as if its whiskers twitched. The second man's mouse, however, was hardly recognizable, poorly worked, with flakes breaking off. The lord was about to declare the first artist the winner when the second craftsman suggested that they let a cat decide which mouse was more lifelike. The lord agreed, and a cat was brought in. The animal ignored the beautiful mouse and immediately pounced on the ugly carving. Everyone was forced to admit that the misshapen mouse was more lifelike if the cat chose it, but they were puzzled as to why. So the second craftsman revealed that he had carved his mouse out of dried fish! The lord was so amused that he gave two rewards, one for the skill of the first artisan, and another for the wisdom of the second.

Here the craftsmen personify two contrasting attitudes—a refined, aesthetic sensibility and crude but effective pragmatism. This parallels the differences between the idealistic book learning common in youth, and the practicality of maturity. Pure beauty and absolute truth inspire young men and women, but by midlife most individuals will settle for what works, however untidy (or fishy!) the solution may be.

Men and women develop wisdom in slightly different ways. Men usually begin with abstract, intellectual, "objective" thinking in youth. They gravitate toward science and philosophy and habitually make universal claims about Absolute Truth, reflecting the expansive and even grandiose spirit of young men. With maturity, men recognize the limits of their understanding and the importance of practical, everyday emotional knowledge.

Women follow a complementary pattern. They usually start with an emphasis on subjective, personal experience, and then later recognize the broader, more universal significance of their insights. This is partly because women are discouraged from displaying their abstract abilities and historically have been excluded from most institutions of higher learning. Even today, girls who do well in math and science are considered unfeminine by their peers. Women also traditionally focus their attention on relationships and feelings, which men consider irrational and unimportant. Yet understanding human relationships requires complex, abstract reasoning. To empathize with another person, an individual must imagine what the other person feels and experiences. This requires constructing complex models of the other person's character. Empathy uses the same abstract thinking that is involved in science, except empathy deals with people and emotions rather than objects and ideas.[5]

A dramatic example of the masculine pattern of development can be seen in the career of Ludwig Wittgenstein, the eminent modern philosopher.[6] He wrote only two books in his career. The first, *Tractatus Logico-Philosophicus*, was as abstract and logical as the title sounds. Written when Wittgenstein was in his late twenties, the work was immediately hailed as a major contribution to philosophy, and considered a paragon of abstract reasoning. Wittgenstein's second book was completed at the age of fifty-nine, shortly before his untimely death. Entitled *Philosophical Investigations*, this later work was also praised as a revolutionary development in philosophy. But the older Wittgenstein rejected his earlier views and particularly his youthful love of abstract thinking and pure logic. Philosophy, the more experienced Wittgenstein concluded, does not offer eternal truth, as he believed earlier. Philosophy is merely a practical tool, whose purpose is to clarify muddled thinking and resolve problems in communicating with other people. Philosophy is pragmatic.

The evolution of women's thinking has been eloquently described by Mary Belenky and her colleagues, building on the work of Carol Gilligan. Belenky's team found that women move through several distinct stages in intellectual development. Women usually begin in a position of *silence*, feeling that they have nothing to say and that no one will listen to them. Women then shift to focus on *received knowledge*, obeying what they are told. Eventually, women reject these external authorities and turn to their own inner experience. This is the stage of *subjective knowledge*. As one thirty-year-old woman put it in Belenky's study, "I can only know with my gut. I've got it tuned to a point where I think and feel all at the same time and I know what is right. My gut is my best friend—the one thing in the world that won't let me down or lie to me or back away from me."[7]

In the fourth stage, women reconcile their subjective truths with those of other people. This is a period of intense and exciting self-reflection, when women recognize that their personal experiences contain insights that apply to other people. What seemed merely subjective turns out to be profoundly and universally human. In the final stage, women balance their initial emphasis on personal, private knowledge with public, universal insights.

Jung offers another way to understand men's and women's complementary paths to wisdom. He described two distinct modes of understanding: Logos and Eros. *Logos* is abstract, universal, logical, and intellectual. It is the stuff of natural science, mathematics, and philosophy, and represents the viewpoint of a disinterested observer. *Eros*, by contrast, involves feeling, intuition, and inner experience. It is the language of myth, dreams, and human relationships, and reflects the perspective of someone engaged in a situation, not watching from a distance. Traditionally, men begin with Logos and then embrace Eros, while women start with Eros and then integrate Logos in their lives. For both men and women, maturity requires the reconciliation of feminine and masculine modes of reasoning.

The present story illustrates the synthesis of Logos and Eros with the soldier's metaphors. When the soldier says that earth is as deep as his grandfather's grave, he links his personal experience with an abstract comment about death. The same integration appeared in The King Who Would Be Stronger Than Fate, where the monarch struggles with fate, an abstract, philosophical issue. Yet the King accepts fate not because of philosophy but through his daughter's marriage to the son of a slave. A metaphysical problem takes the form of a family conflict and is resolved by working through ordinary human emotions—jealousy, pride, and love. Similarly, in The Mortal King, a ruler wrestles with the cosmic issue of death and immortality. But he resolves the matter by accepting practical human reality: just as he received his throne from his father and grandfather, so must he leave it to his children and their successors.

If stories about wisdom feature male protagonists, the issue is not limited to men. Men and women alike must integrate abstraction with pragmatism. To make the point I end this chapter with a humorous tale that celebrates a woman's mature wisdom.

Once upon a time, a near-sighted saint arrived at a new land and saw a crowd of people gathered to meet him. He baptized them all and then later discovered that they were birds, not people. When the birds died, they went up to heaven because baptism gave them the right to enter paradise. Once the birds arrived at the pearly gates, a great dispute broke out as to whether they had souls. The Father, Son, and Holy Ghost assembled with all the doctors of the Church. The men argued and debated, but failed to agree. Finally the men turned to Saint Catherine and asked her opinion. She reflected a moment, and then said, "Oh, give them all a soul, but just a little one!"[8]

The Challenge of Evil

Solomon's Advice
from Italy

nce upon a time, a storekeeper lived with his wife and three sons. One morning, the merchant went to his shop and found a corpse lying on the doorstep. Terrified that he would be accused of murder, he ran away. After traveling many miles, he took a job as a servant to a wise man. The sage was named Solomon, and people came from miles around to pay him for advice. The merchant worked conscientiously and never once asked for his wages. But after twenty years, he yearned to return home and asked Solomon for permission to leave. Solomon agreed, figured out what he owed the shopkeeper, and gave the merchant three hundred crowns.

Then Solomon said, "Everyone comes to me for advice. Are you leaving without any?"

The shopkeeper reflected a moment and asked for a bit of counsel, agreeing to pay Solomon his usual fee. The sage took a hundred crowns and said, "Don't leave the old road for a new one."

"I paid you a hundred crowns for that?" the merchant exclaimed.

Solomon smiled. "And so you will remember it!"

The merchant was dissatisfied, and asked for a second bit of wisdom, paying another hundred crowns.

Solomon said, "Don't meddle in other people's affairs."

"What kind of advice is that?" the shopkeeper grumbled. He

looked at the hundred coins left in his purse, and then decided he might as well spend everything on a last word of counsel. Solomon took the money, and said gravely, "Put off anger till the next day."

The merchant rolled his eyes up in disgust and turned to depart. Solomon stopped him. "I don't want you to leave with nothing at all," the wise man said, and gave the shopkeeper a cake. "Save it until you are back with your family." The merchant thanked the wise man and started out for home.

Along the way, the shopkeeper met a group of merry travelers. They invited him to join them, although they were going in a different direction. The merchant remembered Solomon's first piece of advice: "Don't leave the old road for a new one."

"If I paid a hundred crowns for those words of wisdom," the man thought, "I might as well use them." So he declined the offer and continued on alone. A short while later, he heard gunfire in the distance and saw his new friends murdered by brigands. "Thank God for Solomon's advice!" he exclaimed.

Near nightfall, the shopkeeper found himself in a vast wilderness. He made his way to a lonely cottage, knocked on the door, and asked for shelter. A gaunt man let him in and set another place for dinner. The two men ate in silence. Then the man of the house opened a door to the cellar, and a blind woman emerged. The man picked up a human skull, filled it with soup, and gave the woman a small reed to use as a spoon. When the poor woman finished, he locked her back in the cellar.

"Well, friend," the man asked the shopkeeper, "what do you make of that?"

The shopkeeper remembered Solomon's second counsel: "Don't meddle in other people's affairs." So the merchant said, "You must have reasons for what you do."

The man of the house smiled grimly. "Aye, I do. That wretch is my wife. She took another man as her lover, but I caught them and killed the man. His skull is the bowl she eats from, and her spoon is the reed I used to gouge her eyes out." The merchant felt sickened. "And what do you think of that, friend?" the vengeful husband asked.

The merchant swallowed hard. "If you think you are right, you must be," the shopkeeper said aloud.

"Good," the murderer replied. "Anybody who says I am wrong dies."

Thank God for Solomon's advice! the merchant told himself.

The next day the shopkeeper hurried away and continued his journey. By evening he arrived at his house. Through the window, he saw his wife embracing a handsome young man. The merchant was enraged, and drew his pistol. He was about to shoot his wife and the young man when he remembered Solomon's last piece of advice: "Put off anger till the next day." So the merchant lowered his gun, and rushed to another house on the street. "Who lives there?" he asked, pointing to his own home.

The neighbor smiled. "A mother who is celebrating tonight. Her youngest son was ordained a priest today, and all her family is with her!"

"Thank God for Solomon's last counsel!" the shopkeeper exclaimed. "I might have shot my wife and son!" Then he hurried home and knocked on the door. His wife recognized him immediately and they embraced. All the merchant's family rejoiced at his return. When they settled down for dinner, the shopkeeper took out Solomon's cake. And when he cut into it, out rolled three hundred gold coins!

WISDOM AND EVIL

The tale begins when the merchant discovers a corpse lying on his doorstep. The story never explains how the body arrived at the merchant's shop, but as an unidentified corpse, it conjures up images of murder. The tale thus brings up several motifs familiar from previous stories—death, tragedy, and evil. Confronting this shadowy side of life is a major task of the middle years. The shopkeeper's reaction to the corpse is to flee, and his behavior contrasts sharply with that of young protagonists in fairy tales. The young hero or heroine typically stays to fight evil and eventually wins. The merchant's flight therefore

seems cowardly. But other middle tales, like the Russian story
The One-Eyed Evil,[1] show the same flight. And a closer look at
fairy tales reveals something surprising. Young protagonists
actually *avoid* the problem of evil. They only seem to confront
it. First, young heroes and heroines never do evil themselves,
or if they do, it is only because they were bewitched by the real
villain and acted against their nature. Psychologically, young
men and women project evil onto other people and never acknowledge it in themselves. Youths neatly avoid the most difficult evil of all—within oneself.

Furthermore, fairy tale heroes and heroines always triumph over evil. To them, the dark side of life can be conquered, controlled, or kept at bay. Youths thus deny the power
of evil. George Vaillant found exactly this in his research:
young adults often do not recall childhood traumas, like physical abuse at the hands of an alcoholic father, or the suicide of
a mother. Youths repress and deny evil.

Horror movies, so popular among adolescents, dramatize youthful avoidance of evil. In this genre, college or high-
school students are hacked to death by insane murderers,
digested by alien blobs, or devoured by ghouls. Eventually, the
monster or villain is destroyed—but only apparently. The
source of evil goes underground and emerges later, generally
in a sequel.

The shopkeeper's flight from the corpse dramatizes
youthful avoidance of evil. The reason for this denial is simply
self-protection. Temporarily ignoring death, tragedy, and vil-
lainy helps young men and women to preserve a sense of optimism and hope. If youths were preoccupied with the darker
side of human nature, or with the traumas they suffered as
children, they could easily be discouraged from making their
way in the world.

After twenty years, the merchant decides to return home.
He is clearly now in his middle years. Before he leaves Solomon, the merchant buys some advice from the sage and receives three ordinary proverbs: "Don't leave the old road for a

new one," "Don't meddle in other people's affairs," and "Put off anger till the next day." These are common, even trite, maxims. Solomon's counsel seems all the more mundane because of its high price. The shopkeeper pays a hundred crowns for each bit of advice. Since the merchant received three hundred crowns for twenty years of work, each piece of wisdom represents over six years of his labor!

Solomon also plays the part of the archetypal wise man. Solomon's wisdom is legendary in Judeo-Christian tradition, and Solomon was even said to know the secrets of God. We would expect then, as the shopkeeper undoubtedly did, that Solomon would offer profound insights about life, truth, or destiny. But the merchant receives ordinary proverbs. This recalls the book of wisdom that the god of hermits gave to the man who did not wish to die, in the story of that name. The divine book contained no numinous revelation—just common-sense exhortations to work hard.

Solomon's advice saves the shopkeeper's life not once but three times, so we do not miss the point. His counsel is supremely *practical,* and offers another example of the pragmatic wisdom of the middle years. Here the wisdom applies specifically to the problem of evil.

Solomon's first suggestion is to keep to the old road. In following this advice, the shopkeeper escapes death at the hands of the brigands. So the shopkeeper can avoid evil, which he could not do earlier, when the corpse appeared on his doorstep. Notice that when the brigands attack his friends, the shopkeeper does not go to their aid. Yet he carries a pistol, as we learn at the end of the story when he almost shoots his wife and son. So the shopkeeper's failure to help his new friends seems like cowardice. Young heroes would rush to rescue their friends! The merchant, however, contents himself with avoiding evil and saving his own skin. Self-preservation comes first, and his attitude reflects the realities of midlife. Individuals who risked life and limb for noble causes in youth typically give up their crusades at midlife. The necessity of earning a living and raising one's children takes precedence.

Solomon's advice about sticking to the old road is uniquely relevant to midlife. The shopkeeper is tempted to go off on a new adventure with a band of merry travelers, and such digressions are an ever-present enticement in midlife. Solomon's proverb provides a warning against wandering too far from one's path, experimenting too frequently with new romances or jobs.

In the next episode, the shopkeeper takes refuge at night with the murderous husband who blinded his wife. The story provides gruesome details of the husband's cruelty. Yet the merchant does not run away from the evil situation, as he did with the corpse. Nor does he avoid the evil man, as he did with the brigands. The shopkeeper calmly eats dinner with the husband, and they converse. Symbolically, the merchant comes face-to-face with evil and does not flinch, flee, or fight. He simply heeds Solomon's second bit of wisdom: don't meddle in other people's affairs.

Two points are important here. First, the direct confrontation of evil and tragedy constitutes a major task of midlife. Men and women begin to remember and deal with past traumas, from sexual abuse to emotional deprivation, as George Vaillant found. Author Joseph Conrad offers another example.[2] He suffered many traumas in childhood, but avoided dealing with his memories by becoming a merchant seaman and going on adventures around the world. At midlife, Conrad began writing fiction and focused specifically on evil and tragedy. *The Heart of Darkness,* one of his first works, dwells on the horrors of the Congo under a corrupt colonial administrator and draws on his personal experiences in Africa. Through writing about evil and tragedy in the world, Conrad also confronted the traumas he suffered as a child.

The second point about the merchant's encounter with the murderous husband is that the shopkeeper makes no moral judgment. Even when he hears the hair-raising story of how the husband killed his wife's lover and now feeds her from her lover's skull, the shopkeeper simply says that the husband must be right. This is partly motivated by realism. The merchant needs food and shelter for the night, and it would not do to criticize his host. But there is more here. The merchant exhibits a new attitude toward evil. He is conscious of it, but takes no action and makes no comment. A similar spirit of tolerance emerges in Dante's *Divine Comedy*. At midlife, Dante descends into Hell and confronts progressively more hideous forms of evil, finally meeting Satan. But at every level, Dante stops to converse with the inmates of Hell. He relates to the tormented sinners as fellow human beings, even if he feels horrified by what they did in life. Such a willingness to relate to evil is absent in youth tales, where villains are simply killed. Tolerance of evil is a virtue of midlife. After years of life experience, men and women are painfully aware of suffering and evil, but also recognize that they often cannot change the situation. The wisdom of midlife reflects tragic insight.

In telling the murderous husband "You must have your reasons" and "You must be right," the merchant advocates a form of moral relativism. Other middle tales repeat the theme, like the Grimms' stories Brother Lustig and The Little Peasant and the Hindu tale The King and the Ghoul.[3] By midlife most individuals recognize that their moral judgments can be wrong and that other people hold different ethical principles. Men and women develop greater tolerance for moral ambiguities and accept that there is no one right answer to any ethical problem. They arrive at a pluralistic attitude toward good and evil. Contrary to stereotypes, individuals usually become more tolerant and less moralistic with age. Younger adults are often morally rigid, because of their uncompromising idealism.[4]

The point came home to me in an amusing but humbling way. One day, many years ago, a friend told me that she ran through a red light while driving home from work. She saw a police officer giving tickets to parked cars nearby. The officer jumped on his motorcycle and started off behind my friend. She assumed the policeman was after her and sped away as fast as she could. She escaped the policeman, and as she told me her tale, she laughed with delight. I was shocked and ethically outraged at the time. All my youthful moralism and idealism (and rigidity!) were deeply offended. I had not thought my friend would do such a thing. Certainly *I* would not. We dropped the matter because discussion was impossible; obviously she was wrong and I was right.

Years later, I ran through a stop sign while driving home from work. In my mirror, I saw a police officer run to his car. I feared he would be after me, so I quickly turned down a small alley and parked behind a number of cars the same color as mine. The officer raced by on the main street and missed me. I laughed gleefully until I remembered my friend's story years earlier. So much for youthful morality!

To return to the tale: Solomon's advice about not meddling in other people's affairs counteracts a common temptation of midlife—assuming that one knows what is best for everybody else. His advice reminds men and women at the zenith of authority that there are many situations they do not understand or control.

When the shopkeeper finally arrives at his own home, he finds his wife embracing a young man. The merchant is tempted to kill them, but he forbears. So the shopkeeper is now able to control his own anger and vindictiveness, the darkness in *his* soul. We learn that his tolerance of evil in other people—such as keeping silent with the murderous husband—does not signify a general indifference to moral issues. The merchant knows right from wrong. If he cannot change the world or reform every miscreant, he can at least control his own evil. Notice the tale's unusual richness here. The man who blinded his wife and murdered her lover foreshadows the merchant's own situation. Both men discover their wives in the arms of other men, but the shopkeeper controls himself long enough to find out the reason.

The young man embracing the merchant's wife turns out to be his own son. So we have the classic Oedipal situation in which father and son (apparently) vie for the same woman. The story presents the father's viewpoint, rather than the younger man's, and emphasizes how the shopkeeper must come to terms with jealousy and envy. This reiterates the themes of The King Who Would Be Stronger Than Fate.

The Oedipal situation also suggests another reason that the shopkeeper fled from the corpse many years earlier. The dead body makes a good symbol for the jealousy, rivalry, anger, and lust that emerge in most families—along with love, loyalty, and altruism. The corpse highlights the dark side of intimate relationships and the potential violence that lurks in even the happiest families. The shopkeeper initially deals with these shadowy impulses by avoiding them. Symbolically he flees the corpse. Here we find a meaning for a small detail. The merchant abandoned his family for twenty years. Many fathers do the equivalent, remaining emotionally distant from their families. The story hints that the father's distance can be adaptive and helps him control destructive impulses, such as anger or jealousy. Only after many years of working for Solomon and using the sage's advice does the shopkeeper have enough self-control to refrain from killing his son. By midlife most men and women learn such self-restraint, and teenage children sorely test it.

The theme of using practical wisdom to deal with evil can be found in many other middle tales, like the Japanese story Fortune-Telling Cards.[5] Its remarkable similarity to the Italian tale emphasizes the archetypal nature of the motif.

One winter, a husband left his wife temporarily to find work in a distant city. When spring arrived, the husband started back for home. On the way, he came upon a soothsayer and paid to learn his fortune. The seer gave him a card that read, "A small tree is better than a big one." Dissatisfied with that advice, the husband asked for another prophecy, paid for it, and received a card saying, "Beware of kindness." Still unhappy, the husband demanded a third bit of counsel and paid the rest of his winter's wages for it. This time the card said, "Haste makes waste." Disgusted with himself for squandering his money, the man continued homeward. A storm overtook him and the man sought refuge under a huge tree. Then he remembered the first fortune-telling card: "A small tree is better than a large one." Since he paid so much for it, he thought he should use the advice. So he moved to a smaller tree. Just then, lightning struck the big tree and destroyed it. Grateful for the advice that saved his life, the man resumed his journey and stayed the night at an inn. His hosts were very solicitous, and the husband enjoyed himself. Then he remembered the second piece of advice he paid for: "Beware of kindness." So he remained awake and overheard the innkeeper and his wife plotting to murder him and steal his belongings. The man fled and thanked the gods for the second bit of counsel. Finally, he returned home and saw his wife through the window, having tea with a strange man. Enraged, the husband was about to leap in and kill them both when he remembered the last card: "Haste makes waste." So he announced his return at the door and asked his wife about the stranger in the house. She explained that she felt afraid of being alone with brigands roaming the country, so she made a dummy out of straw and dressed it in her husband's clothes. And there, beside her, was the mannequin!

The farmer does not gain profound metaphysical insight from the oracle, but he does learn practical wisdom that saves his life. Like the merchant in Solomon's Advice, the farmer also deals with tragedy and evil—natural disasters, the murderous innkeepers, and his own violent jealousy. The same themes surface in stories around the world, like the Iraqi tale

A Father's Advice and the Syrian story Tests of Friendship.[6] These middle tales emphasize that the wisdom of midlife does not involve profound spiritual insights about evil or abstract moral principles—simply common sense.

Middle tales also portray evil as something ordinary and all too human. There are no monsters, witches, or dragons in Solomon's Advice—just highway robbers, a man who killed his wife's lover, and the merchant's own jealousy. In Fortune-Telling Cards we have a storm, greedy innkeepers, and again a husband's jealousy. Evil is ordinary and even banal. If benevolent elves vanish in middle tales, as they do in The Elves and the Shoemaker, horrendously evil creatures also disappear. The loss of magic applies to black and to white magic alike. Even when the Devil himself appears in middle tales, like the Grimms' story The Peasant and the Devil, he is portrayed as a mundane figure, wearing a coat and tie and minding his own business.

The importance of pragmatic wisdom came home to me in a poignant way as I was writing this chapter. A man in his early fifties whom I shall call Richard came to me for therapy. After we worked together for some time, Richard told me, "I came to you for million-dollar wisdom, but I get only nickel advice! And I realize that's all I need!" Richard had sought therapy with the hope of hearing deep interpretations of his dreams and discussing the archetypal themes in myths and fairy tales. But it quickly became apparent that his real problem was his inability to assert himself with family, friends, and coworkers, and to deal with his anger. So we focused on those practical, everyday tasks, much to his disappointment. We looked in detail at what inhibited him from saying no to other people, or asking for what he needed. (This was the "nickel advice"!) As therapy progressed, Richard began to assert himself and challenge others, which he had not done previously. His temper outbursts decreased, and he began expressing his anger and frustration in more controlled, effective ways (such as his pointed joke to me about getting only nickel advice).

A remarkable thing happened. Richard began to have profound spiritual experiences, often mystical in intensity. Years earlier, as a youth, he had experienced such moments, but he actively repressed them, fearing that his friends and colleagues would think him strange. As he learned to assert himself in his middle years and deal with anger in practical, everyday ways, his transcendent experiences unexpectedly re-appeared. Richard essentially discovered a wisdom in himself that united the banal and the sublime. Nickel advice turned out to be a priceless spiritual boon.

Important as practical wisdom is, there are other ways of dealing with evil and tragedy. The next middle tale introduces what is perhaps the most surprising approach: laughter.

THIRTEEN

Insight and Humor

The Tell Tale
from Japan

ong ago, a woodcutter returned home earlier than usual. As he was about to shout a greeting to his wife, he saw her through the window. She was drinking wine with the village pawnbroker, kissing him, laughing, and carrying on!

The woodcutter became furious. "I'll kill them both!" he vowed, lifting his axe. Then he caught himself. "That will only make trouble." The woodcutter felt miserable and wandered over to the outhouse to think for a moment. On the way he noticed a knotty piece of wood with a hole in the middle. He suddenly had an idea, picked up the fragment of wood, and went back to his house, making a great commotion to announce his presence.

"I'm home!" he shouted to his wife outside the door.

"My goodness!" his wife whispered to the pawnbroker. "My husband is back early!" She hurriedly hid the wine in a closet, the cakes in a cupboard, and then told the pawnbroker to hide in a large wooden chest. The pawnbroker leaped inside and shut the lid, just as the woodcutter came through the front door.

"You're home early!" the wife observed, trying to seem nonchalant.

"Yes!" the woodcutter exclaimed in an excited voice. "I rushed back to show you what the god of the forest gave me!" The husband reverently pulled out the piece of wood with the hole in it. He bowed to it and then said, "The forest god gave this to me because I work so hard every day."

"What is it?" the wife asked dubiously.

"It is the Tell Tale," the woodcutter said and put it up to his eye. "With it, I can see everything that is hidden!"

"My goodness!" the wife cried out. "Does it really work?"

The woodcutter peered through the hole in the piece of wood and walked around the room. He came to the chest. "Bless me!" the husband exclaimed. "There is something odd in here!" He turned to his wife, "Quickly, bring me a rope." The trembling wife did as she was told, and the woodcutter promptly tied up the chest. "I wonder if the strange object inside is worth any money," the woodcutter said, scratching his head. "I know! I'll take the chest to the pawnshop and sell it." With that, he picked up the coffer and carried it to the pawnshop.

The pawnbroker, of course, was not at the shop, but his assistant was. "I'll sell you this chest for fifty gold coins," the woodcutter said to the assistant. The apprentice looked over the box.

"Don't be ridiculous!" the assistant replied. "It's worth only a few pennies, if that!"

The woodcutter smiled, pulled out a pipe, and stepped outside to smoke. "You think about it a moment," the woodcutter said.

The pawnbroker whispered frantically from inside the chest, "Pay him the fifty gold pieces!"

"Eh?" the assistant exclaimed. He leaned down to listen and recognized his master's voice.

"Pay the woodcutter!" the master commanded. So the apprentice quickly counted out the money and gave it to the woodcutter.

The husband returned home, smiling to himself. "I earned fifty sovereigns today!" he told his wife. "I certainly could use a drink and some dinner. Do we have any wine?" The wife hesitated a second, so the woodcutter took out his Tell Tale and began looking. The wife quickly opened the closet and the cupboard, and brought out the cakes and wine she had hidden.

In no time at all, the story of the magic Tell Tale spread throughout the town. One day, the priests of the village temple called on the woodcutter. "Someone has stolen all the money from the temple treasury!" the priests explained. "We lost five hundred gold coins— everything we saved to repair the temple!" They wrung their hands. "We heard about your magic Tell Tale and so we came to ask for your help in finding the thief."

The woodcutter was too embarrassed to explain his joke, so he followed the priests to the temple. Not knowing what else to do, the woodcutter brought out his Tell Tale, peered around the temple, and nodded. "In three days' time, you will have your money back," he promised, and took his leave.

When the woodcutter went home, he could neither work nor sleep. "How am I to find the thief?" he kept asking himself. The next night, as he lay awake, tossing and turning, someone came up to the window of his house and whispered.

"Mr. Woodcutter, sir!"

"Who is it?" the woodcutter asked.

A man replied, "I stole the temple money. I know you will find out with your magic Tell Tale, so I came to beg you for mercy. I will return the money and do whatever you say, if you will keep my secret! If I were exposed, it would ruin my family! I have never stolen any-thing before." The man was close to tears.

The woodcutter thought quickly and whispered back. "I am glad you came to me. I already knew you were the thief, but I wanted to give you a chance to repent. Take the treasure and bury it beneath the statue behind the temple. And do not steal ever again, because the next time I will not spare you."

The thief thanked the woodcutter profusely and vanished into the night. The next day, the woodcutter returned to the priests, took out his Tell Tale, and searched through the temple and its gardens. When he came to the statue behind the temple, the husband cried out, "Aha! Just as I thought, the money is buried here." The priests dug up the ground and found their five hundred gold coins! They were so grateful to the woodcutter that they put on a great feast in his honor, and rewarded him richly. So the woodcutter and his wife lived in comfort, honor—and fidelity—for the rest of their lives.

HUMOR AND TRICKERY AT MIDLIFE

This tale is delightful and light-hearted, yet it also addresses deep issues about men and women at midlife. The story begins when the woodcutter discovers his wife having an affair with the pawnbroker. Illicit liaisons reflect a stereotype of the middle years, and most people know a man or woman who has a fling at midlife. Surprisingly, statistics show that extramarital affairs peak for men within the first few years of marriage, and for women with the first decade or so—not in midlife. And while divorces do occur in the middle years, they, too, are most common earlier.[1] The stereotype of the middle-aged husband or wife having an affair is more fear than fact, but the fantasy runs deep, and there are powerful reasons for it.

On one side, women normally begin reclaiming their autonomy, power, and sexuality at midlife. Women often begin to enjoy sex more fully and want it more frequently. Throwing off social inhibitions, women feel freer to imagine—and pursue—romantic affairs.[2] On the other side, as their wives embark upon new careers outside the house, husbands often feel threatened and imagine that their wives have affairs with other men. The pattern cuts across cultures. Among the !Kung tribe of Africa, women after menopause are excused from rigid social and sexual rules. They become more assertive and self-confident and often take young men as lovers. Although it is not clear how frequently such affairs occur in real life, !Kung men and women certainly fantasize about them.

When the woodcutter discovers his wife's affair, he comes up with the hilarious ruse about the magic Tell Tale and embarks upon a series of amusing and ridiculous adventures. The story soon resembles a television sitcom. Such humor is a major theme in middle tales around the world.[3]

Youth stories and elder tales, by contrast, usually display an inspired, heartwarming, and moralistic tone, not a humorous one. Tales of youth glorify heroic struggle and therefore cannot poke fun at the protagonists or the villains. Elder tales, for their part, deal with transcendent, numinous revelations, so that humor would border on the blasphemous. Middle tales suffer no such constraints or inhibitions. They mock everything from God to peasants. The reason for this humor is revealed in the woodcutter's tale.

What is striking is how the woodcutter uses humor to deal with his anger. Enraged over his wife's affair, he wants to murder the two lovers, but stops himself. He invents the hilarious story of the Tell Tale instead, tricks his wife, humiliates the pawnbroker, and gains a tidy profit to boot. In psychological terms, the woodcutter sublimates his rage. He brandishes a piece of wood with a hole in the middle, rather than his axe. Psychologists have long noted that humor neutralizes aggression. Jokes and wit provide acceptable expressions for otherwise intolerable, violent emotions. Racial and sexual jokes are permeated with such hostile themes, and many stand-up comedians are notorious for the bite in their humor—the underlying aggressiveness.

The importance of humor in dealing with rage becomes clearer if we compare the woodcutter's story with Solomon's Advice from the last chapter. Recall that the merchant stays one night at the home of a man who blinded his own wife, murdered her lover, locked the poor woman in the cellar, and forced her to eat from her lover's skull. The story is horrifying and warns that without humor, midlife becomes a tragedy. Humor is no laughing matter—it is wisdom.

The same warning about uncontrolled anger can be found in the main story of The Thousand and One Arabian Nights, where a king murders his new wife each morning. The cause of the King's rage was his first wife's affair with a slave. Unlike the wise woodcutter in The Tell Tale, the King lacks humor to sublimate his anger.

Humor is a hallmark of maturity, as a number of eminent psychologists, such as Abraham Maslow, Carl Rogers, and Gordon Allport, have argued. Humor correlates with greater empathy, self-confidence, and creativity. Sigmund Freud even argued that humor is the highest and most mature mode of coping. Research confirms the point. As individuals mature, they use humor more. And the greater a person's psychological well-being, the greater his or her sense of humor.[4]

Middle tales feature more men than women using humor to deal with anger, for several reasons. First, men are usually more aggressive than women and so have a greater need for humor.[5] Second, as middle tales clearly show, a major task for women at midlife is to reclaim their assertiveness and liberate themselves. At this stage humor can be a diversion. Women need to fight for their place in society, rather than make jokes. (Men, on the other hand, usually need to stop fighting and make jokes.) Third, when women assert themselves, midlife typically becomes exhilarating rather than frustrating. This contrasts with the situation for men, who reach the limits of their success, confront decline and limitation, and need humor as a tonic.

Humor is particularly important for individuals in positions of responsibility. When young men and women become frustrated, they can rave about "stupid" authorities and rebel against them. Or they can stalk off, abandoning the situation. Fighting and fleeing are typical events in fairy tales of youth. But middle-aged men and women have no such luxuries. They cannot fume about "incompetent" authorities, since in most cases *they* are in charge. Nor can middle-aged people simply leave the situation, because too many other people, including angry youth, depend upon them for emotional and material security. Hemmed in by responsibilities, men and women at midlife are unable to fight or flee. Humor provides a vital resolution.

Besides its link to aggression, humor is closely allied with illusions and deceit, as The Tell Tale illustrates. The woodcutter pretends that his piece of wood reveals secrets to him, and his deception works so effectively that the pawnbroker pays fifty gold coins for a worthless box. The same hilarious deception appears in tales around the world and reflects a reality of midlife.[6] Men and women attain positions of authority where they are expected to be knowledgeable and confident, whether or not they feel that way. As heads of families, corporations, or institutions, middle-aged individuals must often pretend to possess insights they do not have, and display confidence they do not feel. The Tell Tale sums up the situation: the woodcutter pretends to know hidden truths, but the truth is the pretense!

Frank Baum's fairy-tale classic, *The Wizard of Oz*, offers an excellent example of this midlife phenomenon. The all-powerful Wizard turns out to be an impostor, well meaning but without real magic power. Yet his illusions were essential to Dorothy and her friends. By sending them on various tasks, the Wizard helped the Cowardly Lion find his courage; the Scarecrow, his brains; the Tin Woodman, his heart; and Dorothy, her self-confidence. Baum, I might add, was in his forties when he wrote his first Oz book.

If middle tales show men and women lying, cheating, and deceiving other people at midlife, there is one catch. Individuals can trick their peers and superiors with impunity, but they cannot cheat their inferiors and particularly the younger generation (unless the deception is for the good of youth, as in *The Wizard of Oz*). Selfish men and women who try to exploit children or apprentices are summarily destroyed in middle tales. The stories may advocate deception, but only within the context of generativity, the ruling principle.

The woodcutter's tale emphasizes this point. He does not use his Tell Tale out of greed, and resorts to deception only out of desperation—to avoid murdering his wife and her lover. When he bumbles into his deceit about the temple thief, the woodcutter's trick helps the villain reform. The woodcutter's deceits are ultimately generative.

At midlife, humor also helps men and women deal with the tragic side of life. The theme appeared earlier in The Mortal King where the monarch comes to terms with death through a joke. As Freud noted, humor allows men and women to triumph even over the inevitability of death—to make jokes about dying. A Mongolian story explains how this is possible.[7]

Long ago, a magic bird lived in a mountain forest. Everyone tried to catch it, but no one succeeded. One day, a king went hunting for the bird and caught it without difficulty. When he put the magic creature in a cage, the bird said, "I will tell you a story, but if you sigh at any time, I will escape."

"Once upon a time," the bird began, "a man carried a large treasure in a cart. The wagon broke down in a forest, but a hunter and his dog came by. The rich man asked the hunter to watch the cart and the hunter agreed. The owner went for help, while the hunter guarded the treasure. Night fell, and the hunter worried about his aged mother at home. So he told his dog to watch the cart and went home to check on his mother. The rich man returned, found the dog guarding the cart, and gave the animal a silver coin as a reward for his master. The dog ran home and gave the hunter the coin. The man flew into a rage. 'I left you to guard the cart, and you stole silver from it!' So the hunter killed the dog."

The King heard the story and sighed, "Alas, for the poor dog!" The magic bird immediately escaped from the cage and flew back to the forest. The King returned to the mountain, caught the bird, and put it in the cage a second time. As he left the forest, the bird told another story.

"Once a mother went to fetch water from the well. She told her cat to watch the baby in the cradle. When the mother left, a rat bit the baby's ear off. The cat fought the rat and killed it. Then the cat went back to lick the baby's ear to stop the bleeding. The mother returned, saw the baby bleeding and the cat licking the blood. The mother flew into a rage. 'How dare you bite my child!' The mother killed the cat."

"Ahh!" the King sighed, "what an injustice!"

The magic bird immediately escaped. The King sought the bird a third time, caught it, and started back home. The bird told another story.

"Once there was a terrible drought. A man searched for water and finally found a few drops dripping down from a tall rock. The man collected the water and was about to drink it when a crow flew by and knocked the bowl over. The man was enraged and threw a stone at the bird. The man found the bird dead on top of the rock. And next to it lay a snake sleeping in the sun, with its venom dripping down the rock. The 'water' the man had collected was poison, and the crow had saved his life by knocking the bowl of venom over!"

"Alas!" the King murmured, but before he could complete his sentence, the magic bird flew back to the forest. After that, the King gave up his attempt to capture the bird.

In this Mongolian tale, the King fails to keep the magic bird because he sighs at the tragic stories. He takes the tales too seriously and cannot appreciate their absurdity and black humor. He does not stand back psychologically from the dramas, and it is through such disengagement that humor detoxifies death and tragedy. The importance of distance is particularly clear in self-deprecating jokes. Only individuals who can look at themselves from the outside can make fun of themselves. And, in general, we laugh at situations only if we are not too involved in them. On the other hand, complete detachment breeds indifference and cold objectivity, not humor. Balancing engagement and detachment is central to humor. Here we come to another aspect of wit and midlife—their link to irony.

Irony can be roughly described as asserting or believing something while knowing, at the same time, that it is not completely true. In other words, irony is the ability to hold two different views at the same time. This is what psychologists call *dialectical* or paradoxical thinking,[8] and it is central to humor, because jokes typically involve linking two unlikely viewpoints or events.[9] The capacity for irony develops in the middle years and is a mark of maturity. Young adults typically avoid ambiguities and think in terms of black or white, of either/or categories. They choose one side and ignore the other. Mature individuals learn to tolerate uncertainty and paradox, consciously entertaining contradictory thoughts.[10]

If irony underlies humor, it also animates the moral relativism of the middle years. Men and women follow their own moral principles, but also acknowledge that there are alternatives. They believe and yet do not believe. Such an attitude—seeing through one's own deepest convictions—is a traditional measure of wisdom.[11] Irony also extends to religious beliefs. In his research James Fowler found that young children typically picture God as a good parent, while young adults elaborate more abstract notions of God. At midlife, Fowler observed, an ironic attitude toward God emerges. The individual remains committed to a personal faith and yet realizes that this faith is not absolute truth—that other beliefs are possible. Such an ironic faith, Fowler noted, usually appears only after a midlife crisis.

Besides its connection to irony, illusion, and aggression, humor is linked to one other virtue—healing. As the Bible puts it, "A merry heart does good like medicine."[12] The role of humor in psychological healing is clear: it helps mitigate stress and tragedy. Most professional comedians, in fact, come from unusually traumatic childhoods and survived only because of their sense of humor. Humor also facilitates physical healing, something the late Norman Cousins eloquently described. Crippled in midlife by a painful, debilitating disease, with no cure in sight from medical science, Cousins found that a good laugh gave him more relief from pain than narcotics. So he deliberately immersed himself in funny films and books, and his disease remitted. Comedians intuitively appreciate this, and many explicitly compare themselves to physicians rather than entertainers.[13]

Healing is a major concern at midlife, and middle tales reveal surprising insights on this topic, as we shall see in the next two chapters.

FOURTEEN

Suffering and Healing

The Stoning
a Moroccan tale

nce upon a time, a husband left his wife and home to go on a pilgrimage, as was the custom of their people. Before he departed, the man went to his brother, who was a judge, and asked him to look after his wife.

"Gladly," said the brother. As soon as the husband left, the judge went to the wife. This is my chance! he thought, because he had long coveted his brother's wife. The judge brought a gift with him and knocked at the door. The wife was no fool. She knew what her brother-in-law wanted and turned him away.

Undaunted, the judge returned the next day with an even more costly gift. But the wife only scolded him. "What are you doing?" she exclaimed. "I am your brother's wife! Have you no shame?"

Angered by her words, the judge went to his court. Before the whole village he accused his sister-in-law of being a prostitute. The judge was an eloquent speaker, and his words inflamed everybody. The people stormed the wife's house, dragged the innocent woman out, and threw stones at her until she collapsed. Then the villagers left her for dead.

A little later, a traveler passed by the pile of stones and heard moaning from within. He dug through the rocks and found the wife, barely breathing. The traveler took pity on her, and carried her home to his own wife and family. The kind man and his wife nursed the injured woman back to health and invited her to stay with them.

When the wounded wife recovered, she found she could heal the sick. She cured a neighbor's fever and gave sight back to a blind man. Word of her power spread throughout the land, and people came to her for their ailments. So the wife began a new life as a healer. Every day she received the sick from behind a screen, hidden from view, and asked questions of her patients. Then she advised them on a cure, and all who came to her went away healed.

Meanwhile, far away in his village, the judge succumbed to a grave illness. Ugly sores spread over his body and festered painfully. He summoned doctors and priests, but they could not cure him. The judge tried potions and lotions, and he prayed at all the holy places. But nothing worked. Day by day he grew weaker and more hideous.

The judge's brother finally returned from his pilgrimage. He found his house empty and hurried to his brother. "Where is my wife?" he exclaimed.

"She was stoned to death for being a prostitute!" the judge explained.

"What are you talking about?" the husband demanded. He could not believe his ears. But the judge and the villagers repeated the story.

"She is dead," the judge said. The husband was heartbroken, but there was nothing he could do. Then he noticed how ill his brother was. "On my travels," the husband said, "I heard of a great healer who lives some distance from here. People say she can cure anybody. Let us go to her and see if she can heal you."

The judge agreed, and they set off together. When they arrived, the woman healer saw that the two men were her husband and his brother. But they did not recognize her because she sat behind a screen.

"Tell me about your illness," the wife asked, disguising her voice. The judge recounted his miseries and the remedies he had tried.

"The cause of this malady," the wife declared, "is a grave sin you have committed. Confess this crime, or you cannot recover."

The sick man said, "I am a judge! I have committed no wrong!"

The wife repeated, "Confess your sin, or you cannot be healed."
"I am innocent," the judge insisted.

The husband spoke up. "Brother, whatever it is, confess! Otherwise you will die from your horrible illness!"

Finally the judge stirred. Weeping with shame and remorse, he told his brother, "I coveted your wife, and when she rebuffed me, I accused her falsely of being a prostitute. So the villagers stoned her to death."

With those words, the wife drew aside the screen and stepped forward. The husband was amazed to see her. Then he ran to embrace her. The wife said, "I will cure your brother if you desire it."

The husband thought a moment, and nodded. "My brother has suffered enough, and he has repented. Cure him if you can."

The wife went to the judge and healed him. His sores vanished, and he stood up from his stretcher. The wife and husband returned home in great happiness, while the judge followed behind—chastened and changed.

SUFFERING AND HEALING AT MIDLIFE

This Moroccan story reiterates themes familiar from previous middle tales and then introduces a vital new motif. The drama begins when the wife rejects her brother-in-law's immoral advances. He retaliates by persecuting her. As a judge, the brother-in-law represents a patriarchal figure, and his attack on the wife symbolizes the oppression women suffer in patriarchal society. Indeed, the present story closely resembles The Wife Who Became King, because both tales depict independent-minded wives who reject the illicit advances of a patriarchal figure, and then suffer for it.

The present tale underscores the theme of oppression by having the wife unjustly stoned. What is most daunting is that her attackers presumably include other women, since the tale says that all the villagers participated. Women's oppression does not merely come from men, but from the whole culture, which can turn women against women and neighbor against neighbor.

When the wife recovers from her wounds with the help of the kind man and woman, she discovers that she can cure the sick. Healing appears prominently in middle tales around the world. The Grimms' collection alone includes several stories, like Three Army Surgeons, Brother Lustig, The Three Snake Leaves, and The Godfather. The healing motif emerges in modern middle tales, too. A contemporary version of The Stoning can be found in the 1980 Hollywood movie *Resurrection,* in which a woman (played by Ellen Burstyn) is shot by an angry lover and nearly dies. When she recovers, she finds she has the power to heal the sick.

Healing takes a totally different form in youth stories. The Grimms' youth tale Godfather Death is a good example, and the comparison with The Stoning illuminates the distinctive role of healing at midlife.

Once upon a time, a young man was given the power of healing by Death, his godfather. Death imposed only one condition. Whenever the young man went to cure a sick person, he would see Death in the room. If Death stood at the head of the patient's bed, the young man could cure the person. If Death stood at the feet, the young man had to forgo any cure. The godson obeyed the condition and became a prosperous healer. One day, the young man was offered a great reward to cure the King. Death stood by the King's feet, indicating that the man was to die, but the youth turned the King's bed around and cured the monarch. Death was furious and warned his godson against any further tricks. Sometime later, the King's daughter fell ill, and when the godson went to cure her, Death stood at her feet, claiming her life. But the young man fell in love with the Princess, ignored Death, turned the bed around, and cured the Princess. In anger, Death killed his godson.

This story is typical of youth tales about healing. A young protagonist uses the power of healing to win treasure and true love. To youth, healing is one more way of making it in the world. Healing is subordinated to heroism. But the young man goes too far and loses the power to heal—and his life. In middle tales men and women do not abuse the power to heal. Healing is not a means to power and glory, but a way of coping with traumas and tragedies. Healing supplants heroism. The reason is simple: healing is needed. The young body that served so well and so heroically begins to groan and creak in the middle years. Physical excesses in eating or exertion, which young bodies easily throw off, also take their toll. Injuries are slower to heal, while unwanted fat is faster to accumulate.

Healing, surprisingly enough, is not prominent in fairy tales about *old* people. Although illnesses are more common in later life than in the middle years, the protagonists of elder tales focus on transcendence rather than healing. Instead of repairing the body, elders rise above physical concerns and attain sublime, spiritual insight. Elders withdraw from the material world. Middle-aged individuals, saddled with worldly responsibilities, do not have that luxury. Immersed in material concerns and yet stuck with a body that is slowly declining, men and women at midlife turn naturally to healing.

Many different cultures link healing specifically with midlife. Among the !Kung Bushmen of Africa and the Maori of New Zealand, individuals often take up the vocation of healer in the middle years. Although some men and women train to be healers in their youth, the most highly regarded healers are usually middle-aged or older. The Kirghiz of Afghanistan consider anyone under thirty years of age incapable of being a healer, and in many cultures some of the most powerful healers are postmenopausal women. This is not to say that age itself confers healing powers. Many healers retire in their later years because of the strenuous effort involved in healing rituals.[1]

The Stoning does not explicitly explain how the wife obtains her power to heal, but it is presumably due to her terrible ordeal. Here we come to a theme in folklore around the world, the archetypal image of the wounded healer. The theme is particularly prominent in shamanic traditions, and the wife's experience closely resembles a shaman's initiation. Typically, an individual becomes a shaman when he or she suffers a terrible illness and recovers. Often the malady involves a near-death episode, and the prospective shaman is thought to descend into the underworld and return with the ability to heal. Individuals who do not suffer a spontaneous illness must undergo grueling initiation ordeals, equivalent to a dreadful disease. The example of an Eskimo woman who became a shaman is particularly relevant. Her shamanic initiation began with her being hung from poles stuck in the snow for five days (note the theme of five). The master shaman then shot her, left her for dead, and the next day revived her. She then became a shaman with the power to heal.[2]

There are many reasons why personal suffering and the power to heal are closely connected. On one level, the experience of pain, injury, and illness teaches compassion for others, which is essential to healing. The compassion of maturity also differs from that of youth. In fairy tales, young heroes and heroines typically take pity on sick people and wounded animals. But theirs is the compassion of innocence, filled with the faith that any suffering can be relieved, and any injury or illness healed. Young people have not struggled with the darker side of life, with wounds that do not heal and afflictions that know no cure. Having experienced the tragic dimension of the human condition, men and women at midlife learn a deeper compassion. It is this charity that offers healing at midlife.

On a deeper level, suffering leads to healing through the process of self-reflection and self-reformation. The story dramatizes this point because the judge cannot be cured of his malady until he confesses his crimes. Illness often compels individuals to reflect on their lives and confront their shadow side—their faults, shortcomings, and vices. Ideally, individuals identify and change unhealthy habits that cause or aggravate their disease. Somatic symptoms often have symbolic messages, too, just like dreams. Illnesses can bring up issues that individuals avoid in normal life: the middle-aged business executive who is temporarily disabled by a heart attack, for instance, must come to terms with the relentless ambition and self-seeking that probably contributed to the illness.

The healing process of self-reflection and reformation is really a purging experience. Dante emphasizes the point in the *Divine Comedy*. After descending into Hell at midlife, Dante begins a long journey through Purgatory. There he finds men and women suffering greatly. Yet to his astonishment, they endure their torments gladly. When he asks the reason for their hopefulness, the inmates of Purgatory explain that their suffering helps them grow and develop, until they ultimately can enter Paradise. Each individual, Dante learns, has specific tasks that are tied to past sins. These ordeals do not aim at punishment, but at transformation. Some individuals struggle to change lust into love, others to transform material greed into a desire for wisdom. Experiences of purgatory force men and women to work through the blind instincts that drove them to unhealthy excess in youth. Healing then occurs.

This purging process finds its most dramatic expression in the image of death and rebirth. Individuals abandon their familiar beliefs, social roles, and values. The person's life structures are destroyed, opening the way for new possibilities. In Jungian terms, the *persona* collapses at midlife. This is the poetic term Jung used to describe an individual's public role in life—his or her identity as a parent, worker, citizen, socialist, and so on. (*Persona* derives from the Greek term for the masks used in dramas.) As the persona falters at midlife, the individual is forced to turn inward. Ideally, the person discovers a primordial source of new life deep within. It is this inner energy that is healing and renewing. For some individuals, the deep inspiration involves contact with God, while others call the inner source love, the life force, mystery, or the immortal soul.

The case of Emily offers an instructive example. A business executive who was successful in both career and family, she raised three children and made a reputation in her particular field of marketing. In her late fifties, Emily suffered a deep depression and came to therapy for the first time. She was perplexed by her inner turmoil and self-doubt, because she prided herself on being competent, assertive, and in control—qualities that had led to her success in business. It soon became apparent, however, that beneath her executive self-assurance lurked someone who was frightened, vulnerable, needy, and desperately afraid of being abandoned. Emily had always denied this part of herself and was finally forced to confront it. As she struggled with her depression, she had a remarkable dream, which proved to be a turning point for her.

In the dream, Emily was a child of about five or six, playing alone at home. There was a storm outside, with lightning and thunder, and Emily felt afraid. She went into a cave near her house and found several witches beside a boiling cauldron. The hags cackled, threw horrible things into the pot, and stirred the brew. Emily was terrified but fascinated. Finally one witch drew a healthy baby girl out of the pot. "Isn't she pretty?" the witch muttered to herself, as the baby started crying loudly. "I think she'll do just fine."

Soon after the dream, Emily began making major changes in her life. She started drawing and painting, which she had enjoyed immensely in her youth but had given up. She also began going for long walks in the countryside. Although she had loved the outdoors as a child, it had been many years since she took the time to enjoy nature.

The witches in Emily's dream symbolized her depression. Emotionally, Emily descended into a hellish underworld. Her self-confidence and self-esteem vanished in a maelstrom of turbulent emotions, aptly symbolized by the boiling cauldron. Metaphorically, the life structures she established in youth were boiled away. In Jungian terms, her persona was destroyed, and her familiar identity as a business entrepreneur and a responsible parent broke down. Out of the painful experience, new life emerged for Emily, symbolized by the healthy newborn baby. Emily found renewal and healing in art and nature, reawakening a long-forgotten part of herself. Her experience of death and rebirth, depression and recovery, allowed her to make a more complete connection to her inner self.

The themes of death, rebirth, and healing appeared in my own life a few years ago. I was feeling wounded and vulnerable from a series of personal and professional reversals. But an image came to me in a spontaneous fantasy, and it offered me unexpected comfort and hope. In the drama, I was a child alone in a land devastated by war. In the distance a troop of horsemen approached. They were a dreadful sight, dressed in black and riding black horses. Their leader wore a terrifying mask, and I knew that he was the Lord of Darkness—death and destruction incarnate. The Dark Lord glanced at me, and then motioned to his men. "Bring the boy with us. He will die otherwise. There is no one left in the land." I was astonished, fearful, and yet hopeful. A horseman lifted me onto his horse, and we rode off.

The troop returned to the castle of the Dark Lord, and the horsemen vanished. Only the Lord of Darkness remained, but I dared not address him, nor did he speak to me. Alone in the vast fortress, I grew more despondent, until one evening I walked past a room, deep within the castle. I saw a glow coming from a crack in the door, and I went up to it. I peeked through and saw the Lord of Darkness, kneeling before a great light shining from out of nowhere in the middle of the room. I was astonished. Somehow I knew with that uncanny certainty of dreams that the Lord of Darkness was a servant of this radiance. A beam of the light then fell upon my face, and I was filled with indescribable joy. At that moment, the Dark Lord shifted his position and blocked out the light. I could see nothing more of the numinous light, so I walked away. Yet I found myself feeling new hope and life. My despair had vanished and I felt healed. Later I noticed that I was badly sunburned where the light had fallen on my face. I realized then that the Lord of Darkness had shifted his position and blocked the radiance to protect me from being injured.

This drama was not quite a dream, and yet it was more than a fantasy. In it I journeyed into the underworld, the realm of the Lord of Darkness, just like Emily in her dream of witches. There I discovered a secret power that gave me hope and healing. The image of the Lord of Darkness was deeply therapeutic for me then, and it remains so today. Just as middle tales promise, I discovered that healing and rebirth lie hidden within despair and suffering. The drama came to me before I began working on middle tales, and I did not fully understand the symbolism until I noticed the similarities to middle tales like The Stoning, and to shamanism.

Shamanic themes resonate deeply in popular culture today, particularly among the postwar baby-boom generation. As men and women of this generation enter the middle years, they turn spontaneously toward issues of illness and healing, tragedy and renewal. The Stoning underscores the archetypal links between these themes.

The protagonist of the tale is a woman. But the power of healing is not unique to women. Many other middle tales focus on men gaining the power to heal.[3] A legend from the Chumash tribe in California provides a good example, recounted by Joan Halifax in her book on shamanism. A powerful wizard named Axiwalic became ill and could not heal himself. He finally went off alone to die, but met a spirit who offered him the hope of a cure. The spirit led him down into the underworld, where Axiwalic sat in a great hut and waited. Every kind of animal in the world appeared, from bears to mice. They all defecated on Axiwalic, until he was buried under a pile of feces. Then the animals bathed him, cured him of his illness, and returned him to his people.

Like the wife who symbolically dies when she is buried under the pile of stones, Axiwalic descends into the underworld. There he is covered not by rocks, but by feces! The story adds humiliation and humor to suffering, but the major motif is the same: finding healing in a descent into the underworld.

Women are more closely identified with healing than men, because women traditionally are expected to be nurturing, compassionate, and empathic. Some scholars, like Jeanne Achterberg in her book *Woman as Healer,* have even argued that healing is fundamentally a feminine activity. However, judging from the example of shamanism, probably the oldest form of healing, healers have been both male and female throughout history. In many cultures, male shamans seem to predominate, but even in highly patriarchal traditions, women became shamans. Of course, physicians have usually been male in Western tradition, but physicians are not the only healers. Midwives and folk healers are prominent in other cultures and are usually women.

Healing cannot exclude women or men, because healing requires both masculine and feminine strengths. Compassion and empathy, traditionally feminine virtues, are required to nurse an individual back to health. But bold actions and fierce struggle, two stereotypical masculine qualities, are equally essential. Healers must often force sick patients to take bitter medicine or submit to painful surgery. Healers thus inflict pain. If the wounded healer is a fundamental archetype, so is the wounding healer.[4]

Because healing requires both masculine and feminine qualities, to be genuine healers men must come to terms with their nurturing side, and women with their aggressive strengths. The Stoning suggests the latter point in a subtle way. The wife is independent in the story and resists her brother-in-law's unwanted advances, even to the point of being attacked and stoned to death by the villagers. The wife could have yielded to the corrupt judge and saved her life, but she refused. Like the wife who became King, the wife in the Moroccan tale values her integrity above her life. She insists on her autonomy and assertiveness, even in an oppressive society.

The integration of the masculine and the feminine in healing is charmingly illustrated in the next middle tale, where the collaboration of husband and wife is essential in gaining the power to heal.

FIFTEEN

Renewal and the Underworld

The Bonesetter
from Japan

ong ago, there lived a husband and wife who were both greatly respected in their land. He was a warrior and a physician, and she was famous for her many accomplishments, wisdom, and beauty. One night, the woman went to the outhouse as she usually did. As she undressed to use the toilet, someone touched her on the buttocks.

"Who is it? How dare you!" she yelled, more indignant than fearful. She looked out the window and saw someone run away in the moonlight. She finished her business, returned to the house, and said nothing to her husband.

The next night, the woman went to the outhouse as usual. This time, she took her sword with her, prepared for any trouble. As she undressed, someone brushed her on the buttocks. She drew her sword and cut off the hand touching her.

"Aiee!" Someone yelled from outside and stumbled away into the night.

The woman picked up the hand and stared at it in surprise. It was webbed and looked like a turtle's foot. She calmly finished her business and went to her husband, explaining what happened and showing him the strange hand.

The husband marveled at his wife's courage, and then studied the amputated limb. "What a strange thing!" he exclaimed. Finally he nodded. "It looks like a water demon's hand!" he declared. Then he laughed. "A water demon must have seen you at the toilet and fallen in love with you!"

The woman became indignant. "Don't say such a horrible thing! The demon could have kidnapped me!" She picked up the hand and studied it. "This is surely a rare thing," she murmured.

"Yes," the husband replied, "it might be very valuable." So he and his wife locked the hand in their vault. Then they went to sleep.

In the middle of the night, the man was awakened by whispering at the window. "Please give me back my hand!" a voice pleaded. The man said nothing. He reached over to his bow and arrows and pulled on the bowstring as a warning. The voice stopped abruptly, and someone or something scurried away.

"What was that?" the wife inquired.

"It must have been the water demon!" the man explained.

The next night, the man was awakened again by a whisper outside the window. "Please give me back my hand!" The man picked up his bow, drew the bowstring, and released it, making a twanging sound. The water demon quickly fled.

The third night, the creature returned, and again begged for its hand: "Please give me my hand back."

By this time the man was curious, so he asked, "Why do you want your hand back? It is now dried and shriveled! What could you possibly do with it?"

The water demon showed itself at the window and bowed to the husband and wife. "We water demons know the secret of setting broken bones and healing severed limbs," the creature explained. "So I can rejoin my hand to my arm, and they will both be as good as new!" The water demon pleaded again for the return of its hand.

"Very well," the man said, thinking quickly. "I should kill you for bothering my wife and me, but I will spare you. And I will return your hand, but on one condition. You must show us the secret of setting bones and healing severed limbs."

"That is easily done," the water demon promised. So the husband and wife fetched the shriveled hand from the strongbox and gave it to the creature. The water demon showed the man and woman how to rejoin severed limbs, and fastened its hand to its arm. In a few moments, the demon's hand was healed, and the creature flexed its fingers to prove the point. Then the water demon bowed and disappeared into the night.

The next morning when the man and woman arose, they found two beautiful fish on the porch of their house. They knew the water demon had brought the gift to thank them, so they cooked the fish and enjoyed it immensely. With the water demon's lesson, the husband and wife became great healers. They passed down the art of bonesetting to their children, and to their children's children. Their family prospered, and all their people, too.

HEALING AND THE UNDERWORLD AT MIDLIFE

This Japanese tale is short and apparently simple, yet it is rich with symbolic details. The tale notes that the husband is both a physician and a warrior. This is a rather surprising combination, since the function of a warrior is to kill people and that of a physician is to heal them. This odd detail is symbolic and hints at two important motifs. The first is integrating opposites, in this case, killing and healing. Opposites are prominent at midlife, and especially the duality of masculine and feminine. The latter comprises the second theme. As a healer, the husband takes care of the sick and wounded and draws on his nurturing, compassionate side. The husband has access to his anima, his inner feminine nature. At the same time, he is a warrior, and thus traditionally masculine. So he balances his masculine and feminine sides.

The story notes that the wife was well respected for her own wisdom and accomplishments. The comment is significant, coming from a strongly patriarchal country like Japan, which relegates women to secondary roles. The wife is an individual in her own right, and this implies that she has access to her assertiveness and resourcefulness. The story confirms the point when the woman is molested in the outhouse. She does not run away fearfully, calling for help from her husband, which would be the stereotypical feminine thing to do. Instead, she stands her ground and yells indignantly at the intruder. Later, she does not consult her husband, but relies upon her own counsel. Even more dramatically, the woman takes her sword with her to the toilet the next night. When the intruder touches her a second time, she simply cuts off the offending hand. She is not overly aggressive, however. She warned the intruder the night before by yelling at him and chasing him away. If he returns the second night, he is asking for trouble, and she obliges.

When the woman shows her husband the strange hand, he recognizes that it comes from a water demon. Here the husband and wife complement each other. She makes contact with the creature, and he identifies it as a water demon. In Japanese folklore, these creatures normally live in ponds and rivers. Water, and therefore waterdemons, are common symbols for the unconscious. So, the wife gains access to the unconscious, a function traditionally associated with women. (Women are said to be more intuitive than men.) For his part, in recognizing that the hand comes from a water demon, the husband provides knowledge and conscious discrimination. This is a traditionally masculine function. The husband and wife have complementary roles, which are archetypal and appear throughout world mythology. At the Delphic oracle in Greece, for example, the Sibyl was a woman who made prophecies because of her direct contact with the gods. Her words were usually incomprehensible, so a male priest interpreted her comments. When she contacted the unconscious, he articulated it.

When the water demon appears and asks for its hand back, the husband reaches for his bow and pulls the bowstring. The demon flees, but returns two more times, until the man asks the demon why it wants its shriveled hand back. This exchange between the demon and the husband is extraordinary. The man does not attack the creature, which would be the typical reaction of a young hero. The husband *negotiates* with the demon. Talking things over and communication are traditionally feminine virtues, so we have another suggestion that the husband has integrated his feminine side.

The story confirms the theme with a small detail: the husband pulls on the bowstring as a warning. In medieval Japan, warriors usually slept with their swords near them, rather than their bow and arrows. (If one is attacked at night by intruders, the sword is more useful for fighting at close quarters.) So the husband's action is not realistic but rather symbolic. Plucking the bowstring presumably makes a musical noise, like a lute or lyre. The husband converts a weapon, the bow, into a musical instrument, reiterating the theme of integrating the feminine. There is still deeper symbolism here, because bows and arrows are often used in Japanese shamanism. The bow is plucked like a musical instrument, and the sound is thought to control spirits. Such magic bows are also associated with women shamans.[1]

By complementing each other, the husband and wife reverse traditional gender roles. The wife attacks the demon, cutting its hand off, while her husband, who is a warrior, negotiates with the creature. Role reversals are particularly important for healing. Mircea Eliade, in his classic book *Shamanism,* observed that across cultures, when men become shamans at midlife they frequently dress as women and adopt feminine roles. This occurs among the Chukchee, Kamchadal, Eskimo, and Koryak tribes of Asia and North America, as well as in Korea. Men must gain access to their inner feminine to become healers. The converse holds for women. In Mayotte society, on the Comoro islands in the Indian Ocean, middle-aged women become healers when they are possessed by a *male* spirit. A similar phenomenon occurs among middle-aged Maori women.[2] As these women gain access to their masculine side, they become healers.

Besides the husband and wife, the other crucial character

in the present tale is the water demon. In Japanese folklore, these creatures are malevolent beings who typically lure people, including children, into ponds and rivers. Sometimes the demons simply drown their victims, and sometimes they devour people. If water demons are evil, Japanese tales consistently attribute the power of healing to them. The creatures are paradoxical, at once destructive and healing. This brings us to a major new insight in the story—the association between healing and the demonic.

The theme is perplexing and even shocking, since healing today is usually attributed to positive factors, like optimism or love. However, traditional shamanism makes the demonic aspect of healing overt. As we discussed in the last chapter, shamans are said to descend into the underworld, fight or negotiate with demons, and emerge with the power of healing. Consequently, shamans are often considered demonic themselves. Among the lore of the Buryats and Yakuts of Siberia, the original shaman defied the Supreme God and was punished for it, like Satan in Christian theology. The same link between healing and demonic powers appears in different cultures.[3] Gula, the ancient Assyrian goddess of healing, was also the goddess of death. Hecate, the Greek goddess associated with evil and the underworld, was a specialist in healing children's diseases. And Asclepius, the paramount Greek physician, used the blood of the evil Medusa for healing.

Christianity later split healing from the demonic. Healing was attributed to God, while disease was blamed on sin and the devil. But the demonic aspect of healing could not be suppressed completely. Robert Stewart observed that European folk songs regularly portray demonic underworld beings as a source of healing and renewal. Curative powers were also attributed to relics of Christian saints, which were often gruesome and conjured up images of the demonic—pieces of bone or severed hands.

Fairy stories from Christian cultures make the demonic aspect of healing clear. The Grimms' middle tale The Godfather is illuminating. In the story, a poor man dreamed that he should ask the first person he met on the road to be godfather to his newborn child. The poor man did so, and the first stranger agreed to be godfather. The stranger also gave the poor man a vial of water with the power of healing. The father soon became a famous healer, and after several highly successful years, he sought out the stranger to thank him for the magic fluid.

When the father arrived at the godfather's house, he found a broom and a shovel fighting with each other on the first floor. The man asked them where the godfather was, and they directed him up the stairs. On the second floor, the man found a heap of dead fingers, pointing up to another flight of stairs. On the third floor, the healer came across a pile of chattering skulls, who told him to go upstairs to see the godfather. There the poor man found fish cooking themselves on a fire, and the creatures declared that the godfather was on the next floor. On the fifth level (notice the theme of five again), the man peeked into a room through a keyhole and saw the godfather lying in bed. But the godfather had a pair of horns on his head! The man became terrified and fled.

The godfather is apparently a demon, or the Devil himself. Certainly the whole household reeks of sorcery and black magic, with chattering skulls and severed fingers. Yet the godfather is also the source of healing power. So he is like the water demon in the Japanese story, a demonic figure with the power of healing.

Other middle tales underscore the link between healing and the demonic.[4] Two questions arise: Why is healing linked with the demonic? And what is the significance of the theme for midlife?

The demonic aspect of healing can be explained by a nearly universal human belief that disease is evil and is caused by malevolent spirits. As the cause, evil beings can cure disease, if only by stopping whatever they do to create suffering. More generally, healing requires power of some sort, and such power can kill as much as it can cure, working evil as well as good. This is not as naive a belief as it may seem. In modern medicine, cancer can be treated only by draconian methods—disfiguring surgery, painful radiation, or chemotherapy that causes nausea and vomiting. The cures are almost as demonic as the disease itself. Patients, as Arnold Mindell points out in *Dreambody,* often dream that their physicians are the cause of their diseases as much as the cure.

The power to heal—or to destroy—emerges fully only at midlife. This is because young people normally repress powerful instincts, like rage or lust, which are considered evil. At midlife, as the repression of youth lifts, the wild raw energy surges forth. Although initially frightening, like a volcanic eruption, this primordial libido provides the psychological energy needed for healing. Despite their violence, after all, volcanoes create new land and bring up vital material from the earth's core.

The biblical story of Job illustrates the emergence of such primordial energy at midlife. (Job was middle-aged when his drama began.) God wagered, one day, that Satan could not break Job's faith in God. Satan accepted the bet and, with God's permission, inflicted one calamity after another upon Job. The poor man lost his family, his wealth, and his health. (Notice the theme of a man's midlife downfall.) In anger and agony, Job questioned God's justice and demanded to know the reason God afflicted him so. God appeared as an awesome whirlwind and declared that his actions were beyond all human notions of good and evil. "Who are you to challenge me?" God asked Job, "when I created the heaven and earth!" Chastened by this direct encounter with God, Job ceased his protestations. At the same time, God restored Job to his former good fortune, and healed him of all his diseases.

God is ultimately the source of Job's suffering in the tale. Satan does the actual dirty work, but only with God's consent. And God made a bet with Satan in the first place, which is hardly noble or moral by human standards. So God seems demonic. Yet if God inflicts calamity on Job, he also heals Job, restores his fortune, and reminds Job that he, God, created all things in the world. God is portrayed as the source of life and death, healing and disease, creation and destruction. He represents a primordial power, beyond human notions of good and evil, erupting in Job's world at midlife.

A similar if less dramatic process can be seen in midlife crises, like that of Henri Matisse, the painter.[5] Although a successful artist, Matisse suffered a painful depression at midlife, in which he stopped painting and reexperienced many of his early childhood deprivations. In this tormented period, Matisse moved to the south of France, abandoning his wife and family in Paris. He soon started a series of affairs with young women. Although scandalous by conventional morality, these romances inspired Matisse to begin a new, highly creative period of work. And after recovering from his depression, Matisse later rejoined his wife and family. His passionate affairs gave Matisse contact with a primordial vitality deep within. While the affairs broke traditional notions of good and evil, they were healing.

A similar situation occurred with Jung, who began an affair with one of his young female patients, Toni Wolff, as part of his midlife crisis. The affair violated all canons of professional ethics, but helped inspire Jung to create his own distinctive psychology. Jung explicitly described his midlife experience as contact with "a stream of lava" deep within. The lava symbolized the primordial vitality that generated both his creative insights and his scandalous affairs.[6]

Here we return to a theme discussed before: the moral relativism of midlife. Tolerance for evil allows the mature individual to discover the primal vitality behind what appears to be demonic. Rejecting or fleeing from evil precludes contact with a primordial healing power. But the encounter is dangerous. Abandoning conventional notions of good and evil can be inflating and intoxicating, as Nietzsche's philosophy demonstrates. He urged people to transcend morality and become superhumans. His ideas were much favored by Nazis, who then assumed they were beyond right and wrong. Grandiosity, savagery, and disaster were the result, not healing. Middle-aged individuals avoid this inflation and barbarism by remembering their share of suffering over the years and giving up the heroism of youth for the generativity of maturity. Indeed, when young men and women face the primordial energies of the unconscious, their egos are usually overwhelmed, and psychosis often results. Only after establishing a sturdy ego, usually by midlife, can the individual safely contact the primordial life within. It is no accident that Job is well into midlife, strong and secure in himself, before he meets God face-to-face. Matisse and Jung, similarly, were sucessful individuals before they encountered the primordial power of the unconscious.

Folk traditions from various cultures confirm this warning. !Kung Bushmen of Africa believe that only older individuals are strong enough to handle the powerful spiritual forces that are needed for healing. Among the Kirghiz of Afghanistan, older individuals usually play the role of healer, because only they have the ability to handle powerful djinn, or spirits. Men and women under thirty lack this crucial capacity.[7]

The dark, demonic aspect of healing surfaced in a dream I had a few years ago. In the dream, I was a janitor working outside a small shrine. The building housed a sacred relic similar to the Holy Grail, with miraculous powers to heal. Two young men came up and asked to see the relic. They were tourists, not pilgrims on a religious quest or supplicants seeking healing. I inquired if they had prepared themselves for seeing the relic, and they laughed, insisting they did not need any preparation. I told them I could not let them into the building because it was too dangerous. But they insisted, and became more persistent and vocal. Finally, I gave in and said they could see the vessel, but whatever happened would be their own fault. I unlocked the door to the shrine, pulled the door open, and ducked behind a wall. Then I peeped through a small window. The two men entered the shrine. A light sprang up in the small room, coming directly from the sacred relic. The two men stared at the glowing object and became so fascinated that they could not move, even as the light grew rapidly in intensity. Soon the radiance was blinding and painful, even to me, peering through the window from farther away. As I watched with horror, the two men started to burn up in the overwhelming luminosity. Their bodies disintegrated until only the bones were left, and then the bones themselves turned into dust and vanished before my eyes. I thought there must be some horrendous kind of radiation coming from the relic, like that from a nuclear reactor, and I felt frightened. I hurriedly closed the door, and the light quickly subsided within the shrine. I felt terrible that the two men had been killed, but I told myself that I had warned them.

The danger and demonic power of the healing relic are clear in this dream. The light that offered healing also killed. And it specifically destroyed two young men, underscoring the risk to youth of encountering the primordial power of the unconscious. (This dream occurred some time after my spontaneous fantasy about the Lord of Darkness, described in the last chapter. It also came before I saw Steven Spielberg's movie *Raiders of the Lost Ark,* which has a similar scene. The images are archetypal.)

In retrospect, the dream also conveyed another important message. The young men were cocky and arrogant, as most young men are on some level. They personify the heroic attitude of youth which is overthrown at midlife. The ego is then assigned a new task—to be a janitor!

Making contact with a frightening, dangerous, but ultimately healing source of life is perhaps *the* central task of the middle years. The story in the next chapter elaborates on the theme, and sums up the issues we have discussed so far.

SIXTEEN

The Fountain of Life

The Golden Tree

from a Jewish source in India

ong ago, there lived a great king with five wives. The King loved his youngest wife most of all, so the other queens envied her and whispered evil things in the King's ear. "She has not borne you any children," the queens told the King, and this was true. "It is because she does not love you!" they whispered, and this was false. Finally the King believed the jealous queens and banished his youngest wife, sending her away without any money or food.

The poor Queen did not know what to do, so she simply followed the road. When night fell, she found herself in a great forest and took refuge in a tree. In the morning, the Queen climbed down and found an old man at the bottom of the tree. The Queen took fright and turned to flee.

"Do not be afraid," the old man said, and his voice was so kind and gentle that the Queen stopped. "You are tired and hungry," the old man went on. "Come with me. You can rest and eat at my home." The Queen saw a light shining in the old man's eyes, so she put her trust in him and followed him into the forest.

The old man and the Queen arrived at a small hut, and he prepared a meal, using nuts and berries. The hermit set out a bed for the Queen, woven from rushes, and when she lay down, she fell asleep immediately.

As she slept, the Queen dreamed that she wandered in a lovely garden with a beautiful pool. From the water grew a tree, and it was more marvelous than any she had ever seen, with leaves of gold and blossoms of diamond. As the Queen stared in awe at the tree, an old man in a long white robe came up to her, the very man who had given her shelter! He offered the Queen a golden amulet shaped like the tree in the garden, and the Queen put on the necklace. At that moment, she awoke from her dream. She felt something around her neck, looked down, and found herself wearing a golden amulet! Just then the old man came in from the forest, bearing fresh fruit.

"Good morning," he greeted the Queen. She looked at him with amazement and finally understood that he had been sent to protect her.

"Good morning!" she replied.

The old man smiled and set out another meal. As they ate, the old man asked the Queen about her life and she told him her sad story of being banished from the kingdom. "It is all the more unjust," she lamented, "because I now know that I am pregnant with the King's child."

The old man comforted the Queen. "You can stay here until the King comes to his senses," he said, and the Queen readily agreed.

The old man was a master craftsman. He extracted gold and silver from deep in the forest and fashioned wondrous objects. But the most marvelous things he made were amulets, shaped like the golden tree in her dream. Strangely enough, the old man never tried to sell his work. Instead he melted down his creations and fashioned new ones. This puzzled the Queen and she asked the reason for it. The old man smiled. "It is the creating I enjoy," he explained simply.

The days passed swiftly, and the Queen soon bore her first child, a baby boy. That very night, far away in his palace, the King was troubled by a strange dream. In it, he beheld a magnificent tree with leaves of gold and blossoms of diamond. As he moved closer to the tree, the King saw the face of his youngest Queen reflected on the tree trunk. The King was filled with sorrow, for he bitterly regretted banishing her. He reached out to touch the Queen's reflection, but then everything vanished, and he awoke.

Every night after that, the King had the same dream, and it tormented him. So he called all his sages and asked them the meaning of the dream.

"You are remorseful for banishing your queen," the wise men and women said. "You must send messengers to find her and bring her back." So the King dispatched heralds to all the corners of his kingdom, but no one knew where the Queen was. And every night when the King dreamed of the golden tree, he felt more agony and remorse. In anguish, the King called his soothsayers again. They consulted among themselves, and then spoke to the King.

"If the Queen is lost," they told him, "the golden tree can still bring you comfort. So command the jewelers of the kingdom to make such a tree, and your nightmares will end."

The King summoned all the goldsmiths, and they labored day and night until they created a golden tree more magnificent than anything ever made by human hands. But it was still only a shadow of the golden tree in the King's dreams, and his torment continued. In desperation, the King summoned the sages a third time. They murmured and pondered, and finally turned to the King. "There is only one solution," they said. "You must seek this golden tree yourself." So the King left the palace the next day, disguised as a beggar, determined to find the golden tree.

Everywhere he traveled, the King inquired about the golden tree, but no one could tell him where it grew. He wandered the length of the land, sleeping on the ground, desperate and disheartened. Then one day, the King entered a great forest and came across a hermit. The King asked the old man about the golden tree and the sage smiled.

"Yes," the old man said. "I know about the golden tree. But you are tired and hungry. Come with me to my home. After you eat and rest, I will tell you all you need to know."

The King rejoiced and followed the old man to a small hut. A woman and her child lived there, and they were none other than the King's youngest wife and his new son. The Queen recognized her husband at once, but she wore a veil so the King did not know her, and she said nothing. The old man set out a meal of fruits and nuts, and as the King ate, the sage told him about the golden tree.

"It grows deep within this forest," the hermit said, and the King's heart leaped with hope. "Follow that stream," the old man advised, pointing outside, "and when you reach its source, you will see the golden tree." The old man paused. "But the closer you come to the source, the hotter the stream will be. Its water rises from deep within the earth." The old man closed his eyes and murmured sadly, "Many have tried to reach the tree, and most have perished. Yet there is a way." He bent down and removed his shoes. "If you put on my shoes when you step into the water, the heat will not injure you, and you can make your way to the golden tree. But you must remember to bring my shoes back to me. Otherwise all your effort will be for nothing." The old man added gravely, "This is what I know. The rest is up to you."

The old man gave his shoes to the King and the monarch bowed in gratitude. The King followed the stream deeper into the forest. As the old man foretold, the water became warmer and more violent. Finally the King heard a great roaring, and clouds of steam billowed around him. Through the fog, the King glimpsed a flash of gold, and when he pushed forward, he beheld a luminous tree—the golden tree of his dreams! But the tree was surrounded by a whirlpool of boiling water, and the King despaired. "How can I reach the tree?" he cried out. "I shall die if I step in the water!" Then the King remembered the old man's shoes. He put them on, gritted his teeth, and stepped into the maelstrom.

To his surprise, the boiling water did not burn him, nor did he sink beneath its surface. Carefully, the King made his way to the center of the vortex and stood beneath the tree of his dreams. The King stared in awe, because the tree was a fountain of molten gold. Each spray of liquid metal formed a branch of the tree, and each droplet, a leaf. The form changed constantly and yet always remained shaped like a tree. Hesitantly, the King reached out, as he had in so many of his dreams. This time the tree did not vanish, and he grasped a golden branch. The molten metal did not burn him, and when he withdrew his hand, he took a bough of the tree with him, solid and golden.

The King exulted, for he had fulfilled his dream. He swam to the bank of the river, took off the old man's shoes, and hurried toward the hermit's home. Along the way, the King paused to rest, staring at the golden branch he carried. There on the burnished surface he saw the reflection of his youngest Queen, and he wept, regretting his harsh treatment of her. "Of what use is this golden branch?" he murmured to himself. "I have lost my dearest love!" Sadly the King arose, and resumed his way to the old man's home.

When the King arrived at the hut, he returned the shoes to the old man and thanked the sage for his help. The hermit congratulated the King, but the monarch only sighed. "I have touched the tree of my dreams," he told the old man, "and I have brought back a golden branch. But I cannot rejoice, for I have lost the woman I love most in my life." When the Queen heard those words and saw the remorse in her husband's eyes, she stepped forward and took off her veil.

"You lost me," she said, "but I have returned."

The King recognized his wife at once and fell at her feet, begging for her forgiveness. The Queen embraced the King and forgave him, and then she drew her child forward, so that father and son met at last. The King wept with joy and embraced the boy.

Finally the King and Queen bade farewell to the old man, and made their way back to the palace. When the King returned, he divorced his other wives and made his youngest wife the only queen. Then he planted the golden branch in the garden of his palace, where it grew tall and bright, as tall and bright as the love between king and queen.

THE GOLDEN TREE: TRANSFORMATION AND THE TREE OF LIFE

Focused on two protagonists, the King and Queen, this tale traces out the contrasting paths that men and women take at midlife. The story recapitulates most of the themes we discussed in earlier chapters, and then introduces a new motif, which succinctly sums up the fundamental challenges of midlife.

The story begins with a king and his many wives. Two themes are evident here. First, the relationship between the King and his wives is unequal, as is usually the case in polygamy. The King dominates and the queens must please him. This inequality reflects the historical context of the tale, which is placed in India, and also brings up a familiar theme in middle tales: the oppression of women.

The second motif is the ubiquitous number five. The tale specifically notes that the King had five wives, and the number again symbolizes both excess and integration. The excess is clear enough. The King has an excess of power and privilege over his wives, and the senior wives are excessively jealous of the youngest. The theme of integration is not as obvious, particularly at the beginning of the story. But by the end, integration and reconciliation emerge as prominent motifs.

When the senior queens conspire against the youngest wife, the King believes the malicious gossip. Although only a small detail in the story, the event is symbolic and points to the poor judgment the King exercises in interpersonal relationships. He remains completely naive about the ulterior motives of the senior queens and does not bother to investigate why his youngest wife has not borne him any children, or consider, for that matter, whether childbearing is the sole criterion of a woman's worth. The King's ignorance about human relationships constitutes his flaw. But the King is not grossly cruel or callous, and he is no monstrous Bluebeard. The King is simply like most traditional men and has failed to develop an understanding of human relationships, his feminine side. He spends most of the tale learning, and this is a central task for men at midlife, as The Lute Player and Stubborn Wife, Stubborn Husband illustrated.

The story quickly shifts to the youngest queen. After she is exiled, she suffers great deprivation, and her plight repeats the theme of women's oppression. Instead of living happily ever after, married to a king, the women in middle tales experience humiliation and despair.

The Queen's reaction to her calamity is remarkable. She neither begs for mercy nor despairs, but rather walks bravely onward. Nor does she wait for someone to rescue her. She is a strong, courageous woman. In exile, the Queen reclaims her native power, like the wife who became king, or the Queen in The Lute Player.

The young queen then meets a kind old man, who plays the traditional role of the helpful elder. It is tempting to interpret the old man as a symbol of the Queen's masculine side, her animus. However, the old man is really androgynous rather than masculine. He cooks food for the Queen, sets out a bed for her, and knows how to gather fruits and nuts. Those are all archetypal feminine activities. Moreover, as an elder and a hermit, the old man is more asexual than masculine. He is best considered to be someone who has transcended traditional gender roles and come to an integration of masculine and feminine.

Notice how the Queen finds protection and refuge in nature. The same theme surfaced earlier in Stubborn Husband, Stubborn Wife, where the burning sands of the desert prevent the thief from catching the wife: nature protects her, too. In The Wife Who Became King, similarly, a magic bird picks the wife to be King. Nature, represented by the bird, rescues the wife and bestows power and glory on her. The Golden Tree reiterates the theme in a small detail. The Queen first realizes she is pregnant while in the forest. Nature symbolically gives her new life. Her childlessness in the palace and the reason for her banishment by the King in the first place may very well have been caused by the patriarchal environment of the city.

When the Queen falls asleep in the old man's house she dreams of a golden tree, growing in a beautiful garden. Her dream is peaceful and rejuvenating, in sharp contrast to the King's nightmares of the same tree. This difference reflects the divergence between men's and women's experiences at midlife. As discussed before, men typically go through a grueling experience, which compensates for the honor and glory they enjoy in youth. Women, on the other hand, discover a new sense of strength, autonomy, and identity, which balances the oppression they suffer in youth.

The King's nightmares confront him with his foolish and unjust treatment of his youngest queen and his ineptness in dealing with the feminine. The King's responses to his dreams illustrate how men usually deal with the feminine at midlife.

On the advice of his sages, the King first tries to find the youngest queen and bring her back. Implicit here is the assumption that a man's happiness depends on a real woman. This repeats the romantic dreams of youth, when young men idealize nurturing, beautiful women. Young men project their emotional needs onto such women and expect the women to gratify their needs. At midlife, this arrangement fails. Wives usually tire of doing all the emotional work for their husbands. Men then have a choice. They can look for other women willing to do the feminine work for them, embark on a series of affairs, or remarry. Alternatively, men can develop their own feminine side. The King initially tries the first approach, seeking the Queen and hoping she will give him happiness. But he remains tormented. Simply repeating youthful solutions does not work at midlife.

Next the King's counselors exhort him to have a golden tree made, just like the one in his dreams. The advisors suggest that material achievement will satisfy the King's midlife misery. Notice how the King switches from an *interpersonal* approach to an *impersonal* one. In his dream, he saw both the golden tree and a reflection of his beloved queen, symbolizing a choice between materialistic gain and human relationships. Having tried the latter in searching for the Queen, the King now experiments with the former. He seeks solace in objects. This material interest takes many forms in the middle years. Some men turn to leisure pursuits, new cars, better stereos, or travel to exotic locations. Others redouble their efforts to advance in their careers, seeking greater wealth, power, or prestige. The story explicitly warns against this materialism. The King fails to stop his nightmares with the jewelers' tree.

The King finally accepts the third suggestion of his advisors. He forsakes his palace and seeks the golden tree on his own. Having failed with an interpersonal and an impersonal approach, he tries a *transpersonal* one, searching for the archetypal tree of his dreams.

In leaving his wealth and power, the King experiences a reversal of fortune and suffers the same privation he imposed on the exiled queen. This poetic justice reiterates another major theme in middle tales: men are thrown down from their positions of power and honor at midlife and learn about humility and vulnerability. In his suffering, the King realizes just how much the exiled queen meant to him. He acknowledges the importance of relationships, correcting his earlier insensitivity and ignorance in this area. His suffering is purging.

The King eventually meets the wise old man who offers him shelter and counsel. The Queen recognizes her husband immediately but remains silent. If the Queen revealed herself to the King at this point, he would no doubt ask for her forgiveness, and the two would presumably reconcile. The ruptured relationship between the King and Queen would be resolved, and no further development would occur. The meaning of the golden tree would be ignored, and the King would fall back upon the first suggestion of his counselors—finding resolution to his midlife turmoil in a concrete human relationship.

The Queen's silence brings up a prominent theme in fairy tales about women: waiting.[1] Waiting is often interpreted as a sign of passivity and helplessness, reinforcing feminine stereotypes. The Golden Tree and other middle tales portray a profoundly different picture. The Queen *consciously* chooses to remain silent, and she waits because she presumably knows the time is not right for her to reveal herself. Her waiting is not passive but knowledgeable, and she acts more like a judge than a helpless victim. Yet she is not vindictive. The Queen simply recognizes that the King lags behind her in psychological development, and she waits for him to catch up. This often happens in real life, where one spouse or the other may develop more rapidly. But waiting to reveal herself, the Queen also forces the King to seek out the golden tree and to explore a deeper, archetypal level of meaning.

The old man tells the King how to journey upstream to the golden tree. Here the story adds a charming but highly symbolic detail. The stream, the hermit says, becomes boiling hot near the golden tree, and the only way that the King can survive is by using the old man's shoes. We have already encountered symbolic shoes in previous middle tales. In The Shoemaker and the Elves, shoes symbolized the practical realities of the middle years, the necessity of working and earning a living. Shoes had a similar pragmatic meaning in Stubborn Husband, Stubborn Wife. The parallels with The Golden Tree are literal, because the King needs the old man's shoes to protect him from the heat of the stream, just as the thief needed shoes in the Persian story to shield him from the burning desert sand. The old man's shoes emphasize the importance of remaining grounded in ordinary, everyday experiences when dealing with archetypal themes. Numinous images like that of the golden tree are fascinating and beguiling, but are also psychologically dangerous. An individual can become inflated, or infected by the grandiosity of the experience.

The golden tree is clearly magical and symbolic. Roger Cook describes similar trees in the folklore and mythology of many cultures, from ancient Assyria to contemporary Tibet. Their meanings are complex and many layered. To avoid becoming lost in this symbolic forest, I shall begin my discussion with details about the golden tree and then move outward to more general, archetypal themes about magic trees.

Perhaps the most striking aspect of the golden tree is that it is really a fountain of gold. As the liquid metal shoots into the air and cools, it solidifies to form leaves and branches.

These boughs fall back into the fountain, where they are melted down, thrown into the air once more, and reshaped into new leaves and branches. *This sums up the process of midlife.* The personal convictions, commitments, values, and social roles that individuals establish in youth are destroyed at midlife. These life structures are melted down in the middle years and reforged, just the way the leaves and branches of the golden tree are obliterated and re-formed in the maelstrom. The molten fountain makes a perfect symbol for the primordial source of life that men and women encounter in the middle years.

The tale reinforces the theme of a primordial life energy in a subtle detail. Early on, the story mentioned a puzzling habit of the old man. He spent his time making wonderful objects of jewelry, like the Queen's amulet, but he never kept his handiwork or sold it. Instead he melted everything down and started over. He valued the creating more than the creation. Like the golden tree, the old man symbolizes a ceaseless process of transformation in which old structures are melted down and reforged. The story repeats the image of an inexhaustible source of vitality and creativity.

If the golden tree represents a primordial life source, it must be related to the archetypal Tree of Life. According to Hebrew mythology, which parallels older Babylonian legends, two magic trees—the Tree of Life and the Tree of Knowledge—grew in the Garden of Eden. Against God's express command, Adam and Eve ate from the Tree of Knowledge, and learned about right and wrong. God then banished them from Eden, not only as punishment but also to prevent Adam and Eve from eating from the Tree of Life, and becoming immortal like God.

The golden tree closely resembles the biblical Tree of Life. For one thing, the Queen and the old man live an idyllic life in the forest, enjoying the bounty of nature. The setting is reminiscent of the Garden of Eden, suggesting that the golden tree must be either the Tree of Life or the Tree of Knowledge. A close look at the story suggests the former. Knowledge of good or evil is not the focus of the tale. The Queen knows about right and wrong, and particularly how she was wronged by the King. But the King, too, recognizes his sin. Nor is the thrust of the story about punishment and guilt. Morality, connected with the Tree of Knowledge, is not the issue here. The story focuses on the restoration of life to an injured relationship and the emergence of new life in the Queen's child. These themes are more consonant with the Tree of Life.

The story emphasizes the link between the golden tree and the Tree of Life in a subtle way. Recall that when the Queen first dreams about the tree, the old man appears and gives the Queen an amulet shaped like the tree. The Queen then awakens from her dream and finds herself wearing the amulet. The story implies that she brought back the amulet from her dream. The amulet and the golden tree violate the usual separation between reality and dream, truth and fantasy. This suggests that the golden tree does not involve knowledge, which is based on the distinction between reality and fantasy. So the golden tree must be something more basic than knowledge. And that is surely life itself, since life is the condition of any knowledge or learning. Notice that the Queen has direct access to the golden tree through her dreams, while the King must struggle long and hard to find the tree. As discussed in the last chapter, women traditionally have more direct contact with the vitality of the unconscious. This often makes midlife easier for them than for men.

The golden tree in the story resembles the Tree of Life described in various cultures. Among the Siberian Yakut tribes, the Tree of Life is said to be made of silver, with sap of gold. And the golden sap runs out from the crown of the tree, like a fountain. Magical trees made of silver or gold also figure prominently in European alchemy. These alchemical trees were thought to contain a magical sap, which could turn lead into gold and transform the mortal human body into an imperishable spiritual one. As the key to eternal life, these alchemical trees were symbolically equivalent to the Tree of Life.[2]

In symbolizing a primordial life source, the golden tree sums up the major themes of middle tales. As discussed earlier, the primal source of life includes a demonic aspect. The golden tree reiterates the motif, because the tree grows in a hellish place and arises from deep within the earth. Its heat and subterranean origins imply that it is connected to the underworld. In many mythologies, the Tree of Life is explicitly associated with the demonic and is described as growing in a fiery river that either surrounds or runs through the land of the dead. In Polynesia, the demonic aspect is even more explicit. The coconut is the Polynesian Tree of Life, because the leaves provide material for weaving, the nut furnishes food and drink, while the trunk is used as wood. Yet the beneficent tree, according to Polynesian legend, first sprang from the body of an evil eel monster named Te Tuna. Paradoxically, the Tree of Life originated in something demonic. For the Dayak of Borneo, similarly, the Tree of Life grows from a monstrous serpent in the underworld, and the same link between an evil serpent and the Tree of Life can be seen in ancient Sumerian pottery, as well as in Celtic folk songs. In medieval Christian art, analogously, the cross upon which Jesus was crucified is portrayed as the Tree of Life, with death and sin at its roots.[3]

The golden tree is made of gold, the softest and most malleable of metals, but it has flowers of diamond, the hardest natural substance. So the tree is literally the union of opposites. The story reinforces the integration of dualities when we learn that the tree is a fountain of molten metal. Fluid and constantly changing, the geyser retains the fixed form of a tree. It combines dynamic flux with static permanence. Gold, moreover, does not tarnish, nor do diamonds lose their luster with age, implying that the tree, although a fountain that constantly changes, is also something timeless or eternal. The golden tree beautifully symbolizes the reconciliation of dualities and polarities, which is a feature of wisdom at midlife.

Central to this wisdom is a relativistic outlook, and the golden tree offers a charming metaphor for relativism. Every opinion, fact, or belief is only a branch or leaf of the golden tree. Convictions and faiths may seem golden and glorious for a time, but they soon fall back into the fountain and are melted down, so that new opinions and views can arise. This does not mean that any opinion whatsoever is valid, and that there are no ethical rules for midlife. The golden tree provides a fundamental guideline. As a Tree of Life, it symbolizes creativity and generativity. And those two themes are central principles in the middle years. A person's beliefs, roles, and actions are measured by how much they enrich human life.

Interpreting the golden tree as a symbol of relativism has precedents in the Jewish Kabbalah and Hindu traditions. Since the present tale comes from a Jewish source in India, the cultural context is relevant. In the Kabbalah, the universe is likened to a tree, with God as the root. All beings are the branches and leaves of this mystical tree. An individual's convictions and commitments are only small parts of God's primordial truth. Analogously, in Hindu tradition the various deities of the Hindu pantheon are considered different manifestations of a single, primordial divinity. Particular religious or ethical creeds are inherently partial and relative to a deeper, primordial truth.[4]

The encounter with the golden tree is not the end of the story. Although the King returns to the old man with a branch from the numinous tree, the monarch realizes that he cannot be happy without his youngest wife. The story repeats its emphasis on everyday human life. Numinous experiences, symbolized by the golden tree, are not enough for human fulfillment. The archetypal insights of midlife must be grounded in human relationships. To reinterpret a biblical saying, men and women do not live by the word of God alone.

At this point, the Queen recognizes the King's genuine repentance and reveals herself to him. He begs her forgiveness, and the two are reconciled. But the King also meets his new child, and the event is highly symbolic. In fairy tales, a new child often personifies a new era, a new outlook on life, as Marie-Louise Von Franz noted. Our story quickly confirms the theme. The King and Queen return to the palace with their child, and the King sends away his other queens, making his youngest wife the only queen. The King gives up his patriarchal privileges, symbolized by polygamy, and makes his wife equal to him. Symbolically, he harmonizes the masculine and feminine. Such a reconciliation appears in other middle tales, like Stubborn Husband, Stubborn Wife, The Lute Player, and The Wife Who Became King.

What does the reconciliation motif mean in psychological terms? Androgyny is one possibility and has often been discussed as an alternative to traditional gender stereotypes. Individuals ideally develop the masculine and feminine sides within themselves, whether they are biologically male or female. Although this is a popular interpretation of androgyny, many have raised objections to it.[5] Some critics have emphasized how androgyny assumes that masculinity and femininity are basic elements of human life and easily defined. But those claims are not self-evident. The Golden Tree offers an alternative to androgyny, based on relativism. Simply put, different concepts of the masculine and feminine are like the leaves and branches of the golden tree. They seem solid, eternal, and golden, but are regularly destroyed and reforged, particularly at midlife. Basic though they appear, concepts of the masculine and feminine are only temporary structures. They serve a particular purpose at a particular time, and must be changed to fit new situations. Archetypes of the masculine and feminine are not unchanging, eternal Platonic ideas. They are like any other life structure, elaborated for a period and a purpose.[6] The relativity of gender schemes is clear from historical records, which document drastic changes in masculine and feminine stereotypes over the centuries.[7] But similar changes occur for the individual throughout the life cycle, and especially in the middle years.

Ultimately, I think, the function of the masculine/ feminine polarity is to enrich human consciousness. The male/ female dichotomy offers a framework in which we can compare and contrast every aspect of human life. An analogy may help here. We know right only if we have the concept of wrong, and this basic duality helps us make complex ethical distinctions. In childhood and youth, simple, rigid ethical notions dominate. With maturity, more sophisticated, flexible reasoning appears. Similarly, by classifying things as masculine and feminine, we articulate our experience more precisely. Children begin with simple gender dualities, and tend to have rigid gender stereotypes, even when their parents and teachers encourage more flexible ones. A simplified masculine/ feminine duality helps children cope with the confusing complexity of the world. As they mature, children evolve more complex gender concepts.[8]

Later, in adolescence, when powerful emotions are released by puberty, bewildered teenagers return to simplistic stereotypes of the masculine and feminine. Simple dualities and roles are reassuring. In fact, men's fear of femininity and their need for traditional macho gender roles are highest in youth, when young men are most uncertain of their identity. Conversely, girls often embrace simplistic, restrictive, traditional notions of femininity as they enter adolescence, even when they rejected those stereotypes earlier. Young men and women also exaggerate the differences between them, and this helps them establish a clear, secure sense of identity.

When individuals become parents, they tend to embrace traditional parental roles. Fathers emphasize competition and achievement at work, while mothers focus on nurturing at home, even if husband and wife consciously rejected those traditional roles. Simple, dualistic gender schemes offer a ready-made way of handling the conflicts and emotions triggered by young children. After raising a family, parents generally move to more flexible, androgynous roles. Clearly, different concepts of the masculine and feminine are needed at different times in the life cycle.[9]

In the story, the golden tree is neither masculine nor feminine. Here the tree follows a general pattern in mythologies around the world. The Tree of Life is sometimes masculine and sometimes feminine. The Tree thus differs from other archetypal symbols where gender assignment is fairly uniform across cultures. Heaven, for instance, is usually associated with a male Sky God, and the earth with a female Earth Goddess. Because the Tree of Life does not fit into such regular gender schemes, it is best considered something beyond the masculine and the feminine. The golden tree and the Tree of Life are transpersonal symbols, transcending conventional male/female dualities. Mythology corroborates the point. Among the Ngadju of Borneo, the World Tree preceded the appearance of the two supreme deities—a goddess and a god. Similarly, in Norse mythology, the World Tree Yggdrasil antedated the gods and giants.[10] These numinous trees symbolize what Mircea Eliade called "the inexhaustible spring of cosmic life,"[11] which is neither male nor female.

There is one further theme in The Golden Tree worth mentioning: alchemy. Alchemy frequently used the image of a Tree of Life, suggesting that the golden tree has alchemical connotations. Alchemy appeared earlier in chapter 8, where The Man Who Did Not Wish to Die referred to the Elixir of Life, a traditional goal of alchemy in East and West.

Jung explored the psychological symbolism in alchemy extensively. He argued that alchemical discussions about transforming lead into gold symbolized psychological transformations that commonly occur at midlife. The first step in alchemy is the *nigredo,* or black phase, in which everything is broken down into its primordial constituents. This parallels the midlife experience of depression and suffering, in which a person's comfortable, familiar roles and convictions are melted down. Then comes the *albedo,* or white phase, involving purification of the primordial material. This is analogous to working through the conflicts and issues that were repressed in youth but brought up by a midlife crisis. The third alchemical phase was the *rubedo,* or red phase, involving the reclamation of passion. This symbolizes the encounter with a primordial, healing life force deep within the unconscious. Alchemy thus offers a dramatic metaphor for midlife. The transmutation of base elements like lead into noble metals like gold reflects the challenge of the middle years: to transform the dark side of life—jealousy, death, and suffering—into the wisdom and generativity of maturity.

What does the midlife encounter with the Tree of Life mean in everyday existence? The Tree as a primordial source of vitality and renewal takes a different form for each individual. Jungians might consider the inner source to be the Self. For the religious, it would be God, and for artists, it might be a creative inspiration or passionate romance. Janice Brewi recounts her experience at midlife in *Celebrate Midlife.*

A year after her mother's death, while still grieving, Brewi undertook an exercise in guided imagery. In the drama, she sat beside a beautiful lake, and God appeared in the form of a huge weeping willow, whose leaves created a curtain around Brewi. Sheltered by the tree and overcome with grief, Brewi wept in privacy. To her surprise, her father and mother emerged from the tree, appearing healthy and vigorous. They embraced Brewi, and then, one by one, her brothers and sisters appeared, so the whole family embraced one another. The experience was profoundly healing for Brewi, a turning point in her midlife odyssey and a dramatic example of the Tree of Life.

For most, I suspect, the Tree of Life does not appear in a single, dramatic form, but rather through several sources of vitality and renewal—love for family, love for nature, or love for friends. Certainly this has been my own experience. I have found many small, mundane sources of renewal, rather than a single numinous one. Fairy tales have been one source of inspiration for me in the last several years, and I never cease to be amazed—and rejuvenated—by the insights in apparently simple folk stories. But meditation gives me a different kind of renewal. In meditating, thoughts, worries, and concerns melt away, like the leaves and branches of the golden tree. If I am lucky, a deep and abiding serenity emerges—what I can only describe for lack of better terms as a great and joyful *presence*. Each individual, I think, has many such wellsprings of vitality, which may be overlooked because the sources lack the drama of the golden tree. In a sense, we do not encounter the Tree of Life but a few Shrubs of Life! And that is usually enough.

I end this chapter with one last observation. The golden tree offers a metaphor for all the interpretations in this book. The comments on the stories are simply branches and leaves that will be melted down and reforged in time. After all, middle tales were here before psychological interpretation was invented, and the stories will remain after psychology becomes outmoded. The tales themselves will no doubt evolve. They, too, will be melted down and reforged in the future. The stories spring from a deeper reality—the primordial fountain of imagination and creativity that is the human spirit. And that is the ultimate message of middle tales: in the midst of the reversals and confusion that plague the middle years, insight, renewal, and healing await.

Epilogue:
The Middle Passage

Our journey through midlife comes to an end. Middle tales have taken us past many turns and offered unexpected vistas—often inspiring, sometimes daunting, always provocative. Perhaps the best way to summarize the stories, and what they say about midlife, is to compare middle tales with those about youth. When the two genres are placed side by side, the divergent tasks and distinctive insights of youth and midlife become clearer.

Youth tales begin when the young hero or heroine leaves home. Sometimes this is voluntary, and the youth seeks better fortune in the world. At other times, the departure is fearful and forced—for example, a flight from evil stepparents. Fairy tales mirror reality here, because youths must emancipate themselves from parents. The parting is a willing one for some, like those going off to college, and traumatic for others, like those fleeing a dysfunctional home. On the journey, the heroes and heroines of youth tales seek true love or a great treasure. Their noble quests reflect another task of youth—elaborating ideals and visions that will inspire them as they enter the world. The heroes or heroines then fight with wicked witches or evil dragons, and ultimately defeat their opponents. In real life, youths battle authorities, making them out to be villains, and through these struggles develop a strong will and a secure sense of self. Those are the great treasures of youth.

In fairy tales, the young hero or heroine must be kind,

compassionate, honest, and hardworking to succeed. The exact list of virtues depends on the culture in which the story is told, because youth tales reflect conventional values and aim to instill them in children. Here we come to a subtle irony. Even if young men and women invest much of their energy in rebelling against society, their ultimate aim is still to take a place there. Youth tales portray this paradox. At the end of the quest, the young heroine becomes the beautiful, kind Queen, always deferring to the King—even if she started out as a strong, outspoken young woman. And the young hero becomes a warrior-King, ready to kill if necessary—even if he began as a gentle, introverted young man. Youth tales focus on the triumph of the hero and heroine, but the final outcome is youth's adaptation to society. And this is one of the major tasks of youth—to take a place in society.

Middle tales reverse course completely. What the individual achieved in youth, with such effort and struggle, is destroyed and rebuilt. The first reversal involves giving up the magic of youth. As depicted so poignantly in The Shoemaker and the Elves and The Magic Purse, men and women surrender the utopian visions and romantic dreams of youth when they enter the middle third of life. Forced to earn a living and support a family, individuals compromise their ideals. The innocence of youth becomes work, and idealism turns into pragmatism. The Grimms' tale The Duration of Life makes clear that the middle years are those of the donkey, when men and women often feel like beasts of burden. Still, there is a positive side to this responsibility. Like Atlas holding up the world, middle-aged men and women support all of society, nurturing the young and caring for the old. And there is deep satisfaction in fulfilling these duties.

A second reversal occurs next. As shown in Stubborn Husband, Stubborn Wife and The Lute Player, men and women invert traditional gender roles. Women recognize the oppression they suffer in patriarchal societies, mobilize their talent and assertiveness, and throw off social restrictions. If youth tales portray young women threatened by dangerous villains and rescued by gallant young men, middle tales reveal the charming hero to be another oppressor of women, whom women must overthrow!

Men, conversely, explore their long-suppressed feminine side. They begin to express their feelings, acknowledge their vulnerability, and recognize the importance of relationships. The experience is often painful, and sometimes traumatic or humiliating. Metaphorically, men are cast down from the pinnacle of youthful glory and, as The Lute Player dramatizes, they must wait for a woman to aid them. The gallant Queen rescues the hapless King! This is poetic justice. Men suffer at midlife the vulnerability and oppression that women encounter in youth. But the aim is not punishment; the goal is, rather, balance and integration. By midlife both men and women arrive at a firsthand knowledge of power and helplessness, autonomy and relatedness, triumph and suffering.

By reversing traditional masculine and feminine roles, individuals at midlife come to a deeper, richer understanding of sexuality and human experience. This contrasts sharply with the stark dualities that dominate youth. Adolescents embrace simplistic definitions of the masculine and feminine to help them master unfamiliar and turbulent feelings. As new parents, young adults also turn to traditional roles to allay their anxieties over child rearing. By midlife, most men and women know how to deal with emotional turmoil and can tolerate ambiguity and doubt. They do not need simple dualities, or the comfort of traditional roles. Middle-aged men and women are thus free to develop as unique individuals—to *individuate*. Just as youths leave the comfort and confinement of their families to seek a fortune in the world, men and women at midlife abandon the reassurance and restriction of society for the sake of individuation.

A deeper and more difficult reversal then emerges. This involves a confrontation with death, evil, and tragedy. Stories like The Mortal King, The Man Who Did Not Wish to Die, The King Who Would Be Stronger Than Fate, and Solomon's Advice portray this dark side of life in great detail. Youths typically flee these sobering realities. To them, evil is something that can be conquered and is always "out there," in somebody else. Death and misfortune happen only to other people. In the middle years, most people recognize that tragedy falls upon the virtuous as much as upon the wicked, and that death awaits everyone. Most sobering of all, men and women learn that they are villains, and not just victims, and that evil lurks not only "out there" but in their own hearts, too. An awareness of limitation then supplants the boundless hopes of youth. Fate eclipses faith.

The danger here is despair and cynicism. Having believed too much as youths, middle-aged men and women are tempted to believe too little. In this situation, wit offers comfort and healing, as The Tell Tale and Clever Answers so charmingly illustrate. Humor helps individuals stand outside themselves for a moment. Men and women learn to see from two viewpoints at once—from the inside and the outside. This double vision may be cross-eyed, but it helps people cope with the middle years. At this time men and women run society and cannot abandon their posts. Yet they cannot completely believe in society, having seen through too many illusions. This situation leads to insanity, cynicism—or humor. Ideally, men and women carry out their prescribed roles, but also see through them and laugh at themselves. Humor reconciles the clash between insight and responsibility.

Wit and irony offer a moratorium in the middle years. This situation is analogous to that of adolescence, where long years of schooling offer youths a chance to experiment with life, exempt from responsibility. Individuals at midlife cannot escape their responsibilities—but humor offers an alternative. Unlike the donkey, who can only carry its burdens, men and women can jest and tell stories. And magically enough, the jokes and fables lighten the load. Humor replaces heroism.

Perhaps even more miraculously, men and women find healing in the depths of crises. This is a central promise of middle tales like The Stoning and The Bonesetter. The middle years recapitulate the shaman's initiation into the mysteries of healing. Men and women descend psychologically into the underworld. Stripped of all their defenses, individuals come face-to-face with the core of their being. There they find a primordial source of life, beyond conventional notions of good and evil, male and female. Whether understood as the inner Self, or God, or the life force, this primal source helps men and women reforge their lives. As The Golden Tree dramatizes, the hopes and dreams of youth are melted down and recast into new forms. Men and women emerge from their suffering with deep healing—and the ability to heal others.

Ultimately, men and women gain wisdom from the middle years. But wisdom is not sublime, metaphysical revelation. It is simply practical insight into human life. Pragmatic maxims, drawn from actual experience, take precedence here, as Clever Answers so charmingly illustrates. The soldier's answers are concrete and seem stupid at first, but they are metaphors that express deep insight about fate and death. Midlife unites the abstract, masculine mode of reasoning with the concrete, practical feminine approach. Logos and Eros beget wisdom.

Central to this wisdom is relativism, summed up by Solomon's advice: "Don't meddle in other people's business." Men and women in the middle years abandon the idealism and rigid moralism of youth, when good and evil are clearly defined. Ethical judgments become more complex, ambiguous, and uncertain. The absolute, universal truths that are so important to youth—about politics and ethics, religion and philosophy—are seen to be mere opinions and partial truths. To use the metaphor of The Golden Tree, convictions and commitments are sprays of a numinous fountain, solidifying and taking concrete form for a brief time, and then melting back into the primordial source, into life itself.

Middle tales portray an ideal path through midlife. The

stories ignore the unique problems that individuals confront in real life—coming to terms with one's mother and father, for example, or coping with a spouse. But the goal of the middle years is not merely to resolve childhood problems or relieve private torment. Men and women are called at this time to become fully human—to break from traditional social roles and embrace the whole of human life, light and dark, masculine and feminine. And it is usually only from midlife onward that individuals have the strength and wisdom to deal with the dark side of life and to balance opposites. The challenge is to walk in the middle way.

The different paths men and women take in middle tales are not eternal and absolute truths. Middle tales are not sacred scriptures. And society has changed greatly in the last few years, moving away from patriarchal traditions. Today many women recover their native powers at an earlier age—or never surrender them. And many men develop their gentler, nurturing side in youth. Yet the deeper, archetypal insights of middle tales remain. At midlife, men and women must deal with whatever issues they neglected in youth. For those who focused on power and achievement in youth, whether they are traditional men or liberated women, the task at midlife is to deal with vulnerability, limitation, and relatedness. For those who emphasized nurture and intimacy early on, whether they are traditional women or liberated men, the other side emerges at midlife—assertiveness, autonomy, and power. Balance and transformation are the deeper tasks of the middle years.

What middle tales preach they also practice. They do not merely talk about transformation, they prod individuals toward change. This, in fact, has been the effect of the stories on me. To interpret them, I had to abandon old notions and question cherished principles. As I worked on the stories, they worked on me. The images and symbols in middle tales surfaced in my dreams and fantasies, and the insights in the stories hit home. Ironically, my research on middle tales began as a purely intellectual exercise, but the project soon became a matter of heart and soul. Middle tales awakened my own inner feminine.

These tales will speak in different ways to each individual. Like a good oracle, middle tales adapt themselves to each reader or listener, and point out the issues that he or she avoids. If the issues differ, the end is similar. Middle tales inspire change. They provoke what they preach. Their message is their process.

This book began with The Elves and the Shoemaker and ended with The Golden Tree. I originally chose these two stories for the beginning and end because they seemed to deal with early and later midlife, respectively. After completing the initial versions of this manuscript, I realized that there were deeper links between the two tales. In The Elves and the Shoemaker, the shoemaker loses the magic elves when he sees them and they realize they were seen. The shoemaker gains insight at the expense of magic. Metaphorically, he eats from the Tree of Knowledge, and thereby loses the innocence of youth. Like Adam and Eve, who were exiled from the Garden of Eden, the cobbler is forced to work for his living. This sums up the situation of midlife, when the romantic ideals of youth fade, leaving men and women with sobering realities and responsibilities, grappling like Adam and Eve with work, suffering, and death.

The long struggle of the middle years comes to a climax when men and women encounter a primordial source of life deep within their souls. This is the message and promise of the last tale, The Golden Tree. The King and Queen suffer greatly, but in the midst of their ordeals they come upon the Tree of Life. The numinous tree offers them renewal, healing, and reconciliation. Beyond good or evil, male or female, life or death, tragedy or triumph, the Tree of Life and its primal vitality help men and women integrate the polarities of human existence.

The odyssey of midlife is therefore the journey from the Tree of Knowledge to the Tree of Life—from consciousness and guilt to generativity and creativity. Middle tales complete the story of Adam and Eve after their exile from Eden. These fairy tales trace out the drama of Everyman and Everywoman in the middle years, moving from sobering knowledge to inner vitality.

Yet the Tree of Life is not the final destination. There still remains the last third of life—and its journey toward transcendence and illumination. This is the domain of elder tales—stories about elderly protagonists. The drama of elder tales is as different from middle tales as the latter are from youth stories. But that is a story for another time and another book.

The journey of the middle years is long and complex. Middle tales faithfully reflect the many stages of this journey, but I could not include every important tale here. In particular, I omitted stories that focus on men's encounters at midlife with the deep masculine, and women's contacts with the deep feminine. The tales are too complex and too long to discuss here. So I resort shamelessly to an old fairy-tale trick, the same that Scheherazade used with her 1001 stories: I stop in the middle of a long drama and promise its completion tomorrow, in another book, with further tales, ever more wondrous.

On this note, I end the present volume—in the middle of a journey, not yet finished. But that is surely the message of middle tales and of midlife. It is a time when men and women no longer feel young—but are not yet old; when they struggle to unite masculine and feminine, or good and bad—only to fall into the confusing middle; when they assume leadership over the four quarters of the world, only to discover a fifth direction, in the center, holding everything together; and when they confront, deep within this middle point, a primordial source of life—only to learn that this numinous source is yet another midpoint, one more stepping-stone on a longer journey. Ceaseless exploration is the theme of middle tales and the middle years. And this is the spirit of the middle way—of integration, transformation, and life itself.

Notes

(Full information on all references is provided in the Bibliography.)

INTRODUCTION

1. Bottigheimer's (1986) anthology addresses the importance of fairy tales for adults. Good examples can be found in Courlander (1978) and Abrahams (1983).
2. Examples can be found in Pelton (1980) and Radin (1983).
3. Discussions of the therapeutic uses of fairy tales can be found in Dieckmann (1986), Wallas (1985), and Franzke (1985), as well as the classic by Bettelheim (1976).
4. I describe these in a forthcoming book, *Dragons at the Crossroads.*
5. Hunter and Sundel's (1989) anthology summarizes relevant research.

CHAPTER 1

Tale summarized from Grimms' fairy tales.
1. Mayer (1985).
2. Zimmer (1956).
3. Abra (1989) provides a recent empirical study.

CHAPTER 2

Tale summarized from The Magic Moneybag in Minford (1982).
1. The Man Who Married a Fairy, in Sheppard-Jones (1978).

CHAPTER 3

Tale summarized from Nefyn the Mermaid in Sheppard-Jones (1978).
1. Particularly interesting examples include the African tale The Wonder Worker of the Plains, in Radin (1983), the Japanese story Urashima Taro, in Ozaki (1982), the Iraqi tale A Tale within a Tale, in Bushnaq, (1986), and the Italian story Master Francesco Sit-Down-and-Eat, in Calvino (1980).
2. Longitudinal studies confirming the importance of generativity can be found in Eichorn et al. (1981) and Vaillant (1977, 1989). Cross-sectional studies include Fiske-Lowenthal, Thurnher, and Chiribonga (1975). See also the anthology by Offer and Sabshin (1984).

3. Brandes (1985) offers a sociological perspective on number symbolism, while Von Franz (1974) provides a Jungian approach. Jung's original comments can be found in "The Symbolism of the Mandala" (1953b), and "Concerning Mandala Symbolism" (1959b).
4. Campbell (1959) provides further examples.

CHAPTER 4

Summarized from Mehdevi (1965). The story is Type number 1351 and 1365 in the folktale index by Aarne-Thompson (1961).

1. The Man Who Was Going to Mind the House, in Boos (1984) is very similar to Stubborn Husband, Stubborn Wife. See also Type 1408 in the Aarne-Thompson index (1961).
2. Gutmann (1987), Rossi (1985), and Sinnot (1986) summarize research on gender-role reversals.
3. Jung's main comments are in "Stages of Life" (1960) and "Marriage as a Psychological Relationship" (1954).
4. Jung (1960), 397.
5. In addition to the sources in note 3, empirical studies on role reversals include Fiske (1980), Giele (1980), Holahan (1984), and Eichorn et al. (1981), especially the chapters by N. Haan, and F. Livson.
6. Gutmann (1987) summarizes this cross-cultural research.
7. Cross-cultural anthologies on aging include Brown and Kerns (1985), Kleemeier (1961), and Amoss and Harrell (1981).
8. Recounted in Gutmann (1987). The misogyny implicit in the story must be put in context: the tale comes from a highly patriarchal culture.
9. Excellent discussions of male development include Friedman and Lerner (1986), Satinover (1986), Schafer (1986), Fogel, Lane, and Liebert (1986), Gilmore (1990), Rosaldo and Lamphere (1974), and Chodorow (1987).
10. Examples abound in Campbell (1959), Gilmore (1990), Lidz and Lidz (1986), and Bamberger (1974).
11. Another dramatic example of a man's struggle with the feminine at midlife comes from a gentleman who suffered from schizophrenia since adolescence. In his late thirties, Tom became convinced that the left side of his body was gradually becoming female, making him half man and half woman. Psychologically, Tom struggled with the midlife emergence of his feminine side. Unable to deal with the experience through symbolic concepts and images, he resorted to a concrete, physical expression—the idea that his body became half female.
12. Freud, for instance, discussed his own dreams in *The Interpretation of Dreams*, although he claimed the dreams were from patients. Similarly, Edward Whitmont, a Jungian analyst, confesses in *Return of the Goddess* that the case examples in his first book, *The Symbolic Quest*, were actually autobiographical.
13. Longitudinal research on this point is described in Eichorn et al. (1981), Vaillant (1977, 1989), and Mudd and Taubin (1982). Classic cross-sectional studies are summarized in Fiske-Lowenthal, Thurnher, and Chiribonga (1975) and Neugarten (1964, 1968). More recent research includes Irion and Blanchard-Fields (1987) and Labouvie-Vief, Hakim-Larson, and Hobart (1987).

CHAPTER 5

Summarized from A Woman's Love, in H. Liyi (1983). See also The Wily Dalilah and Her Daughter Zaynab in *The Thousand and One Arabian Nights*. These tales are related to Types 400 and 425 in the Aarne-Thompson index (1961).

1. Gerzon (1982) and Kolbenschlag (1988) summarize the research here. The findings on newlyweds come from Fiske-Lowenthal et al. (1975).
2. Leonard (1982) and Rupprecht (1985) discuss some of these findings.
3. E.g., Three Eyes, in Kawai (1988) and The Queen and the Murderer, in Calvino (1980).
4. These tales are Types 425K, 512A*, 514, 884, 884A, and 884B in the Aarne-Thompson index (1961).
5. The following sources are particularly informative: Brown and Kerns (1985), Gutmann (1987), and Notman (1982).
6. These tales make up Type 881 in the Aarne-Thompson index (1961), and are related to Type 923B.
7. E.g., The One-Handed Murderer, in Calvino (1980) and Three Eyes, in Kawai (1988).
8. Examples include Mankowitz (1984), Douglas (1989), Jung (1976), and Carotenuto (1986).
9. Jung discusses the symbolism of the number five in "Aion" (1959a), and "Paracelsus as a Spiritual Phenomenon" (1953a). See also Campbell (1959).
10. The symbolism of the numbers forty and forty-one are relevant here. Forty usually connotes completion of a large quantity (Brandes, 1985). In the biblical story of the Flood, for instance, it rained for forty days and forty nights. Forty-one thus implies excess, something more than a complete, large number.

CHAPTER 6

Summarized from Lang (1966a). This story is Type 888 and 875c in the Aarne-Thompson index (1961), and is related to Types 880, 880*, and 890.
1. Kolbenschlag (1988) and Hancock (1989) discuss the pattern. Systematic longitudinal data come from Eichorn et al. (1981).
2. See note 1. Good reviews can be found in Sinnott (1986), Tamir (1982), and Boles and Tatro (1982).
3. Overviews of the psychology of menopause are included in Notman (1982b), Reinke, Holmes, and Harris (1985), and McKinlay and McKinlay (1987). See also Hunter and Sundel (1989), Block (1982), Giele (1982), and Brown and Kerns (1985).
4. E.g., The Tsar and the Angel, in Bain (1895), The Beggar King, in Schwartz (1985), The Man among Men, in Radin (1983), The King Who Changed His Ways, in Bushnaq (1986), the Grimms' story The Turnip, and Dreams, in Roberts (1979). See also Type 1962A in the Aarne-Thompson index (1961).
5. Relevant sources include Cath (1980), Soddy (1967), and Tamir (1982).
6. Comparative data are described in Cramer (1986) and Kramer, Kinney, and Scharf (1983).
7. Gutmann (1989) and Sinnott (1986) emphasize this point.

CHAPTER 7

Summarized from Roberts (1979).
1. Besides Elliot Jaques' (1965) paper on death and midlife crises, there are a number of excellent discussions, including Ciernia (1985), Levinson et al. (1978), and Auchincloss and Michels (1989).
2. Empirical research on this point comes from Woods and Witte (1981) and Shulz (1977).
3. The Bedouin's Gazelle, in Bushnaq (1986). The motif is classified as J1577.1, E361.3, and J52.1 in Thompson's *Motif-Index of Folk Literature* (1955–58).
4. Recent discussions on the legacy include Levinson et al. (1978), Erikson, Erikson, and Kivnick (1986), and Kotre (1984).
5. Sherman (1987) and Wrightsman (1988) offer striking cases.

NOTES

CHAPTER 8

Summarized from Ozaki (1982). The story is Type 1935 in the Aarne-Thompson index (1961).
1. Death Corked in a Bottle, in Calvino (1980).
2. Case examples can be found in Nemiroff and Colarusso (1985), Sherman (1987), and Wrightsman (1988). Survivors of near-death experiences report similar aftereffects.
3. Several empirical studies are noteworthy: McMordie and Kumar (1984), Schulz (1977), and Thorson and Powell (1988).
4. Fisher, Wright, and Moelis (1979) noted this in an ingenious experiment.
5. Roberts (1979).
6. Schwartz (1985).
7. Neugarten and Miller (1964) provide empirical data. See also Oldham (1989).

CHAPTER 9

Adapted from Destiny in Laboulaye (1976). The story is type 947B* in the Aarne-Thompson index (1961).
1. These themes are classified as N1370 and N101.1 in Thompson's motif index (1955–58).
2. Bandura (1982) discusses the topic cogently.
3. E.g., What God Wrote Cannot Be Unwritten and What Is Inscribed on the Brow, the Eye Will See, in Bushnaq (1986).
4. From Lang (1903). This story is Type 2031C and 2031B* in the Aarne-Thompson index (1961). See also The Bones of Father Adam, in Bushnaq (1986).
5. Sternberg's (1990) anthology offers excellent discussions of wisdom and the "larger picture." See especially the chapters by M. Csikszentmihalyi and K. Rathunde, and by Robinson.
6. Several studies examine the pattern, using different approaches: Birren (1969), Chinen, Spielvogel, and Farrell (1985), Labouvie-Vief (1990), and Mussen and Haan (1981).

CHAPTER 10

Summarized from Lang (1914). This tale is Type 930 in the Aarne-Thompson index (1914).
1. E.g., The Ismailian Merchant, in Calvino (1980), The Devil with Three Golden Hairs, from the Grimms, To Your Good Health, in Lang (1903), and Three Wonderful Beggars, in Lang (1966).
2. Psychoanalysts and sociologists alike concur here: Myers (1989), Kernberg (1989), and Kotre (1984).
3. Lang (1966a, 1966b).
4. Kohut (1982) emphasizes the point. See also Auchincloss and Michels (1989).
5. Erikson (1963), 268.
6. E.g., the story of Arthur and Gromer Somer Joure, in Zimmer (1956).

CHAPTER 11

Summarized from Afanas'ev (1973).
1. Some of the relevant research includes Abra (1989), Demetriou (in press), Labouvie-Vief (1990), Lehman (1953), and Kohlberg (1984).
2. Relevant studies include Clayton (1982), Cornelius and Caspi (1987), Sternberg (1990), Sinnott (in press), and Cavanaugh et al. (1985).

3. Recent research on metaphoric understanding includes Boswell (1979), Dent (1986), and Labouvie-Vief et al. (1989).
4. Sakade (1959). Other related tales include the Russian story The Potter, in Afanas'ev (1973) and the Tunisian story Just Desserts, in Bushnaq (1986), among others. See also Types 1533 and 1613 in the Aarne-Thompson index (1961).
5. Powell (1980) discusses the point. German philosophers have discussed the topic with the distinction between *verstehen* and *erklären*.
6. Rhees (1984) discusses Wittgenstein's life. See also Chinen (1989a). A similar course of development can be seen in the career of Alfred North Whitehead.
7. Belenky et al. (1986), 53.
8. Attributed to Anatole France, and cited in Von Franz (1972).

CHAPTER 12

Summarized from Calvino (1980).
1. Afanas'ev (1973).
2. Segal (1984). See also Newton (1984) and Silberger (1979).
3. Tawney (1956) and Zimmer (1956).
4. A variety of research underscores this point: Eichorn et al. (1981), Gilligan (1982), and Belenky et al. (1986).
5. The Man Who Bought Fortune-Telling Cards, in Ohta (1981).
6. In Bushnaq (1986). These tales are Types 910A, 910B, 910K, and 992A in the Aarne-Thompson index (1961) and themes J21.2 and J21.5 in Thompson's motif index (1955–58).

CHAPTER 13

Summarized from Ohta (1981).
1. These statistics can be found in Reinke, Holmes, and Harris (1985) and Wrightsman (1988).
2. Hagstad and Janson (1984), Hagstad (1988), and Hallstrom and Samuelsson (1990).
3. E.g., the Russian story Quarrelsome Demyan, in Afanas'ev (1973) and the Bulgarian tale Husband Pour Porridge on My Shoulder, in Nicoloff (1979). See also Types 1358B, 1380, 1381, 1381B, and 1419B in the Aarne-Thompson index (1961).
4. Freud's classic comments are in Humour (1961) and *Jokes and Their Relation to the Unconscious* (1905). See O'Connel's (1976) discussion of Freud. More recent research includes Lefcourt and Martin (1986), McGhee (1983), and Nahemow, McCluskey-Fawcett, and McGhee (1986). Vaillant's (1977, 1989) studies are particularly noteworthy.
5. Intriguing data on this come from Huyck and Duchon (1986) and Barrick, Hutchinson, and Deckers (1990).
6. E.g., the Grimms' tale Dr. Know-all, the Italian story Peasant Astrologer, in Calvino (1980), and the Indian tale Harisarman, in Jacobs (1890). These tales are Type 1641 in the Aarne-Thompson index (1961).
7. The Magic Bird, from Minford (1983).
8. Riegel's (1973) is a classic discussion. See also Rothenberg (1971).
9. Shultz (1976), Suls (1983), Chapman and Foot (1976), and Rothbart (1976) review the research and theory.
10. Data in this relatively new field of research can be found in Labouvie-Vief et al. (1989) and Kramer (1989).
11. The papers in Sternberg (1990) are particularly clear on this point.
12. Proverbs 17:22.
13. Fisher and Fisher (1981), Janus (1975), and Lefcourt and Martin (1986) review the research.

CHAPTER 14

Summarized from Dwyer (1978). The story is Type 712 in the Aarne-Thompson index (1961); cf. Type 899F*.

1. Amoss and Harrell (1981) and Brown and Kerns (1985) offer cross-cultural perspectives on healers and aging, while Doore (1988) and Nicholson (1987) provide many examples of shamanic initiation.
2. Excellent sources on shamanism are Campbell (1959) and the classic work by Eliade (1972). More recent works include Halifax (1981) and Harner (1980). See also note 1.
3. E.g., the Grimms' stories Three Army Surgeons and Godfather Death and the Japanese tales The Kappa Who Played Pull-Finger and Yudaira Springs (Dorson, 1982).
4. Groesbeck (1975) and Von Franz (1972) discuss the theme.

CHAPTER 15

Adapted from Dorson (1982).

1. Blacker (1975).
2. Brown and Kerns (1985).
3. Eliade (1972) and Achterberg (199) provide many examples.
4. E.g., the Grimms' tales Godfather Death, Spirit in a Bottle, The Three Snake Leaves, and The Two Travelers, the Russian story The Bad Wife, in Afanas'ev (1973), and the Italian tale The Captain and the General, in Calvino (1980). The demonic aspect of healing includes motif D1500 in Thompson's motif index (1955–58).
5. Viederman (1981) discusses Matisse's midlife crisis.
6. Staude (1981), Carotenuto (1982), and Beebe (1989) discusses this controversial issue. Creativity, I might add, does not excuse ethical breaches. In fact, when therapists cite a higher purpose as justification for sleeping with patients, this usually means there is none.
7. Amoss and Harrell (1981).

CHAPTER 16

From Schwartz (1985). The story is related to Types 459 and 1525G(II) in the Aarne-Thompson index (1961).

1. Von Franz (1972) discusses the theme.
2. An overview of the symbolism can be found in Cook (1988) and Halifax (1981).
3. Campbell (1959), Doore (1988), and Stewart (1985) provide rich examples. See also note 2.
4. Singer (1989) provides a good discussion.
5. These are summarized in May (1980, 1986), Vetterling-Braggin (1982), and Rowan (1987), among others.
6. This view has been extensively discussed in Vetterling-Braggin (1982), Walsh (1987), Reinisch, Rosenblum, and Sanders (1987), and Sinnott (1986).
7. The historical perspective is discussed in Brittan (1989), Brod (1987), and Kaufman (1987).
8. Basic research on this is reviewed in Reinisch, Rosenblum, and Sanders (1987), May (1980), and Brod (1987).
9. Gutmann (1987), Sinnott (1986), and Wrightsman (1988) review the research here.
10. Cook (1988) and Eliade (1972) discuss the topic.
11. Eliade (1972), 271.

References

Aarne, A., and S. Thompson. 1961. *The Types of the Folktale: A Classification and Bibliography.* Helsinki: Academia Scientarium Finnica.

Abra, Jock. 1989. Changes in Creativity with Age: Data, Explanations and Further Predictions. *International Journal of Aging and Human Development* 28:105–26.

Abrahams, Roger. 1983. *African Folktales.* New York: Pantheon.

Achterberg, Jeanne. 1990. *Woman as Healer.* Boston: Shambhala.

Afanas'ev, Aleksandr. 1973. *Russian Fairy Tales.* Trans. Norbert Guterman. New York: Pantheon.

Amoss, P., and S. Harrell, eds. 1981. *Other Ways of Growing Old: Anthropological Perspectives.* Stanford: Stanford University Press.

Auchincloss, Elizabeth, and Robert Michels. 1989. The Impact of Middle Age on Ambitions and Ideals. In Oldham and Liebert (1989), 40–57.

Bain, R. Nisbet. 1895. *Cossack Fairy Tales.* New York: Frederick Stokes.

Bamberger, Joan. 1974. The Myth of Matriarchy: Why Men Rule in Primitive Society. In Rosaldo and Lamphere (1974), 263–80.

Bandura, Albert. 1982. The Psychology of Chance Encounters and Life Paths. *American Psychologist* 87:747–55.

Barrick, A. L., R. L. Hutchinson, and L. H. Deckers. 1990. Humor, Aggression, and Aging. *The Gerontologist* 30:675–78.

Beebe, John, ed. 1989. *Aspects of the Masculine.* Princeton: Princeton University Press.

Belenky, M. F., B. M. Clinchy, N. R. Goldberger, and J. M. Tarule. 1986. *Women's Ways of Knowing: The Development of Self, Voice and Mind.* New York: Basic Books.

Bettelheim, Bruno. 1976. *The Uses of Enchantment: The Meaning and Importance of Fairy Tales.* New York: Knopf.

Birren, J. E. 1969. Age and Decision Strategies. *Interdisciplinary Topics in Gerontology,* Basel: Karger.

Birren, James, and Vern Bengston, eds. 1988. *Emergent Theories of Aging.* New York: Springer.

Blacker, Carmen. 1975. *The Catalpa Bow: A Study of Shamanistic Practices in Japan.* London: Allen and Unwin.

Block, Marilyn, Janice Davidson, and Jean Grambs. 1982. *Women over Forty: Visions and Realities.* New York: Springer.

Bly, Robert. 1991. *Iron John,* San Francisco: Harper Collins.

Boles, Jacqueline, and Charlotte Tatro. 1982. Androgyny. In Solomon and Levy (1982), 99–130.

Boos, Claire. 1984. *Scandinavian Folk and Fairy Tales.* New York: Avenel.

Boswell, D. A. 1979. Metaphoric Processing in the Mature Years. *Human Development* 22:373–84.

Bottigheimer, R., ed. 1986. *Fairy Tales and Society: Illusion, Allusion and Paradigm.* Philadelphia: University of Pennsylvania Press.

Brandes, Stanley. 1985. *Forty: The Age and the Symbol.* Knoxville: University of Tennessee Press.

Brewi, Janice, and Anne Brennan. 1988. *Celebrate Mid-life: Jungian Archetypes and Mid-life Spirituality.* New York: Crossroad.

Brittan, Arthur. 1989. *Masculinity and Power.* New York: Basil Blackwell.

Brod, Harry, ed. 1987. *The Making of Masculinities: The New Men's Studies.* Boston: Allen and Unwin.

Brown, J. K., and V. Kerns, eds. 1985. *In Her Prime: A New View of Middle-Aged Women.* S. Hadley, MA: Bergin and Garvey.

Bruner, Jerome. 1986. *Actual Minds, Possible Worlds.* Cambridge: Harvard University Press.

Bushnaq, I. 1986. *Arab Folktales.* New York: Pantheon.

Calvino, Italo. 1980. *Italian Folktales.* New York: Pantheon.

Campbell, Joseph. 1959. *The Masks of God: Primitive Mythology.* New York: Penguin.

_____. 1968. *The Hero with a Thousand Faces.* Princeton: Princeton University Press.

Carotenuto, Aldo. 1982. *A Secret Symmetry: Sabina Spielrein between Jung and Freud.* Trans. Arno Pomerans, John Shepley, and Krishna Winston. New York: Pantheon.

_____. 1986. *The Spiral Way: A Woman's Healing Journey.* Trans. John Shepley. Toronto: Inner City Books.

Cath, Stanley. 1980. Suicide in the Middle Years: Some Reflections on the Annihilation of the Self. In Norman and Scaramella (1980), 53–72.

Cath, Stanley H., Alan Gurwitt, and John Ross, eds. 1982. *Father and Child: Developmental and Clinical Perspectives.* Boston: Little, Brown.

Cavanaugh, J., D. Kramer, J. Sinnott, C. Camp, and J. Markley. 1985. On Missing Links and Such: Interfaces between Cognitive Research and Everyday Problem-Solving. *Human Development* 28:146–68.

Chapman, A. J., and H. C. Foot, eds. 1976. *Humor and Laughter: Theory, Research and Applications.* New York: Wiley.

Chinen, A. B. 1989. From Quantitative to Qualitative Reasoning: A Developmental Perspective. In *Research on Adulthood and Aging: The Human Science Approach,* ed. L. E. Thomas, 37–61. Albany: State University of New York Press.

_____. 1989. *In the Ever After: Fairy Tales and the Second Half of Life.* Wilmette, IL: Chiron.

_____. In press. *Dragons at the Crossroads: Fables and Fairy Tales for Mid-passage and Beyond.* Blauvelt, NY: Garber Communications.

Chinen, Allan, Anna Spielvogel, and Dennis Farell. 1985. The Experience of Intuition. *Psychological Perspectives* 16:186–97.

Chodorow, Nancy. 1987. Feminism and Difference: Gender, Relation and Difference in Psychoanalytic Perspective. In Walsh (1987), 249–64.

Ciernia, James. 1985. Death Concern and Businessmen's Mid-life Crisis. *Psychological Reports* 56:83–87.

Clayton, V. 1982. Wisdom and Intelligence: The Nature and Function of Knowledge in the Later Years. *International Journal of Aging and Human Development* 15:315–22.

Commons, M. L., J. D. Sinnott, F. A. Richards, and C. Armon, eds. In press. *Adult Development.* Vol. 3, *Models and Methodologies in the Study of Adult Thought.*

Cook, Roger. 1988. *The Tree of Life: Image for the Cosmos.* London: Thames and Hudson.

Corneau, Guy. 1991. *Absent Fathers, Lost Sons: The Search For Masculine Identity.* Trans. Larry Shouldice. Boston: Shambhala.

Cornelius, S., and A. Caspi. 1987. Everyday Problem Solving in Adulthood and Old Age. *Psychology and Aging* 2:144–53.

Courlander, Harold, and George Herzog. 1978. *The Cow-Tail Switch and Other West African Stories.* New York: Henry Holt and Co.

Cramer, Phoebe. 1986. Fantasies of College Men: Then and Now. In Friedman and Lerner (1986), 163–74.

Dan, A., and Linda Berhnard. 1989. Menopause and Other Health Issues for Midlife Women. In Hunter and Sundel (1989), 51–66.

Datan, Nancy. 1980. Midas and Other Mid-life Crises. In Norman and Scaramella (1980), 3–19.

Demetriou, Andreas. In press. The Relationship between Relational, Experimental/Relational and Meta-cognitive Abilities and Formal, Systematic and Meta-systematic Abilities. In Commons et al. (in press).

Dent, C. 1986. The Development of Metaphoric Competence: A Symposium. *Human Development* 29:223–44.

Dieckmann, Hans. 1986. *Twice-Told Tales: The Psychological Use of Fairy Tales*. Trans. B. Matthews. Wilmette, IL: Chiron.

Doore, Gary, ed. 1988. *Shaman's Path: Healing, Personal Growth and Empowerment*. Boston: Shambhala.

Dorson, R. 1982. *Folk Legends of Japan*. Tokyo: Charles Tuttle.

Douglas, C. 1989. Christiana Morgan's Visions Reconsidered: A Look Behind the Visions Seminars. *San Francisco Jung Institute Library Journal* 8:5–26.

Dundes, A. 1986. Fairy Tales from a Folkloristic Perspective. In Bottigheimer (1986), 259–70.

————. 1987. *Parsing through Customs: Essays by a Freudian Folklorist*. Madison: University of Wisconsin Press.

Dwyer, D. W. 1978. *Images and Self-Images: Male and Female in Morocco*. New York: Columbia University Press.

Eichorn, Dorothy, et al. 1981. *Present and Past in Middle Life*. New York: Academic Press.

Eliade, Mircea. 1972. *Shamanism: Archaic Techniques of Ecstasy*. Princeton: Princeton University Press.

Elliot, Geraldine. 1987. *Where the Leopard Passes: A Book of African Folk Tales*. New York: Schocken Books.

Erikson, E. 1983. *The Life Cycle Completed*. New York: Norton.

Erikson, E., J. M. Erikson, and H. Q. Kivnick. 1986. *Vital Involvement in Old Age*. New York: Norton.

Fisher, S., and R. Fisher. 1981. *Pretend the World Is Funny and Forever: A Psychological Analysis of Comedians, Clowns and Actors*. Hillsdale, NJ: Erlbaum.

Fisher, Seymour, David Wright, and Irwin Moelis. 1979. Effects of Maternal Themes upon Death Imagery. *Journal of Personality Assessment* 43:595–99.

Fiske, Marjorie. 1980. Changing Hierarchies of Commitment in Adulthood. In Smelser and Erikson (1980), 238–64.

Fiske-Lowenthal, M., M. Thurnher, and D. Chiribonga. 1975. *Four Stages of Life*. San Francisco: Jossey Bass.

Fogel, Gerald, Frederick Lane, and Robert Liebert, eds. 1986. *The Psychology of Men: New Psychoanalytic Perspectives*. New York: Basic Books.

Fowler, J. W. 1981. *The Stages of Faith: The Psychology of Human Development and the Quest for Meaning*. San Francisco: Harper and Row.

Franzke, Erich. 1985. *Fairy Tales in Psychotherapy: The Creative Use of Old and New Tales*. Toronto: Hogrefe and Huber.

Frenkel, Else. 1936. Studies in Biographical Psychology. *Character and Personality* 5:1–34.

Frenkel-Brunswick, Else. 1968. Adjustments and Reorientation in the Course of the Life Span. In Neugarten (1968), 77–84.

Freud, S. 1905. *Jokes and Their Relation to the Unconscious*. Trans. J. Strachey. New York: Norton.

————. 1908. Creative Writers and Daydreaming. In *Collected Works*. Standard ed. Vol. 8. London: Hogarth.

————. 1961. Humour. Trans. J. Strachey. In *Collected Works*. Standard ed. Vol. 21. London: Hogarth.

Friedman, Robert, and Leila Lerner. 1986. *Toward a New Psychology of Men: Psychoanalytic and Social Perspectives*. New York: Guilford Press.

REFERENCES

Frye, Northrop. 1957. *Anatomy of Criticism: Four Essays.* Princeton: Princeton University Press.

Gerzon, Mark. 1982. *A Choice of Heroes: The Changing Faces of American Manhood.* Boston: Houghton Mifflin.

Giele, J. 1980. Adulthood as Transcendence of Age and Sex. In Smelser and Erikson (1980), 151–73.

Giele, Janet, ed. 1982. *Women in the Middle Years: Current Knowledge and Directions for Research and Policy.* New York: Wiley.

Gilligan, Carol. 1982. *In a Different Voice: Psychological Theory and Women's Development.* Cambridge: Harvard University Press.

Gilmore, D. 1990. *Manhood in the Making.* New Haven: Yale University Press.

Gilstrap, R., and I. Estabrook. 1958. *The Sultan's Fool and Other North African Tales.* New York: Henry Holt and Co.

Gould, Roger. 1978. *Transformations: Growth and Change in Adult Life.* New York: Simon and Schuster.

Groesbeck, C. J. 1975. The Archetypal Image of the Wounded Healer. *Journal of Analytical Psychology* 20:122–45.

Gutmann, David. 1987. *Reclaimed Powers: Toward a New Psychology of Men and Women in Later Life.* New York: Basic Books.

Hagstad, A. 1988. Gynecology and Sexuality in Middle-Aged Women. *Women and Health* 13:57–80.

Hagstad, A., and P. O. Janson. 1984. Sexuality among Swedish Women around Forty: An Epidemiological Survey. *Journal of Psychosomatic Obstetrics and Gynaecology* 3:191–203.

Halifax, Joan. 1981. *Shaman: The Wounded Healer.* London: Thames and Hudson.

Hallstrom, T., and S. Samuelsson. 1990. Changes in Women's Sexual Desire in Middle Life: The Longitudinal Study of Women in Gothenburg. *Archives of Sexual Behavior* 19:259–68.

Hancock, E. 1989. *The Girl Within.* New York: Norton.

Harner, M. 1980. *The Way of the Shaman: A Guide to Power and Healing.* San Francisco: Harper and Row.

Henderson, Joseph L. 1967. *Thresholds of Initiation.* Middletown, CT: Wesleyan University Press.

Holahan, Carole. 1984. The Relationship between Life Goals at Thirty and Perceptions of Goal Attainment and Life Satisfaction at Seventy for Gifted Men and Women. *International Journal of Aging and Human Development* 20:21–31.

Hunter, Ski, and Martin Sundel, eds. 1989. *Midlife Myths: Issues, Findings and Practice Implications.* Newbury Park, CA: Sage Publications.

Huyck, Margaret, and James Duchon. 1986. Over the Miles: Coping, Communicating, and Commiserating through Age—The Greeting Cards. In Nahemow, McCluskey-Fawcett, and McGhee (1986), 139–59.

Irion, J. C., and F. Blanchard-Fields. 1987. A Cross-sectional Comparison of Adaptive Coping in Adulthood. *Journal of Gerontology* 42:502–4.

Jacobs, J. 1890. *Indian Fairy Tales.* New York: Putnam's Sons.

Janus, Samuel S. 1975. The Great Comedians: Personality and Other Factors. *American Journal of Psychoanalysis* 35:169–74.

Jaques, Elliot. 1965. Death and the Mid-life Crisis. *International Journal of Psychoanalysis* 46:502–14.

Jung, C. G. 1953a. Paracelsus as a Spiritual Phenomenon. In *Collected Works.* Vol. 12. Princeton: Princeton University Press.

————. 1953b. The Symbolism of the Mandala. In *Collected Works.* Vol. 12. Princeton: Princeton University Press.

————. 1954. Marriage as a Psychological Relationship. In *Collected Works.* Vol. 17. Princeton: Princeton University Press.

————. 1959a. Aion. In *Collected Works.* Vol. 9ii. Princeton: Princeton University Press.

—————. 1959b. Concerning Mandala Symbolism. In *Collected Works*. Vol. 9ii. Princeton: Princeton University Press.

—————. 1960. Stages of Life. In *Collected Works*. Vol. 8. Princeton: Princeton University Press.

—————. 1965. *Memories, Dreams, and Reflections*. New York: Vintage Books.

—————. 1967. The Spirit Mercurius. In *Collected Works*. Vol. 13. Princeton: Princeton University Press.

—————. 1967. Symbols of Transformation. In *Collected Works*. Vol. 5. Princeton: Princeton University Press.

—————. 1969. Transformation Symbolism in the Mass. In *Collected Works*. Vol. 11. Princeton: Princeton University Press.

—————. 1976. *The Visions Seminars*. Zurich: Spring Publications.

Kaufman, Michael, ed. 1987. *Beyond Patriarchy: Essays by Men on Pleasure, Power and Change*. New York: Oxford University Press.

Kawai, Hayao. 1988. *The Japanese Psyche: Major Motifs in the Fairy Tales of Japan*. Trans. H. Kawai and Sachiko Reece. Dallas, TX: Spring Publications.

Kerenyi, Karl. 1976. *Hermes: Guide of Souls*. Dallas, TX: Spring Publications.

Kernberg, Otto. 1989. The Interaction of Middle Age and Character Pathology: Treatment Implications. In Oldham and Liebert (1989), 209–23.

Koestler, A., 1964. *The Act of Creation*. New York: Macmillan.

Kleemeier, Robert, ed. 1961. *Aging and Leisure: A Research Perspective into the Meaningful Use of Time*. New York: Oxford University Press.

Kohlberg, L. 1984. *The Psychology of Moral Development: The Nature and Validity of Moral Stages*. San Francisco: Harper and Row.

Kohut, H. 1982. Introspection, Empathy and the Semi-circle of Mental Health. *International Journal of Psychoanalysis* 63:395–407.

Kolbenschlag, Madonna. 1988. *Kiss Sleeping Beauty Goodbye: Breaking the Spell of Feminine Myths and Models*. San Francisco: Harper and Row.

Kotre, J. 1984. *Outliving the Self: Generativity and the Interpretation of Lives*. Baltimore: Johns Hopkins University Press.

Kramer, D. 1989. Development of an Awareness of Contradiction across the Lifespan and the Question of Post-formal Operations. In *Beyond Formal Operations II: Comparison and Applications of Adolescent and Adult Developmental Models*, ed. M. L. Commons, J. D. Sinnott, F. A. Richards, and C. Armon, 133–59. New York: Praeger.

Kramer, M., L. Kinney, and M. Scharf. 1983. Sex Differences in Dreams. *Psychiatric Journal of the University Ottowa* 8:104–8.

Kuhlman, T. 1984. *Humor and Psychotherapy*. Homewood, IL: Dorsey.

Laboulaye, E. 1976. *Laboulaye's Fairy Book: Fairy Tales of All Nations*. Trans. Mary Booth. Great Neck, NY: Core Collection Books.

Labouvie-Vief, Gisela. 1990. Wisdom as Integrated Thought: Historical and Developmental Perspectives. In Sternberg (1990), 52–83.

Labouvie-Vief, Gisela, J. Hakim-Larson, M. DeVoe, and S. Schoeberlein. 1989. Emotions and Self-regulation: A Life Span View. *Human Development* 32:297–99.

Labouvie-Vief, Gisela, J. Hakim-Larson, and C. Hobart. 1987. Age, Ego Level, and the Life-Span Development of Coping and Defense Processes. *Psychology and Aging* 2:286–93.

Lang, Andrew. 1903. *The Crimson Fairy Books*, New York: Longmans, Green and Co.

—————. 1914. *The Brown Fairy Book*. New York: Longmans, Green and Co.

—————. 1966a. *The Violet Fairy Book*. New York: Dover Publications.

—————. 1966b. *The Yellow Fairy Book*. New York: Dover Publications.

Lauter, Estella. 1985. Visual Images by Women: A Test Case for the Theory of Archetypes. In Lauter and Rupprecht (1985), 46–83.

Lauter, Estella, and Carol S. Rupprecht, eds. 1985. *Feminist Archetypal Theory: Interdisciplinary Revisions of Jungian Thought.* Knoxville: University of Tennessee Press.

Lefcourt, H., and R. Martin. 1986. *Humor and Life Stress: Antidote to Adversity.* New York: Springer.

Lehman, H. C. 1953. *Age and Achievement.* Princeton: Princeton University Press.

Leonard, Linda. 1982. *The Wounded Woman: Healing the Father-Daughter Relationship.* Athens, OH: Swallow Press.

Levinson, Daniel, Charlotte Darrow, Edward Klein, Maria Levinson, and Braxton McKee. 1978. *The Seasons of a Man's Life.* New York: Ballantine.

Lidz, Theodore, and Ruth Lidz. 1986. Turning Women Things into Men: Masculinization in Papua New Guinea. In Friedman and Lerner (1986), 117–36.

Liyi, H. 1985. *The Spring of Butterflies and Other Folktales of China's Minority Peoples.* New York: Lothrop, Lee and Shepard.

Luke, Helen M. 1989. *Dark Wood to White Rose: Journey and Transformation in Dante's Divine Comedy.* New York: Parabola Books.

Mankowitz, Ann. 1984. *Change of Life: A Psychological Study of Dreams and the Menopause.* Toronto: Inner City.

May, Robert. 1980. *Sex and Fantasy: Patterns of Male and Female Development.* New York: Norton.

_____. 1986. Concerning a Psychoanalytic View of Maleness. In Friedman and Lerner (1986), 175–94.

Mayer, F. H. 1985. *Ancient Tales in Modern Japan.* Bloomington, IN: Indiana University Press.

McGhee, P. 1983. Humor Development: Toward a Life-Span View. In McGhee and Goldstein (1983), 109–34.

McGhee, P. E., and J. H. Goldstein, eds. 1983. *Handbook of Humor Research.* New York: Springer.

McKinlay, John, and Sonja McKinlay. 1987. Depression in Middle-aged Women: Social Circumstances versus Estrogen Deficiency. In Walsh (1987), 157–61.

McLeish, J. 1976. *The Ulyssean Adult: Creativity in the Middle and Later Years.* New York: McGraw-Hill Ryerson.

McMordie, William, and Anand Kumar. 1984. Cross-Cultural Research on the Templer/McMordie Death Anxiety Scale. *Psychological Reports* 54:959–63.

Mehdevi, A. S. 1965. *Persian Folk and Fairy Tales.* New York: Knopf.

Messner, Michael. 1987. The Meaning of Success: The Athletic Experience and the Development of Male Identity. In Brod (1987), 193–207.

Miller, Alice. 1981. *The Drama of the Gifted Child.* New York: Basic Books.

Mindell, Arnold. 1982. Dreambody: The Body's Role in Revealing the Self. Boston MA: Sigo Press.

Minford, J. 1983. *Favourite Folktales of China.* Beijing: New York Press.

Mudd, E. H., and S. Taubin. 1982. Success in Family Living—Does It Last? A Twenty Year Follow-up. *American Journal of Family Therapy* 10:59–67.

Mussen, Paul, and Norma Haan. A Longitudinal Study of Patterns of Personality and Political Ideologies. In Eichorn et al. (1981), 393–414.

Myers, Helen. 1989. The Impact of Teenaged Children on Parents. In Oldham and Liebert (1989), 75–88.

Nahemow, Lucille, Kathleen McCluskey-Fawcett, and Paul McGhee, eds. 1986. *Humor and Aging.* New York: Academic Press.

Nemiroff, Robert A., and Calvin A Colarusso, eds. 1985. *The Race against Time: Psychotherapy and Psychoanalysis in the Second Half of Life.* New York: Plenum.

Neugarten, B., ed. 1964. *Personality in Middle and Late Life: Empirical Studies.* New York: Atherton Press.

————, ed. 1968. *Middle Age and Aging: A Reader in Social Psychology.* Chicago: University of Chicago Press.

Neugarten, B., and D. Miller. 1964. Ego Functions in the Middle and Later Years: A Further Exploration. In Neugarten (1964), 105–113.

Newton, Peter. 1984. Samuel Johnson's Breakdown and Recovery in Middle-Age: A Life Span Developmental Approach to Mental Illness and Its Cure. *International Review of Psychoanalysis* 11:93–117.

Nicholson, S., ed. 1987. *Shamanism: An Expanded View of Reality.* Wheaton, IL: Theosophical Publishing House.

Nicoloff, Assen. 1979. *Bulgarian Folktales.* Cleveland, OH: Nicoloff.

Norman, William, and Thomas Scaramella. 1980. *Mid-life: Developmental and Clinical Issues.* New York: Brunner/Mazel.

Notman, Malkah. 1982a. Midlife Concerns of Women: Menopause. In *The Woman Patient,* ed. Carol C. Nadelson and Malkah T. Notman. Vol. 2, *Concepts of Femininity and the Life Cycle,* 135–44. New York: Plenum.

————. 1982b. The Mid-life Years and After: Opportunities and Limitations: Clinical Issues. *Journal of Geriatric Psychiatry* 15:173–86.

O'Collins, Gerald. 1978. *The Second Journey.* New York: Paulist Press.

O'Connell, W. 1976. Freudian Humour: The Euspychia of Everyday Life. In Chapman and Foot (1976), 313–30.

Offer, D., and M. Sabshin, eds. 1984. *Normality and the Life Cycle: A Critical Integration.* New York: Basic Books.

Ohta, M. 1981. *Japanese Folklore in English.* Tokyo: Miraishi.

Oldham, John M. 1989. The Third Individuation: Middle-Aged Children and Their Parents. In Oldham and Liebert (1989), 89–104.

Oldham, John and Liebert Robert, eds. 1989. *The Middle Years: New Psychoanalytic Perspectives.* New Haven: Yale University Press.

Osherman, Samuel. 1986. *Finding Our Fathers: How A Man's Life is Shaped by His Relationship to His Father.* New York: Fawcett Columbine.

Ozaki, Y. T. 1982. *The Japanese Fairy Book.* Tokyo: Charles Tuttle.

Pearson, Carol. 1986. *The Hero Within: Six Archetypes We Live By.* San Francisco: Harper and Row.

Peck, Robert. 1968. Psychological Developments in the Second Half of Life. In Neugarten (1968), 79–83.

Pelton, Robert D. 1980. *The Trickster in West Africa: A Study of Mythic Irony and Sacred Delight.* Berkeley: University of California Press.

Powell, Philip M. 1980. Advanced Social Role-Taking and Cognitive Development in Gifted Adults. *International Journal of Aging and Human Development* 11:177–92.

Pratt, Annis. 1981. *Archetypal Patterns in Women's Fiction.* Sussex, England: Harvester Press.

Radin, Paul. 1983. *African Folktales.* New York: Schocken Books.

Reinisch, June M., Leonard A. Rosenblum, and Stephanie A. Sanders, eds. 1987. *Masculinity/ Femininity: Basic Perspectives.* Oxford: Oxford University Press.

Reinke, B. J., D. S. Holmes, and R. L. Harris. 1985. The Timing of Psychosocial Changes in Women's Lives: The Years 25 to 45. *Journal of Personality and Social Psychology* 48:1353–64.

Rhees, R., ed. 1984. *Recollections of Wittgenstein.* Oxford: Oxford University Press.

Riegel, K. F. 1973. Dialectical Operations: The Final Period of Cognitive Development. *Human Development* 16:346–70.

Roberts, Moss. 1979. *Chinese Fairy Tales and Fantasies.* New York: Pantheon.

Rosaldo, Michelle Z., and Louise Lamphere, eds. 1974. *Women, Culture, and Society.* Stanford: Stanford University Press.

Rossi, Alice, ed. 1985. *Gender and the Life Course.* New York: Aldine.

Rothbart, M. 1976. Incongruity, Problem-Solving and Laughter. In Chapman and Foot (1976), 37–54.

Rothenberg, A. 1971. The Process of Janusian Thinking in Creativity. *Archives of General Psychiatry* 24:195–205.

Rowan, John. 1987. *The Horned God: Feminism and Men as Wounding and Healing*. New York: Routledge and Kegan Paul.

Rupprecht, Carol Schreier. 1985. The Common Language of Women's Dreams: Colloquy of Mind and Body. In Lauter and Rupprecht (1985), 187–219.

Sakade, Florence. 1959. *Japanese Children's Stories*. Rutland, VT: Charles Tuttle.

Satinover, Jeffrey. 1986. The Myth of the Death of the Hero: A Jungian View of Masculine Psychology. In Friedman and Lerner (1986), 149–62.

Schafer, Roy. 1986. Men Who Struggle against Sentimentality. In Fogel, Lane, and Liebert (1986), 95–110.

Schavrien, J. 1989. The Rage, Healing and Daemonic Death of Oedipus: A Self-in-Relation Theory. *Journal of Transpersonal Psychology* 21:149–76.

Schwartz, Howard. 1985. *Elijah's Violin and Other Jewish Fairy Tales*. New York: Harper Colophon.

Segal, H. 1984. Joseph Conrad and the Mid-life Crisis. *International Rview of Psychoanalysis* 11:3–9.

Sheppard-Jones, Elisabeth. 1978. *Stories of Wales*. Cardiff, Wales: John Jones.

Sherman, Edmund. 1987. *Meaning in Mid-life Transitions*. Albany, NY: State University of New York Press.

Shultz, T. 1976. A Cognitive-Developmental Analysis of Humor. In Chapman and Foot (1976), 11–36.

Shulz, Carol. 1977. Death Anxiety and the Structuring of a Death Concerns Cognitive Domain. *Essence* 1:171–88.

Silberger, Julius, Jr. 1979. Mourning and Transformation: How Mary Baker Eddy Found in Middle Age a Way of Making a New Life for Herself. *Journal of Geriatric Psychiatry* 12:9–26.

Simonton, Dean. 1989. Age and Creative Productivity: Nonlinear Estimation of an Information-Processing Model. *International Journal of Aging and Human Development* 29:23–37.

Singer, June. 1989. *Androgyny: The Opposites Within*. Boston: Sigo.

Sinnott, Jan D. 1986. *Sex Roles and Aging: Theory and Research from a Systems Perspective*. Basel: Karger.

_____ . In press. Life-Span Relativistic Postformal Thought: Methodology and Data from Everyday Problem-Solving Studies. In Commons et al. (in press), TK.

Smelser, Neil J., and Erik H. Erikson, eds. 1980. *Themes of Work and Love in Adulthood*. Cambridge: Harvard University Press.

Soddy, K. 1967. *Men in Middle Life*. Tavistock Publications/Lippincott.

Solomon, Kenneth, and Norman Levy. 1982. *Men in Transition: Theory and Therapy*. New York: Plenum.

Staude, Jean-Raphael. 1981. *The Adult Development of C. G. Jung*. New York: Routledge and Kegan Paul.

Sternberg, Robert, ed. 1990. *Wisdom: Its Nature, Origins and Development*. Cambridge: Cambridge University Press.

Stewart, Robert J. 1985. *The UnderWorld Initiation: A Journey towards Psychic Transformation*. Guildford, Surrey, England: Aquarian Press.

Suls, J. 1983. Cognitive Processes in Humor Appreciation. In McGhee and Goldstein (1983), 39–58.

Tamir, Lois M. 1982. *Men in Their Forties: The Transition to Middle Age*. New York: Springer.

Tatar, M. 1987. *The Hard Facts of the Grimms' Fairy Tales*. Princeton: Princeton University Press.

Tawney, C. H. 1956. *Vetalapanchavimsati*. Bombay: Jaico.

Thompson, S. 1955–58. *Motif-Index of Folk Literature*. Bloomington, IN: Indiana University Press.

Thorson, James, and F. C. Powell. 1988. Elements of Death Anxiety and Meanings of Death. *Journal of Clinical Psychology* 44:691–701.

Vaillant, George. 1977. *Adaptation to Life: How the Best and Brightest Came of Age*. New York: Little Brown.

——————. 1989. The Evolution of Defense Mechanisms during the Middle Years. In Oldham and Liebert (1989), 58–72.

Van Kaam, Adrian. 1979. *The Transcendent Self: Formative Spirituality of the Middle, Early and Later Years of Life*. Danville, NJ: Dimension.

Vetterling-Braggin, Mary, ed. 1982. *"Femininity," "Masculinity" and "Androgyny": A Modern Philosophical Discussion*. Totowa, NJ: Rowman and Littlefield.

Viederman, M. 1989. Matisse's Nice Period, 1917–1928: A Confrontation with Middle Age. In Oldham and Liebert (1989), 275–282.

Von Franz, Marie-Louise. 1972. *Problems of the Feminine in Fairy Tales*. Irving, TX: Spring Publications.

——————. 1974. *Number and Time*. Evanston, IL: Northwestern University Press.

Wallas, Lee. 1985. *Stories for the Third Ear: Using Hypnotic Fables in Psychotherapy*. New York: Norton.

Walsh, Mary, ed. 1987. *The Psychology of Women: Ongoing Debates*. New Haven: Yale University Press.

Whitmont, Edward. 1969. *The Symbolic Quest: Basic Concepts of Analytical Psychology*. Princeton: Princeton University Press.

——————. 1987. *Return of the Goddess*. New York: Crossroad.

Wittgenstein, Ludwig. 1968. *Philosophical Investigations*. Trans. G. E. Anscombe. New York: Macmillan.

——————. 1974. *Tractatus Logico-Philosophicus*. Trans. D. F. Pears and B. F. McGuinness. Atlantic Highlands, NJ: Humanities Press.

Woods, Nina, and Kenneth Witte. 1981. Life Satisfaction, Fear of Death, and Ego Identity in Elderly Adults. *Bulletin of the Psychonomic Society* 18:165–68.

Wrightsman, Lawrence. 1988. *Personality Development in Adulthood*. Newbury Park, CA: Sage Publications.

Zimmer, Heinrich. 1956. *The King and the Corpse: Tales of the Soul's Conquest of Evil*. Ed. Joseph Campbell. Princeton: Princeton University Press.

Zipes, Jack. 1979. *Breaking the Magic Spell: Radical Theories of Folk and Fairy Tales*. Austin: University of Texas Press.

——————. 1983. *Fairy Tales and the Art of Subversion: The Classical Genre for Children and the Process of Socialization*. New York: Heinemann.

——————. 1988. *The Brothers Grimm: From Enchanted Forests to the Modern World*. New York: Routledge.

Index

229